The Public Management and Leadership series

<u>Series Editor:</u> **Paul 't Hart,** Utrecht University and Netherlands School of Government

Editorial Advisory Group

Public management and, more recently, public leadership have over several decades emerged as increasingly central elements in the study and practice of governance, public administration and public policy.

Around them have developed important new strands of research, debate, education and professional formation. And these in turn have informed a wide range of initiatives in many parts of the world to 'modernize', 'reform', 'innovate', 'de-bureaucratize' and 'professionalize' existing institutions and practices.

The Public Management and Leadership series aims to provide a set of key texts to meet the changing needs of the growing range of graduate, post-experience and other courses in this area as well as concise and accessible reading for busy practitioners.

Genuinely international in scope and conception; accessible in style and presentation; and drawing on empirical information and illustrations from a wide variety of jurisdictions and policy sectors, each title offers an authoritative review of the state of theory and practice in its respective field, and will identify the key challenges and the most promising conceptual and practical tools to tackle them.

The Public Management and Leadership series

Series Editor: Paul 't Hart, Utrecht University and Netherlands School of Government

Published:

John Alford and Janine O'Flynn
Rethinking Public Service Delivery: Managing with External Providers

Martin Lodge and Kai Wegrich
Managing Regulation: Regulatory Analysis, Politics and Policy

Forthcoming:

Richard Mulgan
Making Open Government Work: Accountability, Transparency and Public Management

Mirko Noordegraaf
Perspectives on Public Management

John Uhr
Ethical Public Leadership

In Preparation:

Understanding Public Leadership

The Public Management and Leadership Series

Series Standing Order ISBN 978–0–230–23657–8 hardback
Series Standing Order ISBN 978–0–230–23658–5 paperback

(outside North America only)

You can receive future titles in this series as they are published by placing a standing order. Please contact your bookseller or, in case of difficulty, write to us at the address below with your name and address, the title of the series and the ISBN quoted above.

Customer Services Department, Macmillan Distribution Ltd
Houndmills, Basingstoke, Hampshire RG21 6XS, England

Rethinking Public Service Delivery

Managing with External Providers

John Alford

and

Janine O'Flynn

First published 2012 by
PALGRAVE MACMILLAN

Palgrave Macmillan in the UK is an imprint of Macmillan Publishers Limited, registered in England, company number 785998, of Houndmills, Basingstoke, Hampshire RG21 6XS.

Palgrave Macmillan in the US is a division of St Martin's Press LLC, 175 Fifth Avenue, New York, NY 10010.

Palgrave Macmillan is the global academic imprint of the above companies and has companies and representatives throughout the world.

Palgrave® and Macmillan® are registered trademarks in the United States, the United Kingdom, Europe and other countries.

ISBN 978–0–230–23794–0 hardback
ISBN 978–0–230–23795–7 paperback

This book is printed on paper suitable for recycling and made from fully managed and sustained forest sources. Logging, pulping and manufacturing processes are expected to conform to the environmental regulations of the country of origin.

A catalogue record for this book is available from the British Library.

Library of Congress Cataloging-in-Publication Data
Alford, John, 1950–
   Rethinking public service delivery : managing with external
providers / John Alford, Janine O'Flynn.
      p.   cm.
   ISBN 978–0–230–23795–7 (pbk.)
   1. Public administration.   2. Human services—Management.
   3. Human services—Contracting out.   4. Public welfare administration.
   5. Public–private sector cooperation.   I. O'Flynn, Janine.   II. Title.
JF1525.P6A54 2012
351—dc23   2012012276

10   9   8   7   6   5   4   3   2   1
21 20 19 18 17 16 15 14 13 12

Printed and bound in China

Dedication by John Alford

To the railway workers of Victoria, who got me started on all this.

Dedication by Janine O'Flynn

For Isaac. Never stop asking questions.

Contents

List of Figures and Tables

Figures

Tables

Acknowledgements

As a further proof of the validity of this book's main message, we have to say that we could not have done it without the help and support of numerous 'external' actors.

First, a few people were instrumental in getting us to take on this project. Mark Moore and Linda Kaboolian of the Kennedy School of Government at Harvard University sparked ideas over some years, which eventually came together in this book. Paul 't Hart invited us to write it, and was also a valuable sounding board as the project progressed.

A number of other people also read drafts of the manuscript and proffered insightful comments on the contents of the draft manuscript, including Paul 't Hart, Michael Di Francesco, a very helpful anonymous reviewer and Monica Pfeffer with her 'reflective practitioner' insights – and Janet Tyson with useful editorial suggestions. Thanks also to our publisher, Steven Kennedy, for his astute suggestions and his patience. Others read and commented, often robustly, on drafts of particular chapters: Arie Freiberg, Owen Hughes, Peter Leisink, and Jon Pierre.

Mark Bovens of Utrecht University graciously enabled John Alford to undertake a three-month sabbatical to work on this project, in the course of which he had very productive discussions, informally or in seminars, with Mark himself, Mirko Noordegraaf, Albert Meijer, Sandra Schruijer, and Thomas Schillerman. Alford also benefited from the chance to try out these ideas at seminars at: Erasmus University Rotterdam, where Erik-Hans Klijn and Steven van der Walle gave useful feedback; the Netherlands School of Government (Mark van Twist); the Hertie School of Governance in Berlin, with Gerhard Hammerschmid and Salvador Parrado; the Maxwell School of Government at Syracuse University, New York, with David van Slyke, Rosemary O'Leary and Stuart Brettschneider; and the Kennedy School of Government. Janine O'Flynn had the opportunity to present ideas from the book in seminars and workshops with practitioners from various government departments, and she has benefited from the chance to explore many of them with colleagues, in particular, wide-ranging and detailed discussions with Deborah Blackman. None of those above is responsible for the final product.

Both of us benefited from supportive institutional bases: John Alford at the Australia and New Zealand School of Government (ANZSOG), where Peter Allen, Pauline Clancy and Monica Pfeffer encouraged continued progress, and Janine O'Flynn at the Crawford School of Public Policy, Australian National University. Special thanks go to Allan Fels, Dean of ANZSOG, and Tom Kompas, Director of the Crawford School of Public Policy, the Australian National University, for providing the time, space and resources to enable completion of this work. We also thank our students over recent years, who have allowed us to test out these ideas in class, and helped us in making them sharper and hopefully more relevant to practitioners.

Both of us thank Sophie Yates for her help on this work in its early stages. We especially thank Victoria Musgrove for not only her dedicated administrative support but also her intelligent contribution to the editorial process.

On a personal note, John Alford expresses special gratitude to Sue Harper, who has patiently endured but also supported and been a sounding board for the work on this book, which of course always takes longer than anticipated. And Janine O'Flynn gives special thanks to Frank Ryan for his ongoing encouragement and support.

JOHN ALFORD
JANINE O'FLYNN

The author and publishers would like to thank the following who have kindly given permission for the use of copyright material:

Figure 11.1, which originally appeared as figure 1.1 in OECD (2010) *Handbook on Contracting Out Government Functions and Services in Post-Conflict and Fragile Situations*, Partnership for Democratic Governance, OECD Publishing, http://dx.doi.org/10.1787/9789264091993-en.

Table 2.1, which originally appeared as table 1 'Determinants of service quality' on page 47 (Parasuraman, A., Zeithaml, V. and Berry, L. (1985) 'A Conceptual Model of Service Quality and its Implications for Future Research', *Journal of Marketing*, 49 (4),

41–50). Reprinted with permission from *Journal of Marketing*, published by the American Marketing Association.

Figure 7.1, which originally appeared as figure 2.1 'Example of an enforcement pyramid', in *Responsive Regulation: Transcending the Deregulation Debate* (Oxford Socio-Legal Studies) by Ian Ayres and John Braithwaite (1992). By permission of Oxford University Press, Inc.

Chapter 8 is adapted from John Alford's chapter 'Public Value from Co-production by Clients' in John Benington and Mark H. Moore (eds), *Public Value*, published 2010 by Palgrave Macmillan. Reproduced with permission of Palgrave Macmillan.

Introduction

The devastating earthquake and tsunami that struck northern Japan on 11 March 2011, and their aftermath in the meltdowns at the Fukushima nuclear power plant, were among those moments when the importance of government came dramatically to the fore. In a sense, it was crucial in the advance warnings provided by the Japan Meteorological Agency (JMA). Even though its Earthquake Early Warning System gave people in Tokyo only a minute's notice of severe earth movement, this was enough to save many lives. So too were the early warnings of the subsequent tsunami, which first hit north-eastern Honshu ten minutes after the quake and then spread elsewhere along the coast within the next two to three hours. In the short time before the tsunami hit, government's significance was evident in the frantic efforts of police and fire officers to evacuate citizens to higher ground. And their role became even more noticeable in the aftermath, as they led at times heroic efforts to clear access routes, pull the injured from the rubble, find missing persons, dispense first aid and shepherd shocked and homeless citizens to aid stations and shelter.

When the Fukushima nuclear meltdown dramatically complicated an already appalling situation, it was these same officers who took the lead role in implementing the government-ordered evacuation. These activities, and the agencies performing them, are among the most visible in government. Everyone knows and appreciates that it is government that has the primary role in protecting the public and rescuing people in emergencies. These are self-evidently tasks for public employees.

But what is interesting about these quintessentially governmental functions is that all of them depend on non-governmental organizations and people to achieve their purposes. Put another way, these public sector tasks are all part of a wider web of activities involving private companies, non-profit agencies and members of the public in various capacities. Take the early warning role, for example: this relied on over 1,000 seismographs distributed across Japan and surrounding islands, only 200 of which were maintained

1

and operated by the JMA. The remainder were the responsibility of the National Research Institute for Earth Science and Disaster Prevention, whose cooperation JMA needed. Moreover, Japan benefits from data supplied by other countries' earthquake warning systems. It also utilizes the services of the intergovernmental Pacific Tsunami Warning Centre, based in Hawaii – which was crucial on the day in alerting other countries, as far afield as California and Chile, of the tsunami.

This point is even more forcefully made when we consider the emergency workers. The fire service, for instance, is palpably public in nature; the uniforms worn by its officers symbolize this special status. But it is simply impossible to run a fire service without the contributions of a whole variety of other entities. Some of these are other government agencies, such as the police and ambulance services with whom they coordinate their interventions. These types of inter-dependencies form the basis of a growing trend to inter- and intra-governmental coordination and collaboration.

But the fire service also depends on many private entities. In this particular event, there was a massive outpouring of volunteer assistance, as locals, their neighbours and other citizens pitched in to help the rescue and clean-up efforts. The emergency services simply would not have been able to do what was required by relying on their own employees. In the Fukushima nuclear accident, private contributions of effort were even more essential. Containing the meltdown called for specific actions on the part of the power company and its workers – in the case of some of the latter, quite possibly at the cost of their lives as they were exposed to massive radiation doses. These actions could not have been performed by the fire service, which lacked the requisite knowledge.

While these contributions of private effort were dictated by this extreme situation, they are no less required in the normal operations of a fire service. Obviously, it is important that members of the public promptly report fires. It is also important that motorists give way to emergency vehicles racing to the scene. The fire service also depends on the private companies that supply and maintain their equipment. Importantly, they also rely on those whom they might call their 'clients': the owners and occupants of the buildings where fires and other emergencies might occur. The owners of buildings have to comply with fire codes in their construction and maintenance. Occupants need to be aware of fire safety in their offices and surrounds. In these and many other ways, the purpose of the fire service is fulfilled not only by its employees but also by a myriad of other actors.

In fact, almost every government organization depends on other parties to help implement its policies or deliver services. Very rarely does a public sector agency have sole control over the whole process of producing the public service for which it is responsible. It invariably has to call on effort, information or compliance from other parties. This observation is the fulcrum of this book. Its focus is on the relationship between government organizations and a wide variety of actors, whom we will call external providers.

This is not an original topic. Some significant works have addressed it (for instance, Salamon 1989, 2002; Osborne and Gaebler 1992; Kettl 1993; Bardach 1998; Sullivan and Skelcher 2002; Goldsmith and Eggers 2004; Crosby and Bryson 2005; Agranoff 2007; Donahue and Zeckhauser 2011) and a vast body of scholarship has explored issues such as government contracting, networks, collaboration and public–private partnerships. But what follows is not just another book on contracting, collaboration or network governance. Rather, it offers a broader view of the relationship between government organizations and external providers, in several respects:

- First, it considers a broader range of potential external providers – not just private firms or non-profit agencies, but also other government departments, volunteers, regulatees and individual clients.
- Second, it considers a broader set of mechanisms that might be deployed by government to induce external parties to contribute – not just contracts or collaboration, but also others such as negotiation, supervision or compulsion.
- Third, it encompasses a wider array of motivations that might explain why external parties assist with the achievement of public purposes – not just desire for material rewards or to avoid sanctions, but also non-material motivators such as intrinsic rewards, peer pressure or approval, and normative purposes.
- Finally, it takes into account a broader array of benefits and costs to be considered in weighing up whether and to whom a service might be 'externalized' – not only the benefits of the service and its purchase price, but also issues to do with the nature of the relationship and the strategic impact on the government organization.

Other books have dealt with one or other of these aspects in a similarly broad way, but here we put forward a framework which embraces all four of them together. The intent is to offer a guide to public sector managers on how to think about and manage these relationships. Hence, it is unequivocally a book about management, not about governance. Its focus is not so much about public or stakeholder deliberation about what to do, but rather about actually doing it, in interactions with external parties. This is not to say that governance is unimportant, just that this book is about something else, namely, the involvement of external providers in service-*delivery*.

Nor is the book necessarily advocating the use of external providers (just as it doesn't necessarily argue for production by government employees). It is neither a neo-liberal treatise on privatization nor a Weberian tract on bureaucracy. Instead, it offers a more contingent approach. Its central argument is that whether to externalize a service depends on the circumstances, which vary from one situation to the next. The book offers tools, including a causal mapping heuristic and the benefit-cost framework mentioned above, for making these judgements.

Thus the book is prescriptive insofar as it puts forward propositions about the most appropriate arrangements in specific circumstances. But in our view, this normative bent is not an alien intrusion into the existing landscape. Rather it seeks to make sense of something which, as our account of the fire service and other public agencies makes clear, is already happening. Instead of simply accepting these arrangements, this book calls for purposeful consideration of them. This may lead to some more functions being externalized, and it may also lead to some external functions being brought in-house, but either way, the central concern is what is of value to the public. That, after all, is what we expect from government.

Chapter 1

Mapping the Changing Landscape of Public Service Delivery

The waves of public management reform in developed countries over the last three decades have led to government playing both a smaller and a larger role in our society. It is smaller in that it is now an established truth that public services can be delivered by a wide array of parties external to a given public sector organization as well as by in-house production. Public utilities for services such as electricity, gas, water and transport have been sold off to the private sector. Public sector organizations have contracted out a wide variety of functions, from garbage collection and cleaning to security and employment services. Government agencies establish collaborative arrangements with other government agencies to realize purposes that they cannot achieve on their own. Departments in areas such as human services and conservation enlist voluntary organizations and volunteers in helping deliver some of their services. Agencies responsible for services such as mail or public housing rely on co-productive effort from their clients. And even regulatory organizations seek to call forth voluntary compliance from those they regulate, in the form of positive actions that contribute to organizational purposes. All of these developments have meant that some of the work of delivering public services has been transferred from public sector organizations to non-governmental organizations and individuals – a phenomenon we shall refer to throughout this book as 'externalization'.

But paradoxically, the more government surrenders the role of *producing* public services to external parties, the more its role expands in other respects. This is because public agencies need to interact with those external entities to elicit their productive contributions. This interaction occurs through a wide variety of mechanisms – including contracting, partnering, education, persuasion, incentives, subsidies, 'hard' and 'soft' regulation, and enhancing service information and convenience – which together have important implications for policy making and management. They both alter and expand the work of government organizations and their staff. Not only are they engaged in their own production tasks such as policy advice, service delivery and regulation, but also they are engaged in inducing others outside their organizations to contribute to those tasks through various mechanisms. These additional roles and mechanisms, which pose complex policy and management challenges, are the subject of this book.

The evolution of non-governmental service provision

Historically speaking, the public sector's major role in producing services is a relatively recent phenomenon. It was not until the late nineteenth century that government's functions began to expand beyond a historical norm.

In ancient times, rulers made extensive use of private actors to perform governmental functions. Ancient Egypt and Republican Rome utilized tax farming, in which private individuals shouldered the burden of tax collection in return for a share of the proceeds. Ancient Rome also contracted out nearly all the state's economic requirements, including construction and army provisioning, while in classical Greece the government owned forests, land and mines, but contracted out the work on them to firms and individuals (Levi 1988; Sobel 1999; Megginson and Netter 2003).

For much of the period since then, government's role has typically been confined to the basic functions of defence, foreign affairs, postal services and the making of laws regulating private actors in a patchwork variety of areas of economic and social life. Many activities, widely seen today as core government functions, were undertaken in whole or in part by private interests, including law enforcement, imprisonment, criminal prosecution, and overseas exploration and colonisation (Grabosky 1995a; Sturgess 1996). For instance, 163 of the 197 ships in the English fleet that defeated the Spanish Armada in 1588 were privately owned (Wettenhall 2000). Often the handing out by the ruler of licences and franchises to private parties blurred the line between the public and private spheres. However, in gradual steps from at least the Magna

Carta and through the Age of Enlightenment, notions of the rule of law and of natural rights began to shape and modify the extent to which particularist interests could crowd out the public interest (May 1997).

This had implications for how government dealt with the industrial revolution and its social effects. In the nineteenth century, two factors began to lead to pressures for greater government involvement. One was the expansion of commerce in the Industrial Revolution and in New World frontier expansion. This called for greater government involvement in the provision of infrastructure, such as transport (see Madrick 2009). The other was the reordering of class structures with the expansion of the urban working class and also a lesser increase in the middle classes, which called for government to engage in measures to ameliorate burgeoning social problems, such as poverty, hunger, homelessness and disease (May 1997). The rise of mass working-class parties towards the end of that century generated pressures for government provision of social services such as education, health care, housing and income security – pressures that continued until late in the twentieth century. In OECD nations between 1880 and 1995, for example, the median proportion of GDP spent on state welfare increased from 0.29 per cent to 22.52 per cent (Gough 1979; Lindert 2004). This trend gained added impetus from the aftermath of the Great Depression of the 1930s and expansion of national governments in the Second World War, many of which retained their war powers to tax and spend. The long boom from the 1950s to the 1970s enabled governments to garner revenue without taxing the private sector unduly, while the expectations it unleashed reinforced a popular desire for governments to provide a variety of services to citizens, as well as playing an economic stabilization role in order to avoid a recurrence of the Great Depression.

But as the 1970s proceeded, counter-trends emerged. The combined effects of a growing antipathy to big government, the 'tax revolt', opposition to perceived excessive regulation and tightening fiscal circumstances resulted in a search for non-governmental ways to deliver public services. This manifested itself in a global movement to privatize government functions (Salamon 1981; Savas 1983; Kristensen 1987; Wolf 1988; Hughes 2003). Alongside this, in a lower key, were some initiatives to enlist co-production by citizens, volunteers or clients, together with the hiring of non-profit organizations (Whitaker 1980; Brudney and England 1983; Smith and Lipsky 1993; Alford 2009). By 2000, the types of arrangements involving external providers had proliferated to an extent that would have been unrecognizable forty years before.

Service delivery, implementation and achieving outcomes

Making sense of this proliferation has been a challenge for scholars in the field. For a start, there are different ways of framing exactly what is being externalized. Here it is described as 'service delivery', for the simple reason that this term is widely used in public management. But it should be recognized that service delivery is a subset (albeit the most substantial one) of a larger body of activities the policy literature describes as 'implementation', that is, putting policy into effect (Pressman and Wildavsky 1973; Parsons 1995; Bridgman and Davis 2004; Weimer and Vining 2004). Service delivery is therefore not quite the same thing as implementation. It is typically used to describe the provision of *outputs*, such as welfare benefits, school classes, or roads, rather than of *outcomes*, such as mitigation of poverty, improved literacy or road safety. Moreover, it implies (but doesn't necessarily entail) provision of services to the clients of the government agency, rather than to the agency itself. However, 'service delivery' sits awkwardly with some kinds of instruments, for instance, with applying regulatory constraints or broadcasting advertisements to encourage changes in public behaviour (for example, to use less water) – both of which could reasonably be described as implementation, directed towards achieving particular social outcomes.

In this vein, therefore, we will *mainly* employ the term 'service delivery', conceived as the 'production' of outputs, which includes provision of services to government agencies as well as to their clients. But where the focus is on bringing about outcomes, or on the imposition of obligations, we will instead refer to 'implementation', and in some cases to 'achieving outcomes'.

Terminological confusion

There is a plethora of terms for the act or process of externalization, used in differing ways, such as partnering, partnership, strategic alliance, collaboration, cooperation, network, network governance, joined-up government, whole-of-government, privatization, commissioning, contracting and outsourcing. While there is no such thing as a 'correct' definition of these terms, we need to be clear about what we mean by the words we use in the present analysis.

There are also numerous typologies organized along a wide variety of dimensions, each of them partial in its comprehension of the field. One early attempt was by the former Reagan Administration official, Emanuel Savas (1983, 1987). He put forward a typology of different forms of privatization based on the delineation of three role dimensions: who specifies and arranges what is to be produced, who produces, and who pays. Each of these roles can be played by alternative actors – for example, the role of specifying and arranging can be performed either by an individual consumer, a political authority (for example, an elected government) or a government agency. From these elements, Savas constructed a typology of alternative service arrangements.

But not surprisingly for one who was a crusader for privatization under Reagan, Savas tended to start from the assumption that market solutions are preferable, that is, that government-as-producer is 'guilty until proven innocent'. This mindset meant that his model was prone to a number of shortcomings, such as ignoring the possibility that each of the roles can be *shared* between two or more parties, or assuming that all dealings between parties are either hierarchical or contractual. But classical contracting and hierarchical supervision are not the only types of relationship; others include coercion, negotiation or collaboration (deHoog 1990).

Subsequent typologies classify arrangements in a wide variety of ways. Some of them categorize relationships in terms of the number and sectoral location of the parties involved (Alter and Hage 1993; Mariotti 1996; Exworthy *et al.* 1999; Bovaird 2004; Selsky and Parker 2005). Many of them take the form of continua, in which arrangements vary, for example, in the extent to which they entail closeness between the parties (Lorange *et al.* 1992; Alter and Hage 1993; Huxham 1996; Sullivan and Skelcher 2002; Mandell and Steelman 2003; Agranoff 2007; Sandfort and Milward 2008), or contractual specificity or formality (Hall *et al.* 1977; deHoog 1990; Ring and Van de Ven 1992; Lyons and Mehta 1997; Beinecke and DeFillippi 1999; Bovaird 2004; Donahue and Zeckhauser 2011). Some focus on the level at which interaction occurs – Sandfort and Milward (2008), for example, consider collaborative efforts at the level of policy, organization, programme and client. Some combine two or more of these dimensions into selected ideal-types (Oliver 1990). Skelcher (2005), for instance, identifies public leverage, contracting out, franchising, joint ventures and strategic partnering as specific forms, varying along several dimensions.

Each of these typologies makes sense for the topic or issue to which it is applied. But none of them on its own suits the purposes of this analysis. What is necessary is a framework encompassing all of the phenomena under consideration, but, at the same time, sufficiently discriminating to enable realistic consideration of specific cases. By drawing on the partial insights offered by the existing typologies, we propose a framework that covers the field while enabling useful distinctions to be drawn within it, by addressing three questions:

1 What types of external providers are involved?
2 What are the alternative distributions of roles – such as deciding what to do, funding, or service-delivery – between these external providers and government organizations?
3 What types of relationship are there between these external providers and government organizations? By what alternative modes – such as compulsion, contracts, or collaboration – do government organizations prompt external providers to deliver the desired services?

On the basis of this analysis, we will offer some definitions of key terms, which we argue are clarified by the framework.

Types of external providers

Almost all of the existing typologies conceive of the entities involved as *organizations*, mainly formal ones, such as government agencies, business firms or non-profit/voluntary organizations, and give scant consideration to individuals as external providers. Here we include external providers who are not organizations, such as volunteers, clients and regulatees, in addition to organizations as providers. Table 1.1 sets them all out.

The most well-known type of external provider is *the private for-profit firm*, usually engaged on a contractual basis. They take a variety of forms, ranging from large corporations, such as IT suppliers or defence contractors, through private partnerships such as management consulting or accountancy firms, to small businesses. Almost as well-known is the *voluntary/non-profit/third*

TABLE 1.1 Possible alternative external service providers with which government agencies can interact

External providers	Government agency		
	Local	State/provincial	National
(Other) local government body	Multi-municipality waste disposal facility	Funding for road maintenance	Employment programmes. Early childhood programmes
(Other) state/provincial government body		Disaster recovery programmes	Anti-drugs strategies
(Other) national government body			Services for indigenous people
Private firm	Garbage collection	Engineering maintenance	Defence equipment procurement
Voluntary agency	Primary Care Partnerships	Primary Care Partnerships	Employment programmes
Volunteers	Meals on Wheels	National park conservatorship	Land conservation programmes
Clients	Household garbage collection	School pupils and their parents	Welfare recipients
Regulatees	Cafe proprietors	Polluting companies	Taxpayers

sector organization, also engaged on a contractual basis, usually in areas such as human services or environmental conservation. These also entail a variety of forms, from fully incorporated non-profit companies to less formal associations of volunteer members, such as Neighbourhood Watch or community environment groups. (For the sake of brevity, we will call these entities 'non-profits' throughout this book.) Also commonly known are individual *volunteers*, who donate their time and effort to government agencies in fields such as rural fire-fighting, environmental conservation and community safety, sometimes under the auspices of non-profit/third sector organizations.

Also prominent as external providers, especially in recent years, have been *other government agencies*. In a world where inter-organizational collaboration, 'joined-up government' and 'whole-of-government' initiatives have become commonplace, any particular government organization looks to other government agencies as actual or potential partners. At first sight, it might seem that the lateral relationships typical with the private/non-profit sector partners are less relevant here, since each government agency has the option of going to a political superior to resolve conflicts. But for many inter-agency relationships, this option is not so clear-cut. Often the other agency will be part of a different governmental jurisdiction. Thus a national government agency might find itself dealing with a state or local government organization over which the national government has little formal authority (even though it might have informal power). In a federal system such as that of Australia, Canada or the United States, state or provincial governments are effectively sovereign in respect of those functions and powers guaranteed to them in constitutions. In these circumstances there is no official who has formal authority over the contending parties; they must resolve issues laterally, or take them to a supreme or high court (which can be costly and time-consuming). Even where two or more partnering agencies are within the same government, the lowest level official who has authority over both or all of them is likely to be the political chief executive, such as the president, governor, prime minister or premier. Unless the issue is of great significance, these officials are unlikely to have the time or inclination to get involved in inter-agency dealings. Even more challenging is where the relationship crosses national boundaries, such as those within the multinational military peacekeeping force that intervened in East

Timor to deal with rampaging Indonesian-backed militia following the referendum in 1999, or between national agencies and supranational bodies such as the United Nations. In short, to achieve their purposes, government agencies often need to enlist and engage other government agencies as external providers or partners.

These types are consistent with our commonsense understanding of the term 'providers'. They contribute inputs to the government's production process. By analogy with a private sector production process, they are suppliers rather than buyers. However, we argue that there are other types of external provider who do not conform so readily with this image.

One is the *clients* of public sector organizations – those who receive private value at the 'business end' of the agency's operations, such as welfare recipients, pupils in government schools, road users, public hospital patients or employment programme participants. To the extent that they receive private value, clients differ from citizens, who collectively 'consume' public value, which includes, *inter alia*: law and order and other pre-requisites for the functioning both of the market and of society; remedies to various forms of market failure, such as inability to provide public goods, externalities, or natural monopoly; promoting procedural and distributional equity; and economic stabilization, through macroeconomic management (Moore 1995; Alford 2002; Hughes 2003: 78–80). Public sector clients also differ from the private sector customers who receive private value from firms, with whom they have direct, voluntary economic exchanges. Many of them, such as school pupils, welfare recipients or road users, are *beneficiaries*, who receive a service for which they do not pay any money directly (although they may pay indirectly through taxes, in a different capacity). Unlike the private firm, the agency is not concerned to maximize sales but rather to ration them, according to some notion of equity, through devices such as eligibility rules or waiting lists.

Other members of the public, such as prisoners or those subject to regulatory obligations, do not wish to receive a service, but instead are at least to some extent compelled to do so. These *obligatees* are not engaged in an economic exchange with the agency, so it makes no sense to call them customers. But they have a client-like relationship with the agency to the extent that it seeks to prompt rehabilitation and greater voluntary compliance from them by providing fair, responsive and helpful service to them (Alford and Speed 2006).

Both 'beneficiaries' and 'obligatees' are *roles* rather than categories. Typically, an individual client will constitute some mix of these roles, as well as being a citizen.[1] For example, an unemployed welfare recipient receives income support and job search assistance, but is also obliged to look actively for work and to report changes of income, address or other circumstances.

However, for the purposes of this book, we will distinguish between clients and obligatees, and indeed refer to the latter as regulatees, for three reasons. First, there are many regulatees, and nearly all of them turn out to be contributing to agency purposes when they comply with their legal obligations. Second, many regulatees are companies rather than individuals, and to that extent are not as comfortably encompassed by the term 'client'. Third, regulatees have a rather different relationship to regulatory agencies than client/beneficiaries do to other government organizations. Accordingly, we devote a separate chapter to regulatees as providers.

The essential point here is that clients and regulatees can – and quite often must – constitute external providers to the extent that the agency relies on their contributions of time and effort to achieve its purposes. This phenomenon, sometimes called 'co-production', is more prevalent than appears at first sight. For example, employment services need their unemployed clients to actively seek work or engage in job-relevant training. Schools cannot educate unless students engage actively with learning processes. Doctors cannot bring about a more healthy population unless patients follow prescribed medical therapies and more broadly undertake preventive measures such as better diets and more exercise. In many areas of social life, the success of government programmes depends on the clients doing some work to facilitate it. On the regulatory side, tax authorities find it difficult to ensure the right amount of tax is being paid unless taxpayers comply with their obligations to file tax returns accurately and promptly. Health and safety inspectors seek to prompt voluntary compliance from companies.

Thus, we can identify a considerable range of types of external provider with which a government agency can interact, as set out in Table 1.1. Thinking more broadly in this way enables public managers to imagine alternative means of achieving outcomes.

Distribution of roles

For any service to be delivered, certain things have to happen. Decisions need to be made about what is to be done and who is to do it. Resources need to be devoted to its execution. And someone has to do the actual work. For present purposes, we can group these activities into two broad categories:

- *The deciding role.* This is the set of activities directed towards determining what is to be produced, arranging for someone to produce it, and providing resources to enable it to be done. It is similar to, but we hope slightly broader in its scope, than the 'principal' role in principal–agent theory; the 'purchaser' role in purchaser–provider splits; the 'policy' role in the separation of policy from implementation; or the 'commissioning' role, which has emerged in UK parlance in recent years. These roles tend to entail a more precise form of 'deciding' – namely, the 'specifying of services' – whereas we also include cases where services are not so much precisely specified as broadly determined, and/or fine-tuned or adapted as circumstances evolve, especially in collaborative relationships.

  Related to this is the funding role. The funder is usually but not always the same as the decider. In some circumstances, such as franchising, at least part of the funding role is performed by clients (for example, public transport passengers, postal customers), who pay the purchase price for the service. Another exception is where a private firm provides some of the funding, as happens in many public–private partnerships. The motivation for the private firm in these cases is usually the opportunity to receive a future stream of income or some assets from the project (English 2005; Shaoul 2005). For the purposes of this book, we will generally subsume funding under deciding, but point out exceptions where they arise.

- *The producing role.* This is the set of activities directed towards converting resources into valuable results. It is similar to the roles of, respectively, agent, provider or implementer in the binary distinctions made. It should be stressed that 'production' is here defined very broadly. Although in some minds it conjures up factory production lines churning out material goods, here it refers to any activity that converts resources of any kind into tangible or intangible things of value. Thus it might refer not only to outputs such as public housing construction or postal deliveries but also to outcomes such as improved literacy or reduced crime. The provider is the person or organization who carries out the task that has been decided upon, and can be any of a number of types.

Conceivably, each of these roles could be performed either solely by the government organization itself, or solely by the external party, or by some mix of the two, as set out in all six cells in Figure 1.1. But for the present analysis, we focus on only four of the cells (shaded in grey), since our concern is only with arrangements where the deciding role is at least partly the responsibility of the government organization, and the producing role is at least partly the responsibility of the external party. We therefore exclude cells 3 and 4 from consideration, and focus on the relationships between cells 1 and 2 on the one hand and 5 and 6 on the other. This gives us four permutations, represented by the arrows in the figure:

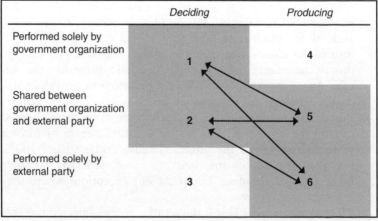

FIGURE 1.1   *Possible allocations of roles*

1 *Government decides, production shared (cells 1 and 5)*. This is the kind of arrangement seen in some public–private partnerships, where both the public agency and the private firm contribute effort, but the arrangement is subject to a government-imposed contract. It is also common in regulatory relationships.

2 *Government decides, external party produces (cells 1 and 6)*. This is the archetypal form of outsourcing (or 'contracting out'), in which government is clearly the principal and the external party is clearly the agent, but also applies to the relationship with volunteers.

3 *Deciding role shared, production shared (cells 2 and 5)*. This is the archetypal form of collaborative partnership, where the government organization and the external party jointly govern the service and jointly deliver it. It is essentially the arrangement seen in some public–private partnerships (different from those mentioned in point 1 above), in partnerships with non-profit organizations, in joined-up government, and also co-production with clients.

4 *Deciding role shared, external party produces (cells 2 and 6)*. This is where an external party delivers a service under a joint governance arrangement where both it and the government organization are represented. It is a relatively uncommon arrangement, but observable in some settings such as primary care partnerships.

However, while this schema is inclusive of all the conceivable arrangements, it does not allow important distinctions to be drawn between certain types that appear to be similar within it but in fact are different. For example, contracting out can be conducted in various ways ranging from transactional to collaborative. This brings us to the third factor in our taxonomy.

Modes of coordination

Identifying the respective roles of entities is a necessary but not a sufficient consideration in understanding a productive relationship. To enable the entities to perform these roles in a useful way, some type of mechanism is needed to ensure that the behaviours or actions by those producing are consistent with what the deciding party wants. Writers such as Savas (1987) and others imply that the only possible types of relationship are either ones based on contract or ones based on formal authority, that is, markets or hierarchies (See for example, Coase 1937; Jensen and Meckling 1976; Milgrom and Roberts 1992). But as discussed above, there is a substantial literature pointing to other modes of coordination between entities. Many put forward a spectrum, which at one end has contractual mechanisms such as precise service-specification, competitive tendering, incentives and penalties, and at the other has collaborative relationships, involving trust, shared goals and mutual commitment, as the means by which the parties coordinate their activities (Ring and Van de Ven 1992; Lyons and Mehta 1997; Beinecke and De Fillippi 1999; Bovaird 2004). Indeed, some of those who focus on the collaborative end of the range propose a continuum of collaboration sub-categories ranging from something like loose coordination through to strong collaboration (for example, Himmelmann 1996). Another mode which attracts less attention is directive supervision[2] – simply put, where a superior gives instructions to someone who acts as a subordinate, as occurs inside a hierarchy, for example, in an employment contract. This receives limited attention in the inter-organizational literature because it is seen as being more common *inside* organizations. But it can be seen in some relationships with external providers – for example, where an organization engages a legal adviser or an IT expert to provide services as required, with specific requests framed as circumstances arise, rather than the work being specified in advance in a contract.

DeHoog points out that even in outsourcing, there can be other modes of coordination besides classical contracting. One is collaboration, as discussed above, but another is a mode that sits somewhere between contracting and collaboration – namely, negotiation or 'relational contracting', where 'a form of consensual and incremental decision making is the norm' (deHoog 1990: 325). Unlike contracting, it does not involve open competitive tendering, but rather invitations to selected bidders, and specific details are then agreed on through negotiation.

The literature on modes of coordination can credibly also be applied to non-organizational external providers such as volunteers or clients. Their contributions to organizational purposes can be elicited not only through incentives and sanctions but also through the building of good relationships, manifested as collaboration. However, this literature has little to say about relations with regulatees, who are also part of our set of potential external

Compulsion	Supervision	Classical contracting	Negotiation	Collaboration
←				→
(Threat of) sanctions	Episodic instructions	Incentives and competition	Flexible agreements	Trust, shared purposes

FIGURE 1.2   *Continuum of modes of coordination*

providers. In this book we take the view that regulatees can be subject to a variety of modes of coordination just as all the other types of external providers can. Nevertheless, compulsion or sanctions loom large in this particular type.

In order to encompass all these aspects, we put forward a continuum traversing five nodal points, as shown in Figure 1.2. At one end is the application of compulsion and at the other end collaborative relationships. In between are directive supervision, transactional contracts, and negotiated agreements. This enables us to distinguish, for instance, between different types of outsourcing arrangements – those based on tightly specified contracts backed up by incentives and penalties, those entailing episodic instructions from the principal, and those that rely on cooperative relationships.

A qualifying factor: the duration of the relationship

One factor to consider is that arrangements can vary in their duration. At one end of the scale would be 'once-off' single transactions which are almost certain not to be repeated – for example, the purchase of banners and bunting for the staging of the Olympic Games in a particular city. At the other end would be interactions of indefinite length such as that between two government departments which work jointly on certain issues – for example, between the police and the mental health service on dealing with psychiatric clients who reside in the community. In between these two extremes, at the shorter end of the scale would be contracts for limited terms such as one year, while towards the longer end would be multi-year franchises, such as those in public transport in the UK, which can run for 12 or 15 years, or public–private infrastructure partnerships, which can be of even longer duration. Also affecting the perceived duration is whether these engagements are repeated.

What makes this factor important is that it affects the expectations of the parties as they establish and maintain their working relationships. If they see the relationship as long-term, it is worth them investing more time and energy in maintaining shared commitment and trust. If, however, they see it as 'once-off' or short-term, they will tend to place less weight on these issues. However, in the interests of parsimony, we will not add this factor as a fourth dimension in our framework, but rather take note of it where it is relevant in the forthcoming pages.

Defining terms

As we noted, there has been a proliferation of terms in this field and, moreover, they are used in many different ways. This means that there is no 'correct' definition of each of the terms under consideration. Instead, all we can do here is put forward what *we* mean by particular terms, and use them consistently throughout the book. The foregoing analysis provides a basis for this. Our key meanings are therefore as follows (see also Table 1.2).

TABLE 1.2   *Glossary of terms*

General terms

External providers: any entities outside the government organization in question that produce all or some of the service.
Externalization: any arrangement in which one or more external providers produce all or some of the service.

Terms relating to the distribution of roles

Outsourcing: any arrangement in which the whole of the production of a given service is handed to an external entity. Another term for outsourcing is 'contracting out' (with the word 'out').
Partnership: any arrangement in which the production of a given service is shared between two or more organizations.

Terms relating to the mode of coordination

Collaboration: where the coordination between two or more entities is primarily through the mechanisms of trust, mutual commitment and shared goals.
Contracting: where coordination occurs through transactional mechanisms such as tight specification, financial incentives, penalties and competitive tendering. Note that this is not the same as 'contracting out'.

External providers are any entities outside the government organization in question that produce all or some of the service. *Externalization* is accordingly any arrangement in which one or more external providers produce all or some of the service. This is the umbrella term for the processes considered in this book; it can cover *either* situations where the whole of the production of a service is handed over to an external entity, *or* where it is shared with an external entity.

Outsourcing will be defined as a particular subset of externalization. It refers to any arrangement in which the *whole* of the production of a given service is handed to an external entity.

Partnership is a term which has had an especial confusion of meanings. One usage refers to the mode of coordination, which confuses it with collaboration. Thus a partnership is said to be a relationship in which the parties interact collaboratively. The other usage, which is the one we use here, is more structural, and refers to the role relationship. It covers any arrangement in which the production of a given service is *shared* between two or more organizations (in this case, one of the organizations would be the government agency in question). Two of the leading authors on partnerships, Klijn and Teisman (2000: 85–6), contrast the terms similarly:

> Contracting-out is characterized by a principal–agent relationship in which the public actor defines the problem and provides the specification of the solution... Partnership, on the other hand, is based on joint decision-making and production in order to achieve effectiveness for both partners.

Thus partnership is contrasted with outsourcing, and is a different subset of externalization. In this definition, a partnership can operate either in a more collaborative fashion or a more transactional fashion.

In a different dimension, collaboration and contracting (minus the word 'out') will be taken to refer not to whether the production is shared between the parties but rather to *modes of coordination*. *Collaboration* is where the coordination between two or more entities is primarily through the mechanisms of trust, mutual commitment and shared goals. In this context, trust is both an antecedent and a consequence of collaboration. As an *antecedent*, it is analogous to (and an alternative to) the other modes of coordination such as contracts or compulsion. But trust is also a *consequence* of collaboration, in that successful cooperation contributes to a 'virtuous spiral' of increasing trust. (This will be explained in detail in Chapter 5.)

By contrast, *contracting* is where coordination occurs through transactional mechanisms such as tight specification, financial incentives, penalties and competitive tendering. It refers to externalization, which is conducted on a transactional or contractual basis rather than through collaborative mechanisms. This is different from *contracting out* (with the word 'out' added) which is here seen in terms of role relationships, as a subset of outsourcing. Each of these terms can be applied to either an outsourcing arrangement or a partnership.

Taxonomy

On the basis of the forgoing discussion, it is now possible to put forward a taxonomy of alternative arrangements between government organizations and external providers, as set out in Table 1.3, which encompasses our three key dimensions. It should be pointed out, at the outset, that this taxonomy does not cover all the possible arrangements conceivable. Rather it is confined only to those cases relevant to the scope of this book: namely where a government organization is at least partly the decider, and an external entity carries out at least some of the provision of the service.

Thus we do not cover arrangements in which government solely performs all three roles, nor those in which an external entity such as a private firm or a voluntary agency or some combination of them performs all of the roles. Nor does it cover situations where government shares the deciding role (for example, through consultation with community organizations) but performs the service-delivery role by itself.

The taxonomy delineates a variety of conceivable types, each representing a different mix of public and private. Some of them are familiar and widespread, such as the several varieties of classical contracting, including commissioning and franchising, and of partnering, such as public–private partnerships and collaborative partnerships. Also increasingly familiar are 'joined-up' arrangements between two or more government agencies.

The classification scheme also allows us to distinguish between different types of public–private partnerships. As will be explained

TABLE 1.3 Examples of alternative arrangements examined in this book

Form		Who produces?	Who decides what is to be done?	Mode of coordination
Outsourcing (Ch. 4)	Contracting out	Private firm, non-profit/voluntary agency, other government organization	Government organization	Contract and/or negotiation
	Public–private partnership (rhetorical)	Private firm	Government organization	Contract and/or negotiation
Partnering (Ch. 5)	Public–private partnership (substantive)	Government organization and private firm	Government organization and private firm	Some by contract, some by collaboration
	Collaborative partnerships	Government organization and non-profit/voluntary agency	Government organization and non-profit/voluntary agency	Mainly collaboration
	Joined-up government	Government organization with other government organizations	Government organization with other government organizations	Mainly collaboration

TABLE 1.3 *(Continued)*

Form	Who produces?	Who decides what is to be done?	Mode of coordination
Volunteering (Ch. 6)	Volunteer	Government organization	Quasi-employment relationship
Regulation (Ch. 7)	Government organization with private firm, non-profit/voluntary agency	Government organization	Compulsion plus negotiation and/or collaboration
Client co-production (Ch. 8)	Government organization and client	Government organization and client	Mixture of exchange, collaboration and compulsion
Multiparty networks (Ch. 9)	Government organization and multiple private firms, and/or non-profit/voluntary agencies, other government organizations	Government organization and multiple private firms, and/or non-profit/voluntary agencies, other government organizations	Various simultaneously

in Chapters 4 and 5, some are truly 'partnerships' in substantive terms, but others are only so in rhetorical terms, in that the producing role is performed solely by the private firm, with varying types of financing arrangements. They are thus more like outsourcing arrangements than partnerships.

Other notions – such as seeing regulatees as external providers – are less commonly framed in this way. But to the extent that regulatees contribute to the achievement of organizational purposes and therefore to creating value for the public, they fit squarely within the logic of this analysis. Consider the notion of co-regulation, in which the agency sets the broad parameters of regulatory obligations, and the regulatee translates these parameters into specific obligations and a plan for meeting them, as well as implementing the plan. The regulatee thus performs some of the work of the regulator, whose role is streamlined to giving expert advice, approving the plan and (infrequent) periodic audits of its implementation (Ayres and Braithwaite 1992: ch. 4; Baldwin and Cave 1999: 39–41).

Similarly, to see clients as co-producers of public services is at odds with the usual way we conceive of clients: as recipients rather than providers. But they fit within this typology as sharing the work of the public sector agency, typically in a collaborative mode.

These are only some of the possible arrangements. In fact, a moment's reflection on the various dimensions and the range of alternatives within each of them would disclose that there are literally hundreds of possible arrangements. The basic point is that there is no simple divide between 'public' and 'private', but rather a vast field of possible intermediate structures in between a notionally purely public and a notionally purely private arrangement. Whilst this is more complex, it is also more useful. It enables consideration of the full range of possible external providers on a comparable basis. It also enables identification of more imaginative alternatives for service arrangements than everyday thinking might allow.

Conclusion

From the 1970s, a long run trend of government assuming increasing responsibility for economic and social activities began to be reversed. But this change of direction did not entail simply handing functions back to businesses across a simple divide between the public and private sectors. Instead, the reallocation of roles is more complex, in that it involves a broader range of parties. Services for the public do not have to be performed only by public sector organizations; they can also be produced by a wide array of other entities, such as private firms, voluntary agencies, clients, volunteers, regulatees and even other government departments. It is also more complex in the variety of relationships these external actors have with government. Not only the mechanisms of markets and hierarchies, but also those of networks and others, play a significant role.

This chapter has sought to map this domain in a framework which aims to make sense of the breadth of possibilities. The remainder of this book will delve into this framework. Chapters 2 and 3 explore what government organizations and external providers seek from each other, considering the benefits and costs to public agencies, and the motivations of external providers and the mechanisms which resonate with those motivations. Chapters 4 to 9 then take each of the main categories of external providers in turn. Chapters 4 and 5 consider organizations (private firms, voluntary agencies and other government departments) as external providers, whereas Chapters 6 to 8 look at individuals (volunteers, regulatees and clients) as external providers or co-producers. Chapter 9 considers multiparty networks of providers, and Chapter 10 brings it all together in a contingency framework, setting out the circumstances in which each type of arrangement is most suitable and the choices that need to be made in managing external providers. Chapter 11 examines how government organizations can best equip themselves to manage external providers, considering, structure, culture and skills. Finally, Chapter 12 provides the conclusion.

Chapter 2

Benefits and Costs: What Government Organizations Seek from External Providers

On 10 September, 2001, US Defense Secretary Donald Rumsfeld declared war on the Pentagon. Describing it as 'one of the world's last bastions of central planning', he called for a wholesale shift from the old defence bureaucracy to a new private sector model. He pledged to 'pursue additional opportunities to outsource and privatize'. In fact, contractors such as Lockheed Martin, Northrop Grumman and General Dynamics already accounted for a major proportion of spending on defence *hardware*, and had done so for decades. But what Rumsfeld was pushing for was the widespread use of private contractors in *all* aspects of the military, including combat, security and protection (Scahill 2007). This was not about external parties making the missiles, bombs or bullets (or the vehicles that carried them), but rather about them firing them in theatres of war.

The next day, the al Qaeda attacks on the World Trade Centre and the Pentagon set the stage for the wars in Afghanistan and Iraq, where Rumsfeld had free reign to pursue his preference for privatization. This preference was based on a deeply held view: that the private sector was *inherently* faster, better and cheaper than the public sector. Rumsfeld himself had long publicly advocated the virtues of privatization. In 1995 he wrote:

The first task is to decide what the core business is... For the federal government, the four basic departments – State, Defense, Justice, and Treasury – have a solid basis for existence. The other departments were either more narrowly based, an afterthought, or both. Some had utility when they were established, but no longer do. Others, in my view, probably should not have been established in the first place... Once one has determined the

27

core functions to be performed by the federal government, all other activities should be scrutinized for elimination, downsizing, reorganization, movement to state and local governments, or privatization. I begin with the conviction that activities should first be undertaken by individual citizens and private organizations.

(Rumsfeld 1995: 3)

This became the guiding spirit of Pentagon policy and practice after he took up the post of Defense Secretary in 2001. Between then and February 2011, at least $177 billion was spent on contractors to provide protection for defence, diplomatic and development missions in those wars, their numbers at times exceeding the number of military personnel there. Among them were the Blackwater corporation, and Military Professional Resources Inc. (MPRI).

By 2010, outsourcing and privatization was seen as the official answer to every military supply problem under the sun. In the words of a 2011 report from a bi-partisan Commission on Wartime Contracting in Iraq and Afghanistan, set up by Congress in 2008:

Contractors have become the default option... In Iraq and Afghanistan, DoD, State, and USAID have contracted for much of what were once considered core functions, mission-critical work, and organic capabilities. The resulting dependence on contractors was driven mostly by external pressures rather than by deliberate decisions about the best way to accomplish agency objectives.

(Commission on Wartime Contracting 2011: 13)

Rumsfeld's enthusiasm for private sector solutions has turned out to be only one of the more spectacular examples of a syndrome which has driven much of the push to privatize since the 1970s. Many governments have enlisted external providers on the basis of an *a priori* assumption that the public sector should be minimized. Encouraging them in this assumption have been the World Bank or other international financing bodies, which often make privatization a condition of financial support, and consultants. During the 1990s, wave after wave of privatization, especially in the former Soviet bloc and in developing countries, was driven by a felt need to mimic other agencies or countries, underpinned by the ideological assumptions mentioned above. In this perspective, the answer to the question 'When does it make sense to hand over government work to external providers?' is: 'Always'.

But other actors – such as some incumbent civil servants, public sector unions or interest groups – vigorously resist any attempts to privatize public functions as a matter of principle. Sometimes this is for converse reasons to those of the privatization advocates: they contend that the public interest is best served by the maintenance of a strong public sector. Sometimes it is because they have a vested interest in retaining jobs in a public agency performing the functions. Whatever the reason, their answer to the question of when externalization should occur is (usually): 'Never'.

However, both positions are deficient. There are many examples of poorly performing externalized services – as we shall see, outsourcing of military combat, security and protection services is a telling instance – just as there are ineffective or inefficient services produced by government. There are several possible reasons, but one important factor is that *public services vary in their suitability for externalization*: some of them are best done by external providers, whereas others work better when produced by government organizations, and still others deliver most value when they are shared between the two.

This is well understood in many government organizations, which take a more pragmatic approach than either the zealous advocates or the diehard resisters of externalization. Broadly, these organizations seek to externalize when it seems useful for the circumstances, but not when it doesn't (see Feigenbaum *et al.* 1998). Their answer to this question of when it makes sense to utilize external providers is: 'It all depends.'

What it depends upon can be simply expressed: *government organizations should enlist external providers when the benefits outweigh the costs of doing so*. But this prescription begs further questions. What are the benefits and costs? And to whom? This chapter examines these factors, then concludes by applying them to the private military contracting case. It shows that, when considered in depth, the costs are more significant than initially appreciated by Rumsfeld and his colleagues, even from his hard-nosed business perspective.

Benefits and costs to whom?

As discussed in Chapter 1, a distinguishing feature of public sector agencies is that they are responsible for ensuring the delivery not only of some private value to individual clients, but also of *public* value, which is 'consumed' jointly by the collective citizenry (Alford 2002). By contrast, private firms only deliver private value to individual customers, with whom they have direct, voluntary economic exchanges. Moreover, the public sector equivalents of those customers – the individuals whom the agency encounters at its 'business end' (Moore 1995) – themselves differ from the private customer ideal-type in varying ways, depending on whether they are beneficiaries or obligatees.

In this context, members of the public have multiple roles: they are both citizens and clients, and they are also one or more different types of client. Their interests in one role may or may not be convergent with those in another. For example, a job search programme recipient would prefer a service that was locally available, of high quality and well-resourced, whereas a citizen might (but not necessarily) take the view that the programme should be more economical and of reasonable but not exceptional quality. A victim of crime might have a different view from a citizen as to how much due process should be upheld, and retribution applied forcefully, in the pursuit and arrest of offenders. Here the citizen is similar to the one portrayed by Rawls as situated behind a 'veil of ignorance', wherein they 'do not know how the various alternatives will affect their own particular case and they are obliged to evaluate principles solely on the basis of general considerations' (1972: 136–7). When a public agency involves an external party, the resultant value may either benefit both citizens and clients, or benefit one without affecting the other, or benefit one at the expense of the other. Similarly, costs may be incurred variously by the different parties. What follows will take account of the distribution of benefits and costs derived from externalization.

Different types of benefits and costs

Usually when we consider the pluses and minuses of engaging external providers, we tend to think only of the service itself and how much it costs. But this fails to encompass the totality of the benefits and costs of externalization. There are two other types that should also be considered.

First, externalized services do not just magically happen by themselves. The very fact that one party is seeking to get the other to do something (or that they are trying to get each other to do something) means there is necessarily some kind of relationship between the two. At the very least, one party must communicate to the other in advance what they want, or signal whether they are happy with it once it is provided. This *relationship* has costs and benefits for both parties, which we will call relationship costs and benefits – for example, the cost of ensuring that providers perform well, or the sense of social connection accompanying a good working relationship.

Similarly, the externalization of a service, even if it improves value for money for that particular activity, may affect for better or worse the organization's standing in its environment, or its overall capabilities. These are *strategic* benefits and costs: ones where the organization's longer-term positioning and competencies are altered by the short-term use of an external provider.

This chapter will consider these three categories – service, relationship and strategic benefits and costs – in turn.

Service benefits and costs from externalization

Service benefits, including service cost-savings, are the increases in the net value provided through the service. This can take the form of either reduced cost, or increased value, or some combination of the two.

Reduced cost

The most commonly mentioned benefit of externalization, especially of contracting out, is that it reduces costs. Up to the 1990s, numerous studies pointed to the cost advantage of private contractors, so much so that something of a consensus view among these analysts was that private contractors were on average between 10 per cent and 30 per cent cheaper than public providers (Millward 1986; Savas 1987; Domberger and Rimmer 1994; Domberger 1998: 40). This was attributed variously to the reduction of the organizational slack endemic in the public sector (Niskanen 1971; Busch and Gustafsson 2002); the impact of competition as a spur to greater productivity (Prager 1994); or the avoidance of the restrictive rules and work practices besetting public service agencies (Domberger 1998). However, the empirical data are contested. In a meta-study of the empirical literature on this question, Hodge (2000) found that 'there was a wide variety of findings, from those reporting no savings from contracting out, to those reporting substantial savings'.

Those studies finding substantial savings tended to focus on particular types of services, namely garbage contracting, cleaning and maintenance services for local government. For other types of services, cost impacts varied from modest savings (8 per cent) to substantial cost increases (24 per cent) (Hodge 2000: 155–6). Boyne (1998) surveyed empirical studies in local service contracting, and also found mixed results. Only half of the studies showed evidence of contracting out leading to higher efficiency, and many of them were methodologically flawed (see also Quiggin 1994; and Brudney *et al.* 2005).

Thus, the impact of contracting out varies, apparently according to the type of service. This lends weight to the argument that the benefits of externalization may be dependent on the nature of the service and the context in which it is delivered.

One argument put forward by lay critics of outsourcing is that private for-profit firms necessarily cost more than public sector organizations because they seek to make a profit, which is included in the purchase price. Logically this is true, but it overlooks the fact that, assuming a fair and rigorous contracting process, private providers can only win the contract – and therefore make a profit – if they submit the lowest bid, or offer the best value for money. The net effect should be that the purchase price is reduced by outsourcing. Of course, not all contracting processes are fair and rigorous, and in such situations private providers are likely to extract excessive profits – as will be discussed in Chapter 4.

Increased value

What constitutes increased value is a complex question. It can comprise, for example, improved effectiveness or enhanced quality, by comparison with that achieved by the government organization. Ultimately, the field of possible increases in value is limitless, since what is valuable is context-dependent and the scope for imagining better service-delivery is vast. What follows is an indicative picture of this field.

- *Effectiveness* is a term much misused. In government, it is typically defined as the extent to which outputs contribute to the achievement of outcomes sought by the organization. Outputs are the services emanating from a particular programme or production process, whereas outcomes are the impacts of those services on social or natural conditions. For example, in education, outputs might be the number of students graduating from a primary school, outcomes would be the improvement in literacy and numeracy in the population, and effectiveness would be the extent to which the former contributed to the latter. External providers, or partnerships with them, can increase effectiveness to the extent that they can deliver services better than government agencies acting alone.
- *Efficiency* is popularly used in various ways, which tend to obscure its difference from other terms. But strictly speaking, it is the ratio of inputs, such as money, labour or raw materials, to outputs. Thus, improved efficiency can entail greater output for a given level of inputs, or less input for a given level of output, or both. Where it involves increased output per unit of input, it can properly be regarded as increasing value. On the other hand, where efficiency reduces the inputs required per unit of output, it can be regarded as lowering costs, as discussed above.
- *Equity* is a multifaceted concept. Stone (2002) explains how equity in one dimension usually means inequity in some other dimension. One broad distinction commonly drawn is that between distributional equity (that is, fairness in outcomes) and procedural equity (that is, fairness in process). Thus, the Scandinavian welfare states, for example, have been very prominent historically in advancing distributional equity (in addition to procedural equity), by establishing systems to facilitate more equitable enjoyment of various services such as education, health services, transport, and so on. By contrast, the United States places less emphasis on distributional equity but a strong emphasis on procedural fairness, especially through its judicial system.
- *Quality*. Thus far, the increased value we have explored has been largely in the realm of public value, 'consumed' collectively by the citizenry, or by a government agency acting on behalf of the

citizenry. But in the course of enabling the creation of public value, government organizations can also create private value, which is consumed individually by clients.

One commonly used term in the field of services management encapsulating the value to clients is 'quality'. This originally emerged in manufacturing, with approaches such as quality assurance and total quality management (TQM). Later approaches advocated starting with customers' needs and wants, and comparing service-delivery against them. As Lewis and Booms (1990: 1) put it:

> Service quality is a measure of how well the service level delivered matches customer expectations. Delivering quality service means conforming to customer expectations on a consistent basis.

Further work focused on identifying the elements of service quality – that is, what exactly was important to customers (see Gaster and Squires 2003). One example is a widely cited article by Parasuraman *et al.* (1985), which identified ten key determinants of service quality as perceived by customers, which they found to be relevant across all types of service (see Table 2.1).

To the extent that involving external providers enables greater attention to one or more of these quality factors, then it can be said to enhance private value – for example, a private parcel service might be able to offer faster delivery than a government postal service.

However, as explained previously, not all clients of public services are the same as private sector customers, and to that extent the notion of quality needs to be amended. To the extent that they are beneficiaries or obligatees, from each of whom the agency is seeking to elicit behaviours such as co-production or compliance, *fairness* is a key aspect of quality (Gaster and Squires 2003). For instance, beneficiaries' perceptions of the fairness of the service will be affected by how much they feel they receive the right level of service, and not feel they are cheated out of something to which they are entitled. Obligatees' perceptions of the fairness of the service will be affected by whether they feel comparable obligatees are being similarly compelled to comply – that is, that they are not 'suckers' who are receiving harsher treatment than their comparators. Both kinds of clients' perceptions of fairness will also be

TABLE 2.1 *One model of the determinants of service quality*

Reliability: consistency of performance and dependability.

Responsiveness: willingness or readiness of employees to provide service (includes timeliness).

Competence: possession of the required skills and knowledge to perform the service.

Access: approachability and ease of contact.

Courtesy: politeness, respect, consideration and friendliness of contact personnel.

Communication: keeping customers informed in language they can understand and listening to them.

Credibility: trustworthiness, believability, honesty.

Security: freedom from danger, risk or doubt.

Understanding/knowing the customer: making the effort to understand the customer's needs.

Tangibles: physical evidence of the service, such as physical facilities, appearance of personnel, tools or equipment, physical representations of the service, other customers in the service facility.

Source: Adapted from Parasuraman *et al.* (1985: 47).

affected by the extent to which they feel they are being treated with respect and consideration.

This relates to a further development of the notion of service quality by Grönroos (1990), who identifies two dimensions, namely, technical quality (referring to the outcome of the buyer–seller interaction – that is, what the customer receives) and functional quality (referring to the process that is, how they receive it) (1990: 37–8). Thus, technical quality for an airline passenger is arriving at the correct destination on time with luggage intact, whilst functional quality is the helpfulness of the cabin service crew or the quality of the food on board.

In a public sector context, applying procedural fairness can be seen as enhancing functional quality – in other words, it concerns *how* clients are treated more than *what* they receive. This is not just a matter of the agency broadcasting catchy advertisements or of its staff saying 'good morning' nicely when they answer phones.

Key elements include: responsiveness and speed of service; information; simplicity; respect and empathy; accessibility; and perceived fairness. These are all features which reduce the costs, tangible or intangible, of the encounter to the client. This is especially important in a regulatory agency, which has little room to move in respect of technical quality. The agency still has to require an outcome in which the regulatee complies with legal obligations, but it may be that this compliance can be prompted by enhanced functional quality in addition to the application of coercion (Alford and Speed 2006).

The effect of externalization on service quality

As with cost savings, the evidence on whether externalization leads to increased value is contested. Noting that critics of contracting out often argue that cost savings are usually at the expense of service quality, Domberger (1998) cited one study of cleaning services which found that competitively tendered services outperformed non-tendered services substantially on cost and modestly on quality. However, Hodge's study cited above found that 'there is no discernible relationship one way or the other' between contracting out and service quality (2000: 156). Again, this indicates that the value gains from outsourcing are variable.

On the other hand, more collaborative forms of externalization may have quality advantages (Podolny and Page 1998). Uzzi (1997) compared long-term collaborative relations with sub-contractors to more arms-length relations, and found that the former facilitated high-quality production by enabling better communication on quality issues.

How does externalization create value?

A variety of mechanisms explains the gains in value or cost savings from using external providers. Some are more related to the capabilities of the *external provider* (Prager 1994; Domberger 1998), whereas others derive more from the capacities of the *partnership*, that is, of the government agency and the external provider acting together (Bardach 1998: 50–1) (see Table 2.2).

Value gains from externalization can be due to any of six sets of factors. The first is *economies of scale*: the provider is able to operate at a scale at which it can spread various fixed and

TABLE 2.2   *Sources of value deriving from externalization*

	Applicable to outsourcing	Applicable to partnership
Economies of scale	√√	√
Economies of scope • unused/under-utilized capacity • by-products • multiple functions • sequencing	√√	√
Specialization • experience curve • knowledge of constituency/ community • legitimacy	√√	√
Flexibility	√√	√
Complementarity • interdependence • exchange		√√
Innovation and learning	√	√√

overhead costs across a larger production volume. One commonly cited example is in the field of garbage collection, which is typically contracted out to private contractors by local municipal councils (Busch and Gustafsson 2002). Often these councils operate at sub-optimal scale, and the contractors are able to offer service at lower unit cost by reaping economies of scale from operating across several adjacent municipalities (Savas 1977; Domberger 1998).

A second is *economies of scope* – the fact that a productive resource can be used for more than one purpose or in more than one way. This has several variants. One is that a government agency may be able to tap *unused or under-utilized capacity* available from an external provider. A common case is where school buildings and facilities, which are only used for classes for part of the day and part of the year, are utilized outside school hours for such activities as after-school care, adult education or as meeting spaces.

Similarly, even where external providers do not have spare capacity, they may be able to offer value in the form of *by-products* of their existing production process or, more elaborately, they may have a production process which can be used for *multiple functions*. For example, in many countries, the child protection agency enlists doctors or school teachers, *inter alia*, in notifying it of suspected cases of child abuse. The doctors and teachers perform this role as part of their jobs of providing medical services or education respectively. Postal service outlets in many countries perform this role for a variety of other agencies handling transactions for electricity, gas and water utilities, and accepting passport applications.

A particular economy of scope is *sequencing*, in which the same client is subject to the activities of each partner, or the same production process is used by each partner, at different times in an order that is beneficial to the client. In Wisconsin, a network of employment, training education and support agencies coordinates services for individual job-seekers, starting with assessment and then placing clients on a four-tier ladder of employment and training options (Corbett 1996).

A third source of value from externalization is *specialization* by the provider, which facilitates the development of skills, technology, market awareness and other capacities enabling it to deliver a better service than the commissioning organization. By focusing on particular services, a contractor can devote more targeted effort to continuous improvement of its service offering, and to learning and experimentation about ways of making the service better. For instance, many government agencies outsource the cleaning of their offices to private cleaning contractors, who have developed expertise in logistics, staff training and technology over time.[1]

Other gains from specialization reside in characteristics of provider organizations, especially in the non-profit sector. One is that an organization may have more *knowledge of a particular constituency or community* in which it is embedded – its issues, desires, fears and political intricacies. Another is that it may have more *legitimacy* in that community, and therefore be able to perform its work with less resistance or indifference from its members, which could be significant if it needs their cooperation.[2] These specialized attributes are virtually impossible for the government organization itself to acquire, because of its structural position (Van Slyke 2002).

Related to specialization is that external providers can have greater *flexibility*, that is, more ability to adjust the scale and scope of production more quickly and/or at less cost. This is especially the case where the public sector agency is able to call on a network of small organizations via contracts, which it can take on or shed as conditions require. This happens in diverse areas, from road maintenance to employment programmes.[3]

It is also claimed by some outsourcing advocates that private businesses are inherently more flexible than public sector agencies, because they are not subject to the same red tape, hierarchical structures and inflexible employment conditions. This argument is overstated to a degree, tending to rely on an outdated stereotype. Three decades of New Public Management have streamlined many public agencies, required them to focus on outputs, and overhauled their employment arrangements – often, incidentally, at the expense of public servants' job conditions and security (Quiggin 1994; Walsh and O'Flynn 2000). The stereotype may have rung true in the past, but is less valid today. And to the extent that public sector structures are still subject to some regulation and centralized control, it is because citizens continue to have expectations that public monies will be spent and public jobs filled with efficiency and probity.

Other factors enabling value gains from externalization tend to be more applicable to the partnership than just the external provider. An important form of this is *complementarity*, in which each partner is able to perform only part of the requisite task but together they can perform all of it and thereby contribute to the provision of a full, effective service. For instance, many urban public transport systems comprising multiple transport modes (for example, subway, bus, surface rail, tram, and so on) can provide a more effective service to the commuter if they coordinate timetables or ticketing systems, which then enable passengers a more seamless transition from one mode to another.

A deeper form of complementarity is *interdependence*, in which each partner's work not only complements but also actually depends on the other's, to the extent that they cannot do their own work without it.[4] Britain's national rail system requires cooperation between the government organization that controls and maintains rail tracks (Network Rail, a hybrid organization closely subject to the Office of Rail Regulation) and the various private operators of intercity and rural train services – cooperation that has been problematic, with dramatic consequences (Flynn 2007: 261).

This interdependence can entail a degree of *exchange*, in which partners each contribute some activity to a joint process, but receive from the process more than they lose. For instance, in wetlands conservation partnerships, common in the US, government agencies rely on landholders, farmers, developers and other private actors refraining from encroaching on wetlands areas and conserving areas already under their ownership, in return for financial incentives and technical assistance.[5]

Finally, a partnership can generate more *innovation*, basically because 'multiple heads are better than one'. Where partners are engaged in more frequent interactions with each other, and trust each other sufficiently to venture 'left field' ideas, they are more likely to cross-fertilize and come up with new ideas for doing things better, and to share those ideas (Lundvall 1993: 59–60; Powell *et al.* 1996). An interesting example is a series of collaborations between government and non-government organizations in Palestine, aimed at improving child nutrition, which led to the development and diffusion of new policies and practices, stemming from high levels of interaction among the parties (Hardy *et al.* 2003).

Similarly, partnerships can foster *learning*, in which each partner imparts to and imbibes from the others greater knowledge and understanding relevant to the service and its delivery, often in a complementary fashion – something they would do less if acting on their own (Alter and Hage 1993; Podolny and Page 1998; Sullivan and Skelcher 2002).

Relationship costs and benefits

So far we have been considering how externalization affects whether the service itself is carried out better or cheaper. But by definition, externalization involves at least two parties, and therefore a relationship between them. This relationship is structured by the fact that the parties must in some way coordinate their actions with each other, but they have at least some differing interests. Getting them to act consistently with the requirements of the relationship, therefore, calls for various 'relationship management' tasks, which have costs attached to them (Kettl 1993; Kavanagh and Parker 1999; Hefetz and Warner 2004). In contracting, these costs are known as 'transaction costs' (Williamson 1981;

Brown and Potoski 2003), but here we use a broader term to
encompass not only transactional dealings but also those occurring
in more collaborative arrangements (White 2005). Each party
seeks to induce the other(s) to behave in ways that are consistent with its interests in the relationship. Doing so calls for at
least some time and effort, which has a cost, either monetary or
psychic. This has been the radical insight of an important strand
of economic thought, variously termed transaction-cost analysis,
institutional economics and organizational economics (Coase 1937,
1960; Williamson 1975, 1985; Jensen and Meckling 1976). Its
essential insight has been that managing the relationship between
service-providers and recipients is not without costs, which must
be factored into judgements about whether to externalize.

On the other hand, if relationships can have costs, they can also
have benefits, in the sense that the relationship itself may be of value
to the parties. Although these are generally not as significant as
relationship costs, they are also considered here.

Relationship costs

Relationship costs are the costs of managing the relationship, in
particular of ensuring that the external party acts in such a way
that the required service is provided. They stem from four types of
relationship management tasks.

The first is *defining the service* – that is, determining what is to
be produced. This task can vary in three inter-related ways. Firstly,
there is the question of who is to define the service. As discussed
in Chapter 1, the service can be specified either by the government agency alone, or by the government agency in deliberation
or negotiation with the external provider about the nature of the
service to be provided. Second, the service can either be specified
all in advance, or be determined in detail along the way, as new
circumstances arise. In classical contracting, the former approach
incurs costs in anticipating actual future requirements in a context
of uncertainty, whereas the latter incurs costs arising from providers
taking advantage of purchasers' vulnerability in mid-production
(Hendry 2002). On the other hand, in collaborative partnerships,
it can take time and effort to agree on service requirements in
advance – although the presence of trust can mitigate opportunism
once the service is in progress. Third, it can either be determined

with detailed specificity – for example, 'the provision of ten community social events of such and such a type for a certain number of people in a particular neighbourhood at $x per head' – or in broad terms – for example, an increase in 'neighbourliness' in a community.

Typically, in classical contracting the service is at least initially specified by the government agency alone (although it may be subject to negotiation), where the specification occurs in advance, and it is tightly defined, with an effort to anticipate potential eventualities in the contract, and measures of performance spelt out, usually in output terms (Donahue 1989; Prager 1994; Kavanagh and Parker 1999). By contrast, a relational contract is likely to be jointly determined by the government agency and the external party, and may be framed in broad terms with details being worked out as circumstances arise.

The second task is *determining who is to produce the service.* How this is done usually depends on how the relationship came into being. At one extreme, the government agency might seek to find and appoint the best available provider through a process of competitive tendering (Cohen and Eimicke 2008). Here the government organization is the initiator of the relationship, to which the provider responds. At the other extreme, a provider may approach a government agency and, hopefully through a process involving probity and due diligence, the government organization agrees to enter into some sort of relationship with the provider. This is not uncommon with major development projects in urban locations. In between these extremes, the parties may enter a relationship because they each have some stake in a situation calling for a partnership of some kind. In these cases, the external parties are to some degree self-nominating.

The third task is *ascertaining whether the service has been provided.* In its most elaborate form, associated with classical contracting, this entails the government agency comparing the performance of the provider against pre-set targets established as part of a performance monitoring regime (Choi 1999; Brown and Potoski 2003). An alternative method might be for the parties to review the progress of the service periodically and exercise judgement about how well it is performing. Another approach might entail the parties simply being happy that no major problems have emerged in the provision of the service, and continuing the relationship on that basis.

The final task is *inducing good performance by the provider*. In classical contracting, the provider is subject to incentives for good performance and sanctions for poor performance. The sanctions can take the form either of financial penalties calibrated to performance measures, or of the ultimate punishment of losing the contract when it comes up for renewal. But other approaches encourage the provider or partner to act consistently with what is required for different reasons. These include the building of trust and commitment in the relationship, through ongoing reciprocal behaviour. Here it is not so much a matter of paying or compelling someone to do something they would not otherwise do, but rather of fostering an active desire to do what is required, or at least a degree of comfort in doing so. To some extent this is about the parties having shared purposes or values, but it is also possible when they have different but complementary purposes.

Whichever way they are performed, these tasks each have costs attached to them, which must be weighed against the benefits from involving an external provider. In the classical contracting model, there are costs in several of its characteristic features, as will be detailed in Chapter 4. First, there are costs in specifying services in output terms – in anticipating uncertainty, mitigating information-symmetry, and disentangling the effects of interdependency (Donahue 1989; Prager 1994; Hendry 2002). Second, there are costs in choosing the best provider through competitive tendering – not only in the tender process but in ensuring that a sufficiently competitive market is available in the first place. Third, there are costs in monitoring performance, such as inspection or data-collection, especially in situations of information asymmetry (Romzek and Johnson 2005). Fourth, there can be costs in applying carrots and sticks to ensure good performance incentives, especially if the ultimate sanction of contract non-renewal is wielded, thereby entailing switching costs.

On the other hand, a relationship based on collaboration also has its costs (Kirkpatrick 1999; White 2005; O'Flynn 2008), as will be discussed in Chapter 5. The initial task of deciding what is to be done can necessitate lengthy deliberation tying up multiple stakeholders (Huxham and Vangen 2005). The process of entering into a partnership may not necessarily have involved the most competent actors being involved. And the relationship itself, while it might engender good performance by the partners, is also vulnerable to dysfunction of various types (Huxham and Vangen 2004;

White 2005). By and large, collaborative partnerships tend to be more costly than classical contracts in respect of defining what is to be done and who is to do it, but then require less effort and cost in ascertaining whether it has been done and in inducing good performance.

Relationship benefits

Relationship benefits are positive factors inherent in the relationship between the government organization and the provider(s). They differ according to whether the mode of coordination is contractual or collaborative.

Contractual relationships can be beneficial in that they clarify the roles of the respective parties. A well-specified contract can give certainty and understanding to both the purchaser and the provider about what is expected of them. This benefit is, of course, subject to the caveats already discussed about the difficulties of precisely specifying contractual obligations.

Collaborative relationships, while not necessarily offering the same degree of specificity as contractual ones, offer a different type of benefit to the parties involved – namely, social connection. To the extent that people value the esteem of others and a sense of belonging, then they may value a collaborative relationship not only for its service and organizational benefits but also for its resonance with their solidary and affiliative motivations (see Chapter 3). Of course, similar benefits can derive from in-house production relationships, but to the extent that they are conducted on hierarchical lines, they may not foster the sense of voluntary cooperation that underpins collaboration.

Strategic benefits and costs of externalization

Strategic benefits and costs are those affecting the government agency's strategic positioning within its environment or its organizational capabilities. Again, the cost side of the externalization ledger is generally more significant here.

Strategic costs

Strategic costs are incurred where externalization leads to the loss of core competencies or adversely affects the public standing of the organization to the extent that the long-term viability of its mission is compromised.

In the private sector, the focus on core competence has tended to legitimize the outsourcing of various functions. The term itself emerged in 1990, when Prahalad and Hamel defined core competence as 'the collective learning in the organisation, especially how to co-ordinate diverse production skills and integrate multiple streams of technology' (1990: 82; but see also the notion of 'distinctive competence', in Selznick 1957). It entered into thinking about outsourcing when Quinn and Hilmer (1994: 43) urged companies to identify and secure core competencies, 'where it can achieve definable pre-eminence and provide unique value for customers', and 'strategically outsource other activities – including many traditionally considered integral to any company' (see also Insinga and Werle 2000).

In the public sector, however, what constitutes 'core' competence is more complicated. In the broad, we can define core competencies as the skills, knowledge and attributes without which the public sector cannot continue to do the things that it is constitutionally, legislatively and/or democratically mandated to do. This means that at the very least, the public sector should not externalize its role as 'principal' (see Jensen and Meckling 1976) – namely, its capacity to define what is to be done, choose who is to do it and ensure that it is done, consistent with its democratic obligations. Boston (1994), for instance, argues against the contracting out of policy advice on this and other grounds.

But beyond the steering role, the public sector has distinctive aspects which can in some circumstances make externalization problematic. One is that *most public sector organizations were originally created to perform functions that the private sector cannot or will not perform.* Consider, for instance, meteorological bureaux, fire brigades, psychiatric institutions, national park services, or naval fleets. Over time, these organizations have developed unique knowledge, experience, capabilities and systems, which are crucial to the successful performance of those functions and which no-one else has in full measure. It is true that private organizations have sometimes undertaken activities in these domains. But they have tended to be in niche functions rather than overall ones. Even where private organizations have taken on whole roles, they have had mixed success in them (the example of privatized railways in the UK comes to mind). Thus, to externalize those functions would be to lose the distinctive competencies they have called forth. Once lost, it would take a lot of time and resources, and a period of sub-optimal performance, to recover them should the shortcomings of the private alternative become apparent.

A second distinctive feature of the public sector is the use of *public power*. It acts on behalf of a state which has a monopoly on the use of legitimate force to compel citizens to comply with public purposes (Weber 1966: 154). This power is indivisible: it is axiomatic that there cannot be competing public powers in the same jurisdiction. More importantly for the present discussion, it is inalienable for all significant functions. To hand the power of the state to private actors is to complicate the accountabilities that surround the exercise of that power (Mulgan 1997). It is true that the state can and does empower private entities to exercise legal authority on its behalf – for example, local motor mechanics conducting vehicle roadworthiness checks, or private school teachers acting *in loco parentis*, or professional bodies overseeing occupational licensing. But these tend either to involve less problematic applications of public power, or to have their usage of that power subject to state monitoring. Where the level of coercion is greater, it is more problematic to externalize the activity. An important example in recent years is the privatization of prisons. While there might be a role for private prison operators in low-security facilities (where the primary service is the provision of accommodation, food and rehabilitative programmes), for higher-security prisons the picture is different (Moyle 1994). Donahue (1989: 176) points to the important rule-making and enforcing role of prison operators:

> The chief of one private detention center... said, 'I review every disciplinary action. I'm the Supreme Court.' This should make us nervous. Will profit-seeking prisons multiply rules during slow periods in order to ensure enough infractions to deny parole to existing inmates until new convicts come to fill the cells? Not necessarily, perhaps not even probably, but it could happen. It is even conceivable that an unscrupulous corrections entrepreneur would perversely rig parole recommendations to release prisoners who are troublesome, dangerous, sickly, or otherwise expensive to detain, while holding onto the more profitable inmates... Public prison officials are at least free of any direct financial temptation to manipulate the prison population.

A third feature relevant to many government organizations is *complexity*, specifically: the inter-dependence between policy making and service delivery; the inter-dependence between parallel programmes or even between ones across different agencies; and the interdependence between agency programmes and external volunteer contributors. This is not only a transactions cost issue, as discussed above, but also a core competence issue. Simply put, where one function is interdependent with another, and the latter is a core competence, then externalization of the former will adversely affect the latter. Thus, a core policy unit, which plays a key steering role, may depend on information from a service delivery role about the changing needs of clients. If the service delivery unit were to be externalized, it would be distanced from the policy unit and the flow of feedback about changing client needs would be reduced. This problem can be especially significant in regulatory roles, where enforcers continuously uncover ways in which regulatees find and exploit loopholes and feed them back to regulatory policy makers and legislators.

Another interdependency is that between the organization and external *volunteers*. An important reason volunteers contribute to organizational purposes is an identification with the mission and values represented by the organization. If the activity is externalized to an organization that represents a different mission, they may be less inclined to volunteer. For instance, if a Meals on Wheels service, hitherto managed by local government, were to be contracted to a private for-profit company, the volunteers who help with day-to-day distribution would be less inclined to assist, since they would see it as contributing to company profits rather than a worthy public purpose.

A final distinctive feature of the public sector is its role as repository and custodian of *values* underpinning an orientation to the public interest. The 'public service orientation', as Clarke and Stewart (1986) called it, is sometimes unfairly seen in terms of stereotypes such as risk-aversion, time-serving, and shirking. But another face of the public service orientation is commitment to public purposes and to values such as probity and fairness. The set of capabilities in public services includes: an awareness of how the broader public interest might be affected by a particular measure; a willingness to 'go the extra mile' for a worthwhile purpose; and an understanding of what is proper behaviour in functions such as public expenditure, recruitment, and procurement. These values and beliefs develop and are infused over time, forming part of orga-nizational memory and culture. To the extent that externalization of functions also divests the organization of the people and systems that maintain these values, a core competence is lost.

The other potential strategic cost of externalization is the *risk of losing public trust or stakeholder support* if the external provider has a poor reputation in one respect or another. This may derive from the fact that the external provider is revealed to have per-formed poorly in a previous contract somewhere else. More seri-ously, it may be that the contractor is seen as undesirable. This has been an issue when governments in the United States and Australia have awarded grants or contracts to religiously based agencies to provide family planning advice, which pro-choice organizations have accused of providing restricted advice to clients. (Conversely, some religious lobby groups have criticized the awarding of such contracts to pro-choice organizations.) As will be discussed in the next section, it also arose as a problem when the Bush adminis-tration handed multibillion-dollar contracts to companies such as Blackwater, to supply armed personnel in Iraq. A series of inci-dents in which Blackwater applied what media and Congressional observers saw as undue or unauthorized force against Iraqi civilians has led to a situation where any government that sought to engage the company would find itself embroiled in controversy (Scahill 2007). In these instances, the issue is not only the ability of the external party to provide the agreed services efficiently but rather a concern that it may distort the definition of services in a way that incurs political opprobrium.

Like relationship costs, these strategic costs – both those to do with core competence and those to do with political standing – will vary according to circumstance. But they can sometimes constitute compelling reasons not to externalize an activity, or to externalize in a particular way such as partnering.

Strategic benefits

One widely cited benefit of externalization is its impact on the organization's *strategic focus*. This is most commonly associated with the notion, inspired by the public choice perspective, of sep-arating purchasing from providing, advocated in Osborne and Gaebler's book *Reinventing Government* (1992) and exemplified in the UK's Next Steps initiative (Jenkins *et al.* 1988) and the National

Performance Review in the US (Gore 1993). This was seen as enabling government organizations to focus on the big picture, and leave operational detail to external providers (Osborne and Gaebler 1992). Moreover, the process of deciding whether to externalize and engaging a provider could lead an organization to more sharply define its purposes, identify opportunities for process improvement, and foster a shared internal understanding of its external context (Quinn and Hilmer 1994; see also Hallam 1995). However, this opportunity is not confined to a contractualist approach. An organization contemplating a partnership with another entity might clarify its own purposes just as well, and understand better its context and operations through such a process.

There may also be *political benefits* in externalization, at least from engaging in its more collaborative forms. A government organization may enhance its standing among key stakeholders if it is seen to have good working relations with highly regarded partners (Baum and Oliver 1992; Podolny and Page 1998). In 1999, the Australian government introduced a new Goods and Services Tax, which was contentious in part because it was feared that businesses would use it as a pretext to pad their prices. In response, the government empowered the Australian Competition and Consumer Commission, which was highly regarded for its strong role in cracking down on unfair trading, to police GST increases (Padula 2004). Moreover, if a government organization is part of an influential network, it may derive power in dealings with other external entities, especially if the network adopts a protective attitude to its constituent groups (Hardy *et al.* 2003).

Military contracting revisited

Let us apply this framework to the case of private military contracting with which this chapter started. It shows what a difference it makes to look at *all* the benefits and costs when considering whether to externalize.

First, even for service benefits and costs, the success of private military contracting in Iraq and Afghanistan has proven to be mixed at best. On the plus side, it had the key benefit of flexibility: it enabled the military to rapidly adjust troop strengths, by providing 'surge' capacity. Additional military forces could be deployed quickly, and just as quickly they could be de-mobilized, unencumbered by political and bureaucratic constraints on flexibility. Private security companies could also hire people with specialist skills, such as language or area knowledge.

But on the minus side, private security contractors were on average more costly than governmental military forces. The high level of turmoil in Iraq and Afghanistan boosted demand for security personnel, while at the same time deterring some potential contractors and therefore reducing their supply. The result was a seller's market: for instance, contract personnel in Colombia were being offered three times their salary to move to Iraq. A further service shortcoming was that, in the estimate of the armed forces on the ground, contractors were less reliable, failing to show up in some critical situations.

Thus, if we confine ourselves solely to *service* benefits and costs, private military contracting in Iraq and Afghanistan seemed a debatable if not entirely absurd proposition. To a degree, the cost issue was submerged, at least initially, in the widespread community view after the events of 11 September that no price was too great to pay to tackle what had taken root in the public mind as the terrorist threat. As the war continued, however, its burgeoning cost began to discomfit citizens and politicians.

But there were several other serious problems with the use of private military contractors, which complicated the balance of benefits and costs. Two of them seemed to be about the quality of the service provided by the private contractors, but on closer examination they turned out to be significant for relationship costs and benefits. One was that private security personnel failed to share information and adjust their actions to unfolding military requirements. The result was frequent episodes of 'friendly fire', where troops shot at security contractors whose identity or mission they did not know. The other problem was even more disturbing: in protecting senior officials as they moved from one place to another, the private contractors behaved in a manner (such as pointing weapons at Iraqi civilians, or driving at very high speeds or without stopping at intersections) that alienated the local citizens with whom the military were trying to build good relationships, in the hope of detaching them from affinity with the insurgents. The contractors' style was directly undermining the coalition's stated strategy for winning the war.

In both cases, although the effects were operational, the cause was a relationship management issue. Basically, the private military personnel were working purely to what was specified in their contracts, pursuing their own narrowly defined mission, such as VIP protection. This meant they were ignoring the need to collaborate with other coalition forces and civilian sympathizers. This problem could have been addressed by either of two changes to the relationship – both of them entailing considerable costs. One would have been to rewrite the contracts to require the private security firms to collaborate better with the official military, as well as to act more carefully in dealings with civilians. But it would have been challenging to specify what kind of behaviours constituted collaboration, and likely entailed extensive and time-consuming negotiation, with attendant costs in time and effort. Moreover, the private contractors – who were palpably concerned about their profits – would have sought additional remuneration to compensate them for the extra obligations in the revised contract.

The alternative solution would have been to reconfigure the relationship as a collaborative one, with the public and private military personnel encouraged and enabled to form cooperative working relationships. Again, even assuming it was feasible, this solution would have entailed costs – of such things as joint training or deliberative processes, and of structural reorganizations to accommodate the collaboration. More seriously, it could have generated further problems, as public and private soldiers began to compare salaries and equipment, and as issues of operational authority began to emerge.

There was also a more extensive relationship management issue: the widespread incidence of waste, fraud and abuse. The Congressional Commission's 2011 report estimated that, of $177 billion spent on contracted military services in Iraq and Afghanistan since they were first invaded last decade, as much as $33 billion (and probably more) had been lost to waste, fraud and abuse. The Commission recommended an extensive series of measures to combat this mis-spending, including measuring officials' efforts to manage contractors, integrating contracting into routine operations, establishing contracting directorates in the office of the Joint Chiefs, and so on, for dozens of further recommendations. Needless to say, these requirements would take time and money, adding to the relationship costs.

Finally, there were both benefits and costs in strategic terms. The main benefit was that it was politically less problematic to send abroad private contractors, who work for profit, than to put enlisted military personnel in harm's way (Avant 2007). This became increasingly attractive as the war continued and the body count began to mount.

On the other hand, there was increasing concern about the use of mercenaries in 'mission-critical' roles. As incidents where mercenaries accidentally or in certain cases deliberately killed or injured civilians in sometimes questionable circumstances increased in frequency, professional military officers were beginning to worry about deploying personnel with the capacity to use lethal force without the appropriate accountabilities. In effect, this was a misuse of what should have been seen as a core competence of the military itself.

In the end, this began to incur another strategic cost: it began to be seen as reputationally harmful to be associated with certain private providers, of which Blackwater was probably the most notorious example (Scahill 2007). It was therefore no surprise that by the end of the decade, there was widespread questioning of the privatization of military force, as illustrated by the establishment of the Congressional Commission on Wartime Contracting.

Table 2.3 sets out the different kinds of costs and benefits, together with examples from the military contracting case.

Conclusion

The original wave of privatization that swept across the world from the 1980s was mainly founded on ideology. It was taken as given that private firms could outperform government organizations in delivering services. However, as public managers grappled with the realities of implementing these reforms, they found a less black-and-white picture: externalization seemed to work well in some circumstances, but not in others. Whether a government organization should externalize an activity, and how, is dependent on contextual circumstances – specifically, on whether the gains from doing so outweigh the costs. Assessing these benefits and costs is not just a matter of comparing the price of in-house delivery with that of external provision. Nor is it enough to also take into account the service gains, in effectiveness, equity or quality – even if these factors can be easily calculated, which is often not the case.

This chapter has canvassed in detail the sources of gains in service or cost-saving that underpin the potential benefits of externalization. But it has also explored two other factors that are important to consider. One is the benefits and costs of the *relationship*

TABLE 2.3 *Benefits and costs of externalization*

Type	Benefits		Costs	
	Generic	*Military contracting examples*	*Generic*	*Military contracting examples*
Service	Effectiveness Efficiency Equity Quality	Flexibility/surge capacity Specialist skills	Purchase price	High cost of personnel compared with government military Contractors less reliable
Relationship	Clarification of the relationship Solidary benefits	—	Costs of defining the service Costs of choosing the provider Costs of ascertaining if service has been provided Costs of inducing good performance by the provider(s)	Specific contracts leading to: • lack of coordination resulting in 'friendly fire' • contractors alienating locals Waste, fraud and abuse arising from: • poor specification and monitoring • lack of competition

TABLE 2.3 (Continued)

| Type | Benefits | | Costs | |
	Generic	Military contracting examples	Generic	Military contracting examples
Strategic/ organizational	Crystallizing strategic focus Political benefits Risk allocation	Politically more acceptable to send contractors to war	Loss of core competencies (unique capabilities, knowledge re public power, interdependency, values) Political standing	Using mercenaries in 'mission-critical' roles Reputational harm from association with wayward contractors

with the external provider. There are some potential benefits of working with and through others, such as solidarity rewards, but realistically, the costs are more significant, for the simple reason that the parties have different interests, and mechanisms need to be put in place to ensure that they act in ways consistent with each other's requirements. These mechanisms have costs which can be significant. More broadly, externalization can affect the *strategic position* of a government agency, its ongoing capability to perform its mission, and its political standing.

Chapter 3

Motivations and Mechanisms: What External Providers Seek from Government Organizations

Who should pay when the weather forecast is wrong? If the Mayor of Moscow, Yuri Luzhkov, had his way weather forecasters would be fined when their predictions were off the mark (Finn 2005). The Mayor had been so unimpressed with the federal weather bureau's predictions that he funded the creation of a local bureau in 1999, but when they failed to predict the *exact* timing and severity of a major snow storm which caused mayhem in Moscow in 2005 he threatened to start fining them for incorrect predictions. In retaliation, the head of the weather bureau said he would be happy to pay the fine if the Mayor would agree to give them a bonus every time they got it right, some 90–99 per cent of the time.

The Mayor's suggestion and the weather chief's response reflect the everyday assumption that applying rewards and sanctions will affect behaviour and performance, but they also point to the practical problems of doing so. If the assumption holds, applying a fine or shelling out financial rewards should result in more accurate weather forecasting by the bureau. In our case, it assumes the Moscow bureau was holding back its efforts in crafting forecasts and, therefore, that fining them would increase the likelihood of them getting it right. But could imposing fines *really* combat what is still an imperfect understanding of the weather? By the same token, would paying bonuses encourage the weather bureau to get it right more often, and how could they actually do this?

In this chapter we consider how government agencies induce external providers to engage in service delivery. This entails the exercise of influence, about which there has been much research. An influential early example was by French and Raven (1959), who identified five 'bases of social power', namely: *reward* power; *coercive* power; *legitimate* power, where the less powerful person believes he should comply because the influence attempt is seen as appropriate; *referent* power, based on the attractiveness of the power figure; and *expert* power. This schema has been very useful in analysing power situations, but it is prone to two types of shortcomings for our purposes. First, its focus is primarily on the inter-personal or intra-organizational; its bases of power tend not to embrace all the elements of *inter*-organizational dealings. Second, French and Raven's model does not tell us a lot about the *mechanics* of influence: how its bases of power – or what we will call 'organizational instruments' – result in behaviours on the part of those influenced. We offer here a more intricate account, in which the impact of organizational instruments on providers' behaviour is mediated, firstly by how the instruments are framed, secondly by providers' motivations, and thirdly by organization-level factors.

Broadly, the argument is that external parties' propensity to contribute is a function of their *willingness* and their *ability* to do so (see Figure 3.1). Willingness is affected by the external parties' *motivations* to contribute – the fundamental drivers of their behaviours – which in turn are influenced by *motivators* employed by government agencies to encourage individuals and organizations to provide services. Thus we distinguish between motiv*ators* – the instruments wielded by the public sector organization – and motiv*ations*: the attributes of those being motivated. External parties' ability to contribute is enhanced by *facilitators* – the ways government organizations can make it easier, at any given level of willingness, for external providers to contribute to agency purposes.

However, this is not the end of the story. Foundational work by Simon (1957) and others on people as 'cognitive misers' who satisfice rather than optimize, and related recent thinking on how to 'nudge' citizens and organizations into socially requisite behaviours

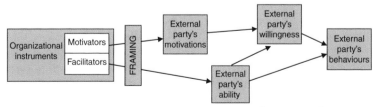

FIGURE 3.1   *Key constructs concerning why external parties co-produce*

has highlighted how the impact of motivators and facilitators is mediated by the way they are 'framed' – that is, how they appear to the providers (Tversky and Kahneman 1981; Thaler and Sunstein 2008). For example, the same incentive might appear differently depending on whether it is framed as a 'gift' or an obligatory payment. There is, therefore, not a precise correspondence between motivators and their effects on motivations. Understanding how they interact to affect behaviour is central to understanding relationships with external providers. For the most part we will consider the motivations of individuals, and how they are affected by framing. However we also delve into how these motivators are mediated by organizations.

Why consider motivation?

Motivation is critical to understanding the behaviour of actors in any system (see Perry and Porter 1982: 89; Frey and Jegen 2001; Le Grand 2003; Fehr and Gintis 2007), and especially important when government organizations rely on external parties to co-produce public services. First, the very fact that providers are 'external' means that the management tools of hierarchy and those common to the employment relationship – such as supervisory instructions, organizational restructuring, work redesign, promotion or reassignment – are less available to the government agency. Instead, different forms of influence may be needed to activate the motivations of the parties that work with government.

Second, motivation is much more complex than the carrots and sticks of popular mythology, and for that matter of economics-based schools of thought that have had such a powerful influence on public policy and management in recent times. To make sense of what actually motivates external providers we need a more sophisticated and nuanced understanding of motivation and motivators. Without it the risk is not just that performance by external providers may be less effective than it could be, but also that it might actually be *worse* than through in-house delivery.

Third, different providers have differing mixes of motivations, and will respond to different appeals and mechanisms in a variety of ways. Rather than relying on one all-purpose approach, it is important to tailor the mix to the circumstances, to ensure a 'fit' between the person and the organization (see Leisink and Steijn 2008). If we think that external parties are all self-interested, for example, then competition, sanctions and rewards will encourage them to do as the government organization wants. However, if we think that external parties come to a relationship from a more public-spirited motivational base then collaborative, partner-style approaches will be more much important in designing and operating service delivery systems (see, further, Le Grand 2003). The interaction of motivations and motivators is, therefore, a complex puzzle.

Homo economicus, self-interest and extrinsic motivation

The default setting of public service management over the last decades has been to assume people are self-interested maximizers of their own benefit. This assumption draws strength from a key strand of Western rationalism. As Adam Smith wrote in *The Wealth of Nations*, 'It is not from the benevolence of the butcher, the brewer, or the baker that we expect our dinner, but from their regard to their own interest' (1986: 119). The archetype that best represents this way of thinking is *homo economicus*, a 'mythical species' upon whose shoulders the discipline of economics has been built (Levitt and List 2008: 909).

Homo economicus is central to neo-classical economics and rational choice theory. She is perfectly rational because she seeks to maximize her utility function, that is, her 'preferred mix of benefits and costs'; she is self-regarding in that she makes her decisions as an individual; and she effortlessly calculates the gains and losses associated with different courses of action (see Frederickson and Smith 2003; Talbot 2005; Fehr and Gintis 2007; Levitt and List 2009). This model of human behaviour has affected our understanding of public administration over the past few decades and influenced public sector reform in many areas.[1]

Getting *homo economicus* to behave in the desired fashion is a matter of appealing to her extrinsic motivations. In this account, acting in the desired fashion (for example, by performing a contracted task) is a 'disbenefit' for the person being motivated. She suffers a loss of time or amenity, for which she needs to be compensated to an extent that she sees as outweighing these losses. Thus the reward is *extrinsic* to the task at hand. For instance, a factory worker might see his pay as the reason he spends 40 hours a week enduring the drudgery of the production line. With that pay, he can enjoy his life outside work with his family or pursue his myriad leisure interests, activities that increase his utility.[2] A school pupil might spend large amounts of time diligently studying because she knows it will give her the reward of a higher grade in her upcoming exam. Both are engaging in this work to gain a reward extrinsic to the actual task they are performing.

Moreover, there is a scalable relationship between reward and effort: the greater the reward, the greater or more diligent is the supply of effort from *homo economicus* (Reeson and Tisdell 2008; Airely *et al.* 2009). All economic thinking about incentives and sanctions is basically about anticipating or managing this relationship, in which the essential question is: how much effort will be prompted by what level of reward? This raises a further question, that behavioural theorists call *expectancy*. Rewards need to not only be *valuable* to the person being motivated, but also to be certain. The provider needs to see what might be called a 'clear line of sight' between their action and the reward. If the provider can't be sure that a particular valued reward will result from doing a task, then the motivation will be attenuated.

Three critiques

The strength of this model – its simplicity – is also its weakness. Whilst *homo economicus* is a great asset in the design of economic models, this 'ideal being has a crippling defect: [she] does not exist!' (Oullier and Sauneron 2010: 39). What if individuals are not rational, self-interest seekers, and are instead or in addition motivated by other factors? These questions have driven a critique *of homo economicus*, pointing to the narrowness of its account of human behaviour (Frey and Meier 2002; and see Ng and Tseng 2008). And whilst the field of economics has at worst ignored them, or at best underestimated them, scholars in other disciplines have focused considerable attention on the broader range of motivations (Oullier and Sauneron 2010). Here we canvass three main criticisms, each of which undermines this ideal. None of them, in and of itself, solves the puzzle of motivation; each is limited in its own way. We therefore conclude this section with a fuller schema.

Work as a pleasurable activity

At the heart of the theory of extrinsic motivation is the assumption that the behaviour being sought from the provider is inherently unpleasant. The mere offering of material rewards signals that we have to 'bribe' people to undertake this boring, arduous, unpleasant or demeaning activity – activity that has 'disutility'. But the fact is that work is not necessarily unpleasant. Many people enjoy their work in itself and gain satisfaction from it; for them pay is not the *most* important driver of their actions. This phenomenon is what psychologists call *intrinsic* motivation,[3] which involves satisfying needs for personal worth or accomplishment, or for personal growth and development.[4] Where jobs are more interesting, where work is varied and meaningful, where employees are granted more autonomy, where they get frequent feedback, and where they are able to exercise knowledge and skill, their developmental needs are more likely to be met (Hackman and Lawler 1971). And just as jobs within organizations can be intrinsically motivating, so too can the roles of *external* providers who, all else being equal, are more likely to be committed to their tasks if they help satisfy intrinsic needs. For example, the staff of the Moscow weather bureau find satisfaction in the application of forecasting techniques, the emergence of weather patterns as the aggregate data from observation stations comes in, and successfully calculating weather outcomes. The forecasting success is its own reward.

The idea of intrinsic motivation challenges the assumption that *homo economicus* is motivated solely by extrinsic rewards; she is much more complex. But this notion has its own challenges: how, from observation, can we determine which *behaviours* might be linked to intrinsic rather than extrinsic motivation, for example (Frey and Jegen 2001)? Think back to our diligent student; is she motivated by the prospect of a higher grade (extrinsic motivation), or does she want to learn for the sake of learning (intrinsic motivation) (Kreps 1997: 361)?

But just because it is not easy to determine whether motivation is intrinsic or extrinsic does not mean it does not exist. However, it does not account for the full picture and we need to consider other factors to gain a more nuanced understanding.

Social context and peer approval or pressure

The self-regarding and self-interested picture of *homo economicus* ignores her social context. In fact, social structures have an important influence on how people behave. Most people tend to begin relationships from a position of conditional reciprocity – I'll be nice and if you are nice then, in return, I'll be nice again – and build norms through repeated social interactions (Rege and Telle 2004; Fehr and Gintis 2007). The influence of external factors gives rise to an alternative model to *homo economicus* which explains human behaviour differently. *Homo sociologicus* attaches considerable weight to the social approval of those around him; he enjoys the respect, esteem and fellowship of others, and tries to avoid being disliked or shunned (Bénabou and Tirole 2006). Thus people may participate in collective endeavours not to pursue self-interest, but because of a desire for social belonging and esteem – they want to be liked and accepted, regardless of any 'costs' of time and effort involved in participating (Olson 1965). So people external to a government organization may be motivated by social affiliation or peer pressure to participate in an activity even though it is detrimental to their material self-interest.

Other-regarding behaviour and purposive values

From their social milieu, people also acquire and hold norms and values, which are purposive or expressive in nature and prompted by concern for others or purposes beyond self – such as the beliefs that the environment should be protected, poor people should be supported, war should be waged on terrorism, or that the Moscow public should be forewarned of bad weather (Reeson and Tisdell 2008). People can subscribe to these purposive values even though it is contrary to their self-interest to do so. For example, a high-income earner might support progressive taxation on equity grounds, even though she personally pays more tax than otherwise. Etzioni (1988) calls this 'the moral dimension'.

Not surprisingly, most economists struggle with this phenomenon, since it strikes at the very heart of their behavioural model. They characterize it as 'altruism', which they describe as the '"warm glow" effect which comes from doing social good' (Besley and Ghatak 2003: 241). Some writers devalue the significance of purposive values and altruism by recasting them as a form of selfishness, arguing that individuals get psychic benefit from their actions (Downs 1957). With volunteers, for example, 'one can perceive altruistic motives simply as a case where an individual donor is better off because he/she receives utility from the happiness of others' (Ferris 1984: 329). But this is a circular argument where self-interest is attributed to any behaviour (Talbot 2005; see also Fehr and Gintis 2007; Alford 2009): it 'is just a fancy way of saying that individuals do what individuals do... By definition, there is no such thing as an individual who does not maximise his utility' (Thurow 1983: 217) (see also Batson 1991). Others employ altruism in a binary fashion to encompass everything except self-interest, creating an inverse relationship between one's selfishness and one's altruism (Margolis 1982; Le Grand 2003).

Lurking in the background is the suspicion that this is a less robust motivation than hard-nosed incentives and sanctions. The implication, *sotto voce*, is that it is only realistic to expect that given a choice between a material gain and the nice feeling that comes from doing the 'right thing', people will opt for the material benefit.

But framing altruism in this way fails to comprehend all its nuances (Hoggett *et al.* 2006). First, the allocation of resources between oneself and others may not be the main consideration at issue in purposive values. Instead individuals might be focused on the allocation of resources *among others* – for example, concern about the gap between rich and poor in third world countries. Nor is *resource*-allocation necessarily the primary concern; rather it may be about the ideal *relationships* between the self and others, or more significantly about those among others. People care about whether due process is applied in judicial proceedings, whether citizens are consulted in the taking of decisions about those affecting them, or whether human rights are upheld in other countries.

Second, different people have different purposive values, and these are shaped by factors such as social class, professional occupation or ethnic background. Thus a medical doctor may, as a result of professional training and interaction with her occupational group, subscribe to the principles of the Hippocratic Oath, and from that derive a particular set of beliefs about what the priorities of the public health system should be. This may run counter to her own economic self-interest, and it may also diverge from the purposive values of other citizens.

Third, purposive values are not always benevolent or 'nice' things. Take, for example, patriotism. Pride in one's country involves a positive commitment to a collective entity, and in times of war can go as far as putting one's life at risk by enlisting in the military. But it is not for nothing that patriotism has been called the 'last refuge of the scoundrel', since in addition to other-regarding acts for one's fellow citizens, it can also involve insulting, persecuting or even killing the citizens of other countries (Johnson 1775 in Agassi 1974). 'Others' are not an undifferentiated mass of recipients of goodwill.

Fourth, to lump together everything that is not self-interest under the heading of altruism is to miss important distinctions between purposive values, intrinsic motivation and the need for social belonging, which are actually different phenomena.[5] Purposive values are made up of complex and varying mixes of concerns, only parts of which can be characterized as altruism. Moreover, they are not the same as other motivations such as intrinsic or social ones.

In fact, while some scholars argue about the theoretical possibility of altruism and purposive values, there is more than enough evidence that these concerns loom large in people's day-to-day motivations. This has long been recognized in disciplines such as psychology, sociology, anthropology, and political science, but interestingly it is also being explored in the field of behavioural economics, and even beyond the social sciences, in fields such as biology and neurology.[6]

A schema of motivation

Our critique of *homo economicus* has found it wanting: it is too narrow a conception of the complex motivations embedded in human beings. We have unearthed three other bases of motivation in addition to material self-interest. Thus a more complete schema recognizes four types, in each of which people attach value to something different:

- *Material self-interest*, in which people value extrinsic material rewards or conversely the avoidance of sanctions.
- *Intrinsic motivation*, in which people gain satisfaction from the act of doing the work or carrying out the task itself.
- *Sociality*, in which people gain satisfaction from a sense of social affiliation or approval from one's peers.
- *Purposive values*, in which people attach value to purposes beyond their own self-interest.

Each of these motivations in itself, however, only partially explains individual behaviour. Very rarely is an individual a creature of only one of them. Rather, we tend to be complex bundles of motivations which sometimes co-exist peacefully, sometimes jostle with each other and often vary over time (Talbot 2005). The question, therefore, is: what mixtures of them influence us in our behaviours, and under what circumstances?

One way of thinking about this is that people's motivations are 'lexically ordered': they need to have one motivation satisfied before another can be addressed (Ayres and Braithwaite 1992). A provider of services to clients with a disability might in the first instance seek to empower his clients to gain meaningful employment and only then pursue profit maximization beyond that.[7] Most famous in this vein was Maslow's hierarchy of needs, which posited that lower order needs needed to be met before people focused on higher order ones: from physiological needs (survival), through security (shelter and protection), belonging (group affiliation) and psychological needs (self-esteem and respect) up to self-actualization (Halachmi and van der Krogt 2005).

Just as importantly, motivations are amenable to change, in response to external influences. This brings us to the subject of *motivators*.

Motivators: transforming motivations into effort and action

When we focus on motivators we are concerned not with people's inner drivers of behaviour but rather with the various instruments with which government organizations can tap those drivers, most notably in external parties. Public sector organizations deploy a wide range of devices with individuals or organizations to prompt their behaviour or effort. We identify five types of motivators relevant to external provision, each obviously relating to one of the motivations set out above.

The first are *sanctions*, which involve the threat or actual application of a punishment, lightly or heavily. This was the Mayor of Moscow's motivator of choice, when he threatened the weather bureau with fines if they don't get their forecasts 'just right'. But sanctions need not be material; they can also be in-kind, such as barring from practice, banning from a specific location, or cutting people off from services or denying welfare payments.

The second are *material rewards*, which involve tangible benefits. Money is the most typical of these, applied in a variety of forms, such as performance bonuses tied to achievement of results, or premiums related to availability of inputs, but they could also include in-kind benefits such as free or discounted service or ancillary benefits.[8] For example, the Conservative–Liberal Government in Britain devised a scheme with local governments to reward householders for recycling (Garvey 2010; Pickles 2010). It involved giving people a little 'nudge' in the right direction by providing a small reward for increasing the amount of recycling they left at the kerb:

> The beauty of this scheme is its simplicity. It's just like collecting loyalty card points. People sign up, their bin gets weighed, and points are added onto their account. Those points can then be cashed in at over a hundred local businesses including Marks & Spencer, Coffee Republic and Cineworld, or donated to local schools. Residents earn up to £135-a-year worth of points. That's a big boost for the local economy. That means the council doesn't have to pay so much in landfill tax, which in turn, helps to hold down council tax. Everyone benefits. And it works. Recycling rates in the pilot area went up by 35 per cent.
>
> (Pickles 2010)

The third are *intrinsic rewards*, which involve arranging the task so the provider finds it interesting, challenging, meaningful and respectful of his competence and/or autonomy, enhancing either a sense of competence or self-determination in the external party, or the enjoyment of the task or activity with which they engage.[9] These effects are prompted by measures such as structuring services to enable providers to exercise autonomy. They send a signal of trust to the other party (Bénabou and Tirole 2003), and can increase motivation.

The fourth are *social* motivators, such as conviviality, approval and disapproval. While sociality as a motivation is basically a concern to be well-regarded (or avoid being poorly regarded) by others, the range of social motivators varies with how we understand 'the social.' The provider is concerned with how she is regarded by a variety of others. Most narrowly, the relevant 'other' is the government agency with whom the external party interacts, where sociality responds to things like friendliness or mutual respect. How those on the front counter at an employment agency interact with jobseeker clients can affect the clients' willingness to exert effort. Most broadly, the relevant 'other' may be the broad general public, where our provider is concerned about reputation; here the government agency can use praise or criticism of performance as a powerful motivator. One form of this is 'competition by comparison', in which the relative performance of providers is periodically published in numerical terms. This occurs in public transport systems, school education, and hospitals, among other services. In each case, there may or may not be a material reward attached to the performance, but rather a reputational effect: no provider wants to be at the bottom of that list. (Of course, these 'league tables' of providers can also prompt a focus purely on the ranking to the detriment of other values, as discussed below.)[10] In between these two extremes are specific 'others', such as a particular ethnic or geographic community, a profession, an industry or a set of clients, in all of which approval or disapproval will be important, but also aspects of conviviality or opportunity to participate or belong.

Interestingly, social motivators are extrinsic rather than intrinsic in nature because they come from outside those whom they motivate. The difference is that they involve non-material rewards; it is other people's attitudes towards one that count, rather than how much money they offer. In this case social approval can be considered a substitute for money (Van de Ven 2001).

The final motivator has to do with the legitimacy of the task, typically a function of its *perceived contribution to the public good*: appealing to the provider's purposive values by conveying to them that the activities they are undertaking are worthwhile in terms of those values. There are two main ways to do this. One is for these activities to actually have a purpose that is valued: what has been called 'mission alignment' (Besley and Ghatak 2003). The other is to seek to persuade the provider of the importance of that value, through education or publicity. In the British recycling example, critics of the use of material rewards argued that whilst it might encourage more recycling, it did not act to convey the broader importance of this activity because it relied on 'reactions not reasons' (Garvey 2010):

> It rewards people to produce more recyclable waste, rather than take steps to reduce the amount they produce in the first place . . . The point of recycling has to do with understanding the importance of reducing waste in a finite world. It costs energy and resources to make a plastic bottle, fill it with water, package it and ship it to your local shop. We currently get almost

all of that energy by burning fossil fuels and doing damage to our climate. The resources which go into the bottle's production, distribution and disposal might have been used in other, better ways. Once empty, the bottle might take up space in a landfill or end up in the ocean. If you understand the value of reducing waste in a finite world – if you want to avoid a hand in wasting energy, causing climate change, squandering resources, poisoning oceans – you might think twice about buying a bottle of water. If you recycle because you earn reward points for doing so, you might just buy a lot of plastic bottles.

Thus, using other motivators such as educating people about the importance of recycling due to its broader public benefits can motivate them to change their behaviour in the longer term.

Matching motivators with motivations

To a considerable degree French and Raven's bases of power map onto these motivators: reward power onto material rewards; coercive power onto sanctions; legitimate power onto perceived legitimacy; referent power onto part of sociality; and expert power onto parts of both intrinsic rewards and legitimacy (as well as onto ability to contribute, discussed below). But here we also consider the mediating role of motivations.

We can identify some obvious pairings where a motivation is mobilized by a particular motivator (see the shaded boxes in Table 3.1). For example, material rewards and sanctions should register most clearly with material self-interest; intrinsic rewards with intrinsic motivation; peer approval or disapproval with sociality; and mission alignment with purposive values. But this story is only *partly* valid because each of these possible pairs holds under certain (not all) conditions, each motivator has an effect on others, and it matters how each motivator is 'framed' in this relationship. In this section we consider these pairings and their complexities.

Sanctions/material rewards and self-interest

Sanctions and material rewards are two sides of the same coin, constituting negative and positive material incentives. Material self-interest lies at the heart of what has been described as 'the

TABLE 3.1 *Relationships between motivations and motivators*

		Motivations			
		Material self-interest	*Intrinsic motivation*	*Sociality*	*Purposive values*
Motivators	*Sanctions*	✓✓	✗✗	✓/✗	✗✗
	Material rewards	✓✓	✗✗	✓/✗	✗✗
	Intrinsic rewards		✓✓	-	-
	Peer approval or disapproval			✓✓	
	Perceived legitimacy or contribution to public good				✓✓

Key: ✓✓ = motivator has strong positive effect; ✓ = modest positive effect; ✗✗ = strong negative effect; ✗ = modest negative effect.

most fundamental economic "law": raising monetary incentives increases supply' (Frey and Jegen 2001: 590). People understand very clearly through these incentives that if they work more they will receive more of something they value. Similarly, the threat of sanctions tells them clearly that they will be punished if they do not supply the desired behaviours and effort. Sanctions and material rewards, then, are 'high-powered' incentives because there is a direct relationship between the provider's effort and the pecuniary benefit; this contrasts with 'low-powered incentives' where there is a more diffuse relationship (Frant 1996).

Clearly, material rewards and sanctions do have some positive effect on providers' supply of requisite behaviour, and examples of this abound.[11] But although they 'work', the effect on effort or performance is not necessarily as universal or as strong as its proponents would argue. One reason is that it can be hard to engineer the conditions where this will be most effective.

First, spelling out the behaviours required of the provider in terms specific enough that monetary rewards can be attached to them may mean casting them in ways which diverge from the ultimate value the agency is seeking to have delivered to it, resulting in goal displacement.[12] Rewarding teachers for the average test scores of their pupils provides a convenient metric to which monetary incentives can be tied, but the test scores may not direct effort toward the education authority's ultimate purpose of instilling creativity or critical thinking into students, which teachers may neglect in favour of 'teaching to the test', or at worst it may encourage cheating.[13] Indeed, the linkages between performance pay and outcomes are quite mixed, with evidence showing it improves retention rates, but not *necessarily* academic achievement or even attendance (Eberts *et al.* 2000).

On the other hand, if we try to specify services in ways that encompass all the performance dimensions the government agency cares about, it can create the opposite problem: goal diffusion. This is where we give providers far too many 'top priority' goals, which in the end is tantamount to having no goals at all. And where performance goals diverge from each other then the situation gets even more complicated. Of course, this can often be the case in public service delivery of complex non-standard services. Complicating the problem even further are situations where the provider is responsible to more than one agency: the 'multiple principal' problem. In a world where government agencies deal with a variety of wicked problems, or even just complex ones, and where networked governance is assuming increasing importance, these situations become more and more common.

A second challenge is where factors outside the providers' control affect their behaviour and performance. Whilst the Moscow mayor might like perfect weather forecasts, it is a simple fact that the weather is not always predictable. This variability makes it hard for anyone to be able to anticipate the weather without error. Understandably, the provider will seek compensation for the inherent risk attached to this. More importantly, if providers feel that their efforts alone are not going to make much difference to whether the required results are achieved, they may become demotivated and reduce effort. In the case of educational outcomes for students, for example, teachers are just part of the story of student performance – parents, the principal, the school, and socio-economic background all matter (Harvey-Beavis 2003).

Third, how do we know whether the provider has performed the required behaviour? If a mental health programme was run by a non-profit organization which received payments tied to the number of people who emerge from it in a better state of mind, how could we tell whether each individual has a 'better state of mind'? One answer might be that no episodes of psychiatrically problematic behaviour have been observed. But over what period of time should we measure? If it is less than a year, it is quite unlikely to confirm longer-term stabilization. If it is more than one year, it exceeds the usual budget period, and a proxy measure indicating some sort of progress might have to be fashioned – a challenging task. This is a classic case of information-asymmetry because we cannot really know what is going on in the mind of a patient. Employing experts such as psychologists or psychiatrists to make assessments can help, but this is time-consuming and costly.[14] Other challenges emerge where work is performed out of sight of the government agency, for instance in aged care facilities, foster homes, or in unemployment programmes. In most of these cases, after-the-fact monitoring is possible, but it does not prevent mishaps, nor is it cost-free.

Thus, the effectiveness of material rewards is constrained by factors such as goal displacement, goal diffusion, non-controllable external factors, and information asymmetry – factors that lead providers to disdain financial rewards as being either too small to matter or irrelevant to the type of work carried out (Steele 1999: 10). Worse still, these can make actual performance *worse*, because high-powered incentives can induce gaming behaviours such as the misrepresentation of performance to access rewards, or the concealment of non-compliance to avoid sanctions.

All of this suggests that material rewards are only likely to work where they are focused on simple behavioural tasks (Jochelson 2007). However, *even where all the conditions for their effective operation are met*, they can have perverse effects. Sometimes this is due to the time horizons built into arrangements (for example, a three-month reporting period) which encourage short-termism: such as, educators teaching to the test rather than providing a broader education. At other times, material rewards encourage only temporary compliance rather than long-lasting behavioural change because using them signals that tasks are unattractive and, sooner or later, the power of such rewards evens out, or the material rewards themselves run out (Kohn 1993: 62). On the other side of the coin, sanctions tend to have a dampening effect on creativity and innovation, all else being equal, and therefore they can produce risk aversion (Smith and Lipsky 1993).

In summary, material rewards and sanctions can have a powerful effect on self-interest as a motivation, but only in particular circumstances, and sometimes that impact can be perverse. As we shall see later, they can also have perverse effects when they interact with other motivations and motivators.

Non-material motivators

Just as material reward had its logical partner, each of the non-material types of motivators resonates strongly with its logical pair. First, *intrinsic rewards* are strong motivators of work performance, resonating with intrinsic motivations (Deci 1975; Lepper and Greene 1978; Deci *et al.* 1999; Grant 2008). Employees who seek to fulfil higher order needs respond to intrinsic rewards such as having jobs that offer variety, autonomy, task identity and feedback.[15] Importantly for this book, it is not just employees who respond in this way, but also external providers (Alford 2009).

Second, social approval, disapproval and belonging are powerful motivators (Fehr and Falk 2002) of helping behaviours, and strongly influence donation behaviours.[16] Experiments have shown that peer punishment enforces cooperation and acts as a powerful non-material sanction, even where people do not know each other:

> Both punishing and rewarding seem to be facets of the deep-seated human propensity to reciprocate good and bad, a propensity guided by reasoning and emotions, and based on heuristics and cues ... Fear, shame, guilt and their converse, the elation and inner glow after a generous action, work to keep humans from cheating. Being cheated arouses anger, indignation and moral outrage, and often causes individuals to inflict costly punishments on defectors.
>
> (Sigmund 2007: 597–8)

Although punishment can increase cooperation, it can be counter-productive: adding the threat of punishment can decrease the menaced player's willingness to cooperate. Peer punishment is actually relatively rare because it is so costly in social terms. In small-scale societies, or village life, reputation might have a more pervasive role; it is easier to gossip behind the back of a bully than to confront him. Undermining a good reputation is an inexpensive but ominous form of sanctioning, which might eventually lead to ostracism – that is, exclusion from the market for trustworthy partners. In large societies, peer punishment is also rare, and is repressed by the institutions upholding law and order.

Expressions of approval or disapproval need not be actually voiced by others, especially where social norms have been internalized. Once this happens a breach of these norms can automatically produce feelings of guilt or shame, and compliance a feeling of self-respect. Consider the case of public littering: people will not litter even when there are no others in sight, and where they must go out of their way to dispose of the litter, because norms are so strong they will feel guilty for dropping their rubbish. This brings us to the third non-material motivator: legitimacy or *perceived public benefit*.

It is well established that within an organization, when people buy into its mission they will work harder and generally be more productive. Indeed, mission can replace the profit motive in some settings, motivating people to exert effort, and work harder in pursuit of something less tangible (Besley and Ghatak 2003). Take the example of a firefighter pursuing the mission of the firefighting service:

> Why do I risk my life by running into a burning building, knowing that at any moment ... the floor may give way, the roof may tumble on me, the fire may engulf me? ... I'm here for my community, a community I grew up in, a community where I know lots of people, a community that knows me.
>
> (firefighter cited in Grant 2007: 393)

Likewise, there is a public-service motivation amongst contractors that can be harnessed to pursue public interest, for example, defence contractors working with government in long-term, interactive relationships are motivated to create the technology to provide national, and international security (Jolley 2008).

As foreshadowed above, one reason that providers might 'buy in' to the mission of a government agency is that the *actual* mission is consistent with their purposive values. Volunteers are typically mobilized by purpose; they will donate time and effort in pursuit of these goals.[17] The importance of this is seen most powerfully in emergency situations. When a hurricane, bushfire or flood strikes, there is often a massive mobilization of volunteer support which derives from a mixture of material self-interest (people want to protect their property), sociality (it is simply the done thing to contribute to the emergency response effort), and identification with the mission of the emergency organization. Similarly, the military finds it much easier to recruit when the country is under direct threat from foreign powers, or where a war is seen as 'legitimate' in the public's mind.[18]

Of course, providers can also have values that diverge from the purpose of the government organization and often this reflects different interests. How might a government organization respond to this? Changing the mission to make it more amenable to providers may reduce the value that the programme offers to the public as a whole. But pursuing mission *compatibility* might be a possibility and this can be done in two ways. First, the organization could focus on mission *content* and seek to find synergies, compromises or trade-offs between its purpose and the values adhered to by providers, and second, it could focus on mission *process* and involve providers in devising mutually valuable missions.

Another strategy might be to try and persuade providers of the legitimacy of the existing mission through education and publicity.[19] Many jurisdictions have run extensive campaigns to persuade motorists to drive more safely, and particularly not to drink and drive. The Transport Accident Commission of the Australian state of Victoria, the government agency with a monopoly on third-party accident insurance, relied on motorists driving safely to achieve one of its core goals of reducing the road toll. It joined with the police and the roads authority from the 1970s onwards to work on reducing road accident deaths. Over two decades, the number of people killed on the roads went down from 762 in 1988–9 to 295 in 2009 – a decrease of 61 per cent (see O'Flynn 1999; and TAC 2009).

Effects on other motivations

In summary, each of the motivators resonates with its logical pair among the motivations to influence providers to contribute, with some qualifications. However, each motivator also has implications for motivations other than its logical pair, some positive, but many of them negative.

Material incentives can, in very particular circumstances, reinforce intrinsic motivations, while financial incentives combined with education can have both widespread and rapid effects.[20] But more typically, the effects of material incentives on non-material motivations, especially on intrinsic ones, are negative (Deci 1975; Frey 1997b; Bénabou and Tirole 2003). In particular, they can diminish or crowd them out. Cognitive social psychologists in the early 1970s discovered that if people are paid to do something they would otherwise have done out of interest, they will be less likely to do it in future without being paid (Deci 1975). If a child is told he will receive $5 if he does his homework, when normally he enjoyed doing it for nothing, then in future he is unlikely to do it without receiving the money. These 'hidden costs of reward' (Lepper and Greene 1978) produce both short and long-term effects on motivation and organizational performance:[21]

> Once a reward is offered, it will be required – and 'expected' – every time the task has to be performed again – perhaps even in increasing amounts. In other words, through their effect on self-confidence, rewards have a *'ratchet effect'* .
> (Bénabou and Tirole 2003: 503, emphasis in original).

This motivational crowding effect, where intrinsic motivation is displaced by material incentives, is produced by two psychological mechanisms.[22] One is that people see an external intervention such as a material reward or sanction as reducing their self-determination – they are being *forced* to behave in a particular way, which reduces their intrinsic motivation. The other is that a material reward or sanction signals that their own intrinsic motivation is not important or valued and this can undermine it over time:

> An intrinsically motivated person is deprived of the chance of displaying his or her own interest and involvement in an activity when someone else offers a reward, or orders them to do it. As a result of impaired self-esteem, individuals reduce effort.[23]
> (Frey and Jegen 2001: 594)

Thus, material rewards or sanctions have negative effects on intrinsic motivation where individuals see them as controlling, but can reinforce intrinsic motivation if they see them as supportive (Frey and Jegen 2001: 594–5). This is now supported by plenty of evidence from both economics and psychology.[24] It is also the case that material rewards and sanctions have similar effects on the other two types of non-material motivations: sociality and material values. Often these motivations are treated as forms of intrinsic motivation, but here we consider them separately.

Sanctions and material rewards have complex effects on *sociality*, arising from the fact that it is also an extrinsic motivation. On the one hand, material rewards can reinforce sociality; a provider might be positively motivated by a performance-contingent bonus not so much for the material benefit it can bring, but because it conveys a strong message about how well they have performed, it signals this to others, and consequently raises the esteem in which he is held, or at the very least boosts his self-esteem. Much the same point can be made about sanctions. For some providers, the reputational damage of being punished can be much more significant than the material loss.[25] Thus corporate shaming can have a strong influence on regulating business behaviour.[26]

On the other hand, material rewards may undermine the 'reputational value of good deeds, creating doubt about the extent to which they were performed for the incentives rather than for themselves' (Bénabou and Tirole 2003: 1654). Because social approval is given to self-sacrificing acts, 'rewarding gift-giving deprives the agent from the opportunity to realize social approval. This latter effect reduces the incentives to give and makes the end outcome ambiguous' (Van de Ven 2001: 17).

The landmark work identifying what we can now describe as the crowding out of purposive values is Richard Titmuss' book *The Gift Relationship* (1970), where he argued that blood donors would be *less* willing to donate if they were paid for doing so. This crowding out breaches the fundamental law of demand and supply in economics, but paying for blood undermined the social value of donating to contribute to the common good. As with the broader work on intrinsic motivation, this theory was initially criticized for lack of evidence; however, his key points now have strong empirical support.[27] Further, we now have plenty of evidence to show that sanctions and material rewards crowd out purposive values in a similar manner to the way they crowd out intrinsic motivation. In extreme cases not only does such action crowd out voluntary contributions, it can destroy established norms and reduce contributions in the long-term (Janssen and Mendys-Kamphorst 2004).

In summary, different motivators have differing effects on motivations, as shown in Table 3.1. In particular, sanctions and material rewards have a less unequivocally positive impact on most of the motivations than we might at first assume. Moreover, the particular impacts vary according to circumstance. This suggests that managers in government organizations need to consider the context in determining how to influence external providers; using carrots and sticks is not quite as simple as it might seem.

Framing

A well-known optical illusion is a picture that could be seen either as an elaborate candlestick or as two heads facing each other in close proximity, depending on whether the observer assumes he is looking at a substantive object or two silhouettes. This is an example of the phenomenon of 'framing' which also affects how motivators are perceived. The ground-breaking work of Nobel-winning economist Kahneman and his colleague Tversky (1981) showed that the 'frames' people adopt influenced the decisions they took, and that these decisions often violate the notions of rationality, consistency and coherence that underpin much economic thought. Frames are heavily influenced by the norms, habits and personal characteristics of individuals. Four aspects of framing are relevant here (see also Thaler and Sunstein 2008).

First, the impact of an intervention will vary according to whether it is perceived as a sanction or a reward, even if in other respects they are of equal weight. Experimental games in which participants can choose whether to collaborate in the production of public goods show this:

> Investigations comparing negative with positive incentives (i.e. the carrot with the stick) show that rewards are considerably less efficient than punishment, at least for the games considered here, in which the public good is a linear function of the number of contributors. Positive incentives become costly, and negative incentives become cheap, if success is fully achieved – that is, all cooperate.
>
> (Sigmund 2007: 598)

Second, the impact of a reward, material or otherwise, will be different depending on whether it is perceived as a gift or an obligation. In tax administration some authorities frame the issuing of tax refunds in a speedy manner as a gift, even though it is merely returning to taxpayers money which is rightfully theirs and which they have effectively lent to the public purse during the fiscal year. More generally, the building of trust in the process of collaboration between organizations and/or individuals is facilitated by mutual giving of 'gifts', tangible or intangible offering of things perceived as valuable to the other party, given over and above the previously agreed terms of the relationship. Chapter 5 discusses this in more detail.

Third, the value of a more complex non-material reward may be enhanced if it is conveyed through peripheral cues rather than direct expression. Whilst monetary rewards focus people's attention on precise calculation of benefits and costs, indirect rewards such as being treated respectfully are mentally processed by people in a less deliberative fashion, known as 'peripheral processing' (Petty and Cacioppo 1981). They take in cues which are outside the more explicitly stated obligations, making the latter less salient. Faced with direct persuasion, people subject it to scrutiny and seek to devalue it, whereas peripheral cues evoke a normative response – for example, a liking for the organization as a result of being treated respectfully (see also Rege and Telle 2004).

Finally, the power of an offer or threat varies according to how certain it is seen to be, in a non-linear fashion. Kahneman and Tversky (1979) unearthed a version of this they called 'prospect theory' through review of numerous experiments. They found that people evaluate different-sized probabilities, and different prospects of gains and losses, disproportionately and in general in a loss-averse fashion. Another variation on this idea concerns reciprocity – a significant factor in collaboration between organizations or with individuals. If person A believes that others will cooperate and contribute, then the 'best' strategy (if they are rational) is to contribute; however if person B believes that others will not contribute, then the best strategy is not to contribute. These beliefs are subject to similar framing biases as those discussed by Kahneman and Tversky impacting on individuals' beliefs about how others will behave, thereby influencing their own actions.

More recently, framing has been central to the notion of 'nudge' which has captured a lot of attention in public policy circles for its potential to influence the behaviour of individuals in ways that can be beneficial for broader society.[28] The main point from this literature is that governments can change 'choice architecture' which will encourage people to make better decisions; that is, they can give them a little 'nudge' in the right direction.[29] This has inspired 'nudge' strategies in areas such as health (that is, tackling obesity and reducing smoking) and environmental issues (such as, making rubbish bins smaller and recycling bins larger; encouraging shorter showers during water shortages) and put such ideas at the centre of government. There is a 'nudge unit' in the British Cabinet Office and Richard Thaler, one of the authors of the book *Nudge*, has advised the government in that country. In the United States, President Barack Obama has been advised by Cass Sunstein (Thaler's co-author) who was appointed the head of the Office of Information and Regulatory Affairs in 2009 or 'nudger in chief' as his co-author described him.[30] In France too there is increasing interest in using neuroscience to influence the behaviour of individuals in a range of areas, but especially in public health (see Oullier and Sauneron 2010). Despite all the attention, recent critiques of the approach in Britain stress that nudge strategies are not, of themselves, likely to be effective without broader structural changes.[31]

Motivation at the organizational level

So far we have been considering how *individuals* might be motivated to contribute productive effort to public purposes. But the fact is that many of the external parties considered in this book are *organizations*. How then do we extend these notions of motivation to them? The answer, at one level, is that we don't: only people can be said to be motivated. Organizations do not have motivations; they have interests. But at another level, organizations have significant effects on the motivations of the individuals within them, and also mediate the impacts of motivators. Here we consider four factors.

The first is the *mission* of the external organization. In the short term, when it is at odds with the motivations of organizational members, the mission tends to prevail. This is especially the case when organizational survival is at stake. An organization under threat which emphasizes the significance of staying afloat may moderate the extent to which members subscribe to other non-material values. This is often an issue for non-profit organizations dependent on government contracts: their staff experience a tension between their normative purposes and the agency's financial need to bid for business that demands, for example, accountability regimes at odds with their principles.

In the longer run, the relationship between organizational mission and employee attitudes is fairly indirect. The mission functions as a focusing device, albeit asymmetrically. Insofar as it articulates the values of organizational members, it tends to reinforce them. But the reverse is less true: to the extent that it diverges from those values, it has a minimal effect on them. Of course, many organizations do not have an articulated mission. Instead they have a more implicit one, which may or may not reflect members' values.

A second factor is the distribution of *power* in the organization. Simply put, the more powerful the individual within the organization, the more likely that her motivations will dominate the way the organization responds to a government organization in the externalization process. This power will most likely be a function of the individual's position within the organization, but could also be due to her having valued knowledge or skills, or being deferred to as an informal leader within the organization.[32]

A third factor is the *structure* of the external organization. Not only will structure affect the distribution of power, it will also affect the pattern of interactions with the government organization. The motivations of those dealing directly with the public sector organization, or engaging in boundary-spanning activity, will be much more important than those of the people staffing back-office functions. Structure will also affect the configurations of motivations within the organization, giving prominence to some at the expense of others. For instance, an external provider that has a structure based on functions may privilege those motivated by concern for production values, whereas one based on categories of clients may tap into a different set of motivations.

The final factor is the *culture* of the external provider. Culture is based on shared core beliefs and values, which powerfully influence those in the organization (Schein 2004), and hence organizational members' motivations. Thus, a road construction authority hiring an engineering firm to build a bridge can expect an allegiance to robust construction standards within the firm, just as a government welfare department is likely to find that duty of care will be an important motivation for staff in a social work agency.

The motivations of individuals, therefore, are likely to be shaped and mediated by a range of features of the organizations that act as the linkage between individuals and government organizations.

Ability

Of course, a provider may be perfectly willing to contribute to a government agency's purposes, but be unable to do so. This may be because the task that the agency seeks from the provider is too difficult to perform, or too hard to understand, or inconvenient in some other way. In these circumstances, no matter how much the agency threatens sanctions, offers rewards or appeals to underlying values, the provider still cannot perform the task because it is just too hard. Increasing penalties or rewards is like talking more loudly to someone who doesn't understand the language, in the hope that increased volume will prompt understanding – which of course it doesn't. Government agencies can employ two types of measures to enhance providers' ability to perform their role. First, they could try to increase the providers' awareness or understanding of what is to be provided and how to do so; these we can call education and information strategies. Second, they could try to make it easier for the provider to undertake the task; these we can call convenience strategies. These strategies can significantly enhance the contribution to agency purposes of different types of providers, both organizational and individual, as will be discussed later in this book. But what is interesting for present purposes is that they also have an effect on two of the motivations we have been considering and therefore on providers' willingness to contribute.

For a start, increasing task convenience and understanding usually benefits providers materially, primarily by reducing the time or effort it takes them to do the task, thereby resonating with their material self-interest. Second, by enhancing the providers' sense of competence, it appeals to their intrinsic motivations – not least by mitigating the frustration they might feel in dealing with bewildering systems.

However, there is a limit to the second effect: offering 'too much' help and guidance to external parties can undermine their sense of competence, thereby creating strong dependencies, which ultimately undermines self-esteem and intrinsic motivation (Bénabou and Tirole 2003). Such patterns can be seen in those services to the unemployed where jobseekers are treated as passive recipients rather than active participants in co-production (see Alford 2009).

Conclusion

In this chapter we have reviewed the motivations and motivators that have the potential to affect external providers, and found that the model of people as self-interested utility-maximizers is too simplistic to account for the multitude of factors at stake:

We are neither as intellectually heroic nor as instrumentally villainous as a narrow focus on the microfoundation assumptions of modern economics and rational choice theory would imply. Given what we know about peoples' mixed motivation, cognitive limits and variable social framing of situations, to assume that they will react in a predictable way to policy interventions and incentives simply as a result of their rationality and self-interestedness is incongruous tending towards absurd.

(Stoker and Moseley 2010: 15)

Instead, government agencies need to exercise sophisticated judgement about which particular mixes of motivators to employ, and when to do so. None of this is to imply that providers are somehow motivational ciphers, to whom government agencies apply various influences and thereby have them dancing to their tune. Providers contribute to public purposes for their own good reasons, including how they perceive the interventions government agencies make. In the end, provision by external parties is difficult to sustain unless there is at least some voluntary impulse informing and animating their contributions.

Thus, just as government agencies seek something of value from involving external providers, as discussed in Chapter 2, so too do external providers expect something. The challenge for government agencies is to help to fashion the terms of this exchange so that they are value-creating for both sides.

Chapter 4

Outsourcing and Contracting to Other Organizations

In June 2004, the Department of Justice in the state of Western Australia took back control of the holding cells at the Supreme Court, following a dramatic breakout by nine violent prisoners. It pointed the finger at 'systemic failure' of the private firm it had contracted to deliver security at the courthouse, including guards propping open steel-plated doors to enable freer movement of staff, cell keys and perimeter keys being kept on the same key ring, failure to activate the alarm following the breakout, and not complying with the minimum number of staff prescribed (Taylor 2004). In the aftermath of the breakout there were calls for the Minister to resign and for a major investigation into contracting practices to work out just how these prisoners managed to escape. But was this as simple as a lazy or sneaky contractor? A series of reports and investigations identified a litany of problems: the publicly owned infrastructure was outdated, costs were blowing out, the contract failed to adequately specify the treatment of high security prisoners, and the relationship between AIMS, the provider, and the Department of Justice was 'turbulent'.[1] This was a case where it seemed that contracting was causing headaches rather than providing solutions.

In this chapter we focus on a particular distribution of roles between government organizations and external parties, and a particular mode of coordination between them. We call the distribution of roles in this case *outsourcing*, where an external party produces the whole of a service, while the government organization decides on and usually pays for it. We call the mode of coordination *contracting*, which involves specifying, monitoring and the use of incentives, penalties and often competition between

TABLE 4.1   *Key dimensions of outsourcing to organizations*

Distribution of roles	*Outsourcing*
Who decides?	Government organization
Who produces?	Private firm
	and/or non-profit/voluntary agency
	and/or other government organization
Mode of coordination	Classical contracting (usually)
	or
	Collaboration (sometimes)

providers. Thus 'outsourcing' and 'contracting' have distinctively different meanings here, even though they may be used somewhat inter-changeably in daily discourse (see Table 4.1).

Governments have long relied on contracts to engage with external providers, but there has been a major expansion in both the scale and scope of contracting over the last few decades. In the Australian context it has been argued that contract 'has become the most significant mechanism for the ordering of public resources and the delivery of services, both to the public and to the government itself' (Seddon 2004: 32), and in the United States the large-sale contracting undertaken by all levels of government is described as 'government by proxy'. Indeed for every federal government employee in the US there are now six government-by-proxy employees carrying out the work of government under contract (Dilulio 2003). This increased prevalence however has not meant that contracting has become any easier. As Kettl (2010) puts it, of all the strategies used to shrink government, 'contracting out poses the most fundamental, ongoing governance and public management puzzles' (p. 239). In this chapter we: examine the meaning of contracting, distinguishing it from other forms of engagement (for example, partnering, which is covered in Chapter 5); consider the nature of private firms, non-profits and other government organizations as contracting parties; explain the benefits and costs of contracting out; and canvas options for eliciting good performance from contracted providers.

The meanings of outsourcing and contracting

For our purposes, outsourcing ('or contracting out') is where a government organization (the 'principal') engages another party (an 'agent') to carry out work on its behalf (see Jensen and

Meckling 1976; Moe 1984; and Donaldson 1990). The principal hopes to benefit from the relationship because it presumes that the agent is better at doing the work in question. But at the same time, the principal faces a problem: that the agent has different interests, and if possible may take the opportunity to benefit at the principal's expense. The prison breakout case shows this clearly: the government wanted the contractor to manage the holding cells, whereas the contractor wanted to make a profit with the minimum cost, and therefore engaged in practices that were beneficial to it (ease of movement, lower wage costs) but which were detrimental to the government organization (escaped prisoners, public outcry, media attention) when an *actual* breakout occurred.

The usual device for handling this agency problem is a contract – a binding set of commitments between the principal and the agent. Typically it contains a specification of the services to be delivered, some measures of performance of those services, the amount of remuneration the agent will receive for delivery (either for the whole work or in parts tied to delivery) and the conditions under which the contract might be terminated. The design of the contract turns out to be critical in motivating agents to work in the interests of the principal (Lane 2000). Thus contracting is the mode of coordination between the principal and the agent.

Contracts can be highly formalistic or more relational.[2] Classical contracts or 'black letter law' agreements are very formalized and transactional: short, often anonymous, self-liquidating, economic exchanges. At the other end of the spectrum are relational contracts where norms, such as preservation of the relationship, participation in exchange, reciprocity or trust, develop to govern the parties. In this chapter, we will focus specifically on classical style contracts because these have tended to dominate the practice of outsourcing – although we also acknowledge that many of the assumptions of classical contracting, including those relating to motivations, hold to only a limited extent. Relational contracts (and more broadly, collaboration) will be considered in Chapter 5 because these models have underpinned partnering approaches to working with external parties.

Contracting forms

In recent practice, there has been a variety of government outsourcing arrangements, but two major forms have dominated: the contracting out of services and public–private partnerships

(PPPs) for infrastructure. Both have tended to be more classical than relational, despite the use of the term 'partner' in the PPP version, and both have motivational roots in the *homo economicus* view of the world.

Contracting out

Contracting out is the transfer of activity from the public sector to external parties, and involves government organizations entering into contracts with others, usually private or non-profit organizations and in some cases, other government organizations. In engaging another party to carry out the activity, government *usually* retains the responsibility for determining what will be provided and the financing for delivering of the service or function (Ferris 1986). Contracting out is generally considered a form of privatization because it involves a reduction in government involvement and an increase in private activity (see Savas 1987; Fairbrother *et al.* 2002; Van Slyke 2002, 2007; Aulich and O'Flynn 2007).

(It is important to note here that we use the term 'contracting *out*', not just 'contracting'. Contracting (with the 'out'), refers to the distribution of roles. It is *different* from just 'contracting', which refers to the mode of coordination.)

Contracting out encompasses both the externalization of public services where providers deliver services directly to clients on behalf of government (for example, employment services or refuse collection), and those services delivered directly to government organizations themselves (such as, cleaning or information technology services). Within the OECD, the most enthusiastic adopters have been the English-speaking and Nordic countries, with the continental European countries less likely to engage in contracting out (Blöndal 2005). International patterns show that governments tend to start with the contracting out of 'blue collar' or support services, such as cleaning or waste management, then move into non-core professional/ancillary services such as information technology or legal services, and then finally into what we might think of as 'frontline' government services such as fire-fighting, prisons, or child welfare services.

Contracting out has long been championed as a means of addressing the dysfunctions of bureaucracy, especially overcoming inefficient resource allocation. Its incentives and controls are

seen as encouraging, motivating or inducing the contractor to provide goods or services which are less costly, higher quality or more
responsive. The cost promise, along with the ability to access expertise not held in-house, and the potential to replace underperforming
internal providers has made outsourcing increasingly popular with
governments. An extreme example comes from Maywood, a small
city of around 28,000 people in Los Angeles County in the United
States. In 2010 the City fired *all* of its employees and outsourced *all*
its functions – from policing to crossing guards to city planning –
in an attempt to cut costs, improve quality, get rid of underperforming and corrupt employees, and bring it back from the brink
of bankruptcy. Many saw it is an act of 'municipal genius' with a
member of a local advocacy group arguing:

> Remember the Soviet Union? They had a lot of bureaucracy, and
> they lost. Maywood was like that. Now people know that if they
> don't work, they will be laid off. Much better this way.
>
> (Streitfeld 2010)

The promise of cost savings was a powerful force driving this
practice, especially competitive tendering and contracting out,
which expanded rapidly through the 1980s and 1990s as many
government came under pressure to cut costs. When a study
in the United Kingdom (Cubbin *et al.* 1987) showed that savings of 20 per cent could be made when refuse collection was
contracted out, the practice of outsourcing exploded. When subsequent studies (see Domberger 1989, 1993, 1994) suggested this
was the case across a range of areas – from defence contracting
to cleaning – the scale and scope of outsourcing grew. Despite
cautions regarding the variability of savings (Hodge 1996) and
the importance of a combination of competition and monitoring (Hefetz and Warner 2004), the cost-cutting promise has been
central to driving governments toward outsourcing. But this is a
two-edged sword: there is emerging evidence that municipal governments in the United Kingdom are increasingly *in*-sourcing in
response to budget pressures – some 60 per cent of respondents
in one survey explained they were bringing services back into
government to increase efficiency and reduce service costs (UNI-
SON 2011).

The implementation of contracting out has been facilitated
by the separation of *purchasing* and *providing* functions within

government organizations and the use of competition to choose providers (O'Flynn and Alford 2008; Bevir 2009). Driving this separation has been the idea that self-interested bureaucrats who are responsible for both the production and consumption of services have incentives to maximize budgets rather than control costs or enhance quality (Downs 1957; Niskanen 1971; Ostrom and Ostrom 1971; Savas 1982). Separating these functions would help to clarify who was responsible for what, enabling clearer lines of accountability, control and responsibility, and it would also stimulate competition in areas traditionally monopolized by government (Ferris 1986).

The experience of contracting out, however, has been mixed. When it works well it helps to clarify mandates, drive efficiency gains, flexibility, and innovation, and improves spending decisions. On the other hand, contracting out can also create complexity, strip away those parts of public purpose and services that cannot be easily specified, and costs can increase (Donahue 1989). Many writers have pointed to the transparency and accountability issues that surface under contracting regimes, especially where there are commercial-in-confidence arrangements which reduce levels of scrutiny (see, for example, Mulgan 2000b; Seddon 2004; Blöndal 2005).

Public–private partnerships

The second major form has been public–private partnerships (PPPs). Across the volumes written on the topic of PPPs, several 'families' of PPP arrangements can be discerned ranging from long-term infrastructure projects through to development projects with civil society organizations.[3] The result is considerable ambiguity and debate about what a PPP *actually* is.[4] Here we focus on a specific form of PPP which accounts for much of the confusion: infrastructure partnerships, also known as PFIs (private finance initiatives) in the United Kingdom and further afield. What makes these arrangements ambiguous is that they usually do not involve partnerships in the sense that we use the term here, in that typically the producing of the service is *not* shared by the government and external provider, but rather all performed by the provider, usually under a long-term contract.[5] Arrangements which are much more about *partnering* are the subject of Chapter 5. Our focus is on the use of the private sector to 'design, build, finance, maintain, and operate . . . infrastructure assets traditionally provided by the public sector' (Blöndal 2005: 19). In a PPP the role of the public sector organization is to:

> define the scope of business; specify priorities, targets and outputs; and set the performance regime by which management of the PPP is given incentives to deliver . . . The essential role and responsibility of the private sector in all PPPs is to deliver the business objectives of the PPP on terms offering value for money to the public sector.
>
> (Gerrard 2001)

However, this description begs a question, which should be asked of most PPPs: how can they be called 'public–private partnerships' when they are neither 'public' nor 'partnerships' – that is, the government does not do any of the producing, all of which is performed by the private party in the arrangement? Hodge and Greve (2008: 95) argue that 'Infrastructure finance deals are no more partnerships than the contract made when citizens take out a house mortgage with their local bank.' Teisman and Klijn (2002) specifically noted that the PFI scheme in the UK was a form of contracting rather than partnering.

Take for instance one of the most commonly used types of PPPs: the build-own-operate-transfer (BOOT) scheme, as applied for instance to the construction and maintenance of a freeway. Here the private provider performs the work of building the facility, and then owns and maintains it for, say, 25 years. Tellingly, the remaining task is to *transfer* the facility back to the public sector, a role which underscores the fact that it has been in private hands until then. A similar logic applies to another common device, the sale-and-lease-back arrangement, in which government sells public assets to private firms, then leases them back, while the private firms operate and maintain them.

The misuse of the term 'partnership' in these types of cases has been attributed by Hodge and Greve to a 'language game ... designed to "cloud" other strategies and purposes' (Hodge and Greve 2005: 7; see also Linder 1999; Savas 2000; and Shaoul 2005). In particular it is seen as a more palatable term than the 'privatization' it replaced, in part because it includes the word 'public' and in part because it involves 'partnership', which is generally seen as a positive. Coming after a decade or more in the Anglo-American democracies of growing public disillusionment about, and interest group resistance to, the extensive handing over of public assets and programmes to the private sector, 'public–private partnerships' were offered as kinder, gentler alternatives to privatization, even though in many cases they amounted to much the same thing. We will call these arrangements '*rhetorical* public–private partnerships', to distinguish them from more genuine PPPs where the production task is shared, which we will call '*substantive* PPPs' and explore in Chapter 5.

PPPs comprise various bundles of design, construction and maintenance tasks, whereas contracting out is usually focused on single or specific services (for example, refuse collection, or delivery of meals to the elderly) (Webb and Pulle 2002). These arrangements can have various combinations, for example, PPPs may take the form of a DCM (design, construct, maintain) where the private firm designs, constructs and then maintains the asset; a BOO (build, own, operate), where a private firm/consortium builds the infrastructure and then owns and operates it for a fee (either paid by government or users); or a BOOT (build, own, operate, transfer), where the asset is transferred to government at the end of the contract.[6]

The contracts that govern PPPs tend to be long, complex, legalistic, and highly specified; in other words, they tend toward the classical rather than the relational end of the spectrum. According to Hodge (2005), the full set of contracts governing the CityLink toll road in Melbourne, Australia, stood several meters high and required a team of lawyers to interpret them.

The range of projects undertaken using PPPs is broad and take-up across the developed and developing world progressed rapidly. The use of a PFI model in Japan, for example, began in 2001 following legislative changes to allow for longer-term contracts between government and the private sector (previously a law prohibited contracts longer than five years). Between 2001 and 2007 more than 90 PFI projects were launched – from waste facilities, to accommodation for public employees, to educational facilities, and Japan's adoption of PPPs outstripped that of the UK (Confederation of British Industry 2007).[7]

There have been many PPP success stories. In England, studies have shown that PFI-funded hospitals are cleaner than those built with public money, and receive higher patient ratings. In India, the 90.4 kilometre six-lane expressway built between Jaipur and

Kishangarh in Rajasthan was completed six months ahead of its 30-month schedule, demonstrating that PPPs can deliver ahead of time.[8]

Governments have been attracted to PPPs for several reasons, all loudly advocated by proponents: they structure incentives for private firms to deliver on time and under-budget; they bring forward large infrastructure projects that debt-shy governments are not prepared to fund; they transfer risk to private firms; and they enable governments to shift costs 'off the balance sheet'.[9] However, in some cases PPPs do not represent a strategic choice, but rather a government or funder requirement. In the UK, for example, it was government policy in the early 2000s that all new prisons would be built under PPP arrangements (Sturgess 2002). And in Africa, projects funded through the International Development Association have required a PPP model: for example, a project for rural water supply in Rwanda stipulated that ten per cent of the supply had to be managed by local private operators (Alexander 2008).

Whilst PPPs have increased in popularity they have not been without their detractors, raising questions about whether they are actually cheaper, whether risk is really transferred, and how these are actually paid for in the longer-term.[10] Serious concerns have been raised in the UK and elsewhere about whether PFI projects really reduce costs and time over-runs, with some writers arguing that positive evaluations have come from pro-PFI governments. Others[11] have questioned how risk is calculated and costed and whether it is actually transferred to the private sector through this model.[12] There have also been serious concerns raised about the lax performance monitoring of these schemes; a 2010 UK National Audit Office report, for example, found a failure to collect objective performance data, an over-reliance on self-report data, a failure to audit returns by private contractors, and insufficient resources for monitoring (Pollock *et al.* 2011).

Outsourcing and PPPs have been positioned nearer to the classical contracting end of the spectrum, and have had mixed success around the world. In some circumstances there have been appropriate matches between the service and the instrument for governing the relationship between the parties, whilst there has also been extensive evidence to show that mismatches create considerable problems, not just technically but also politically.

Understanding contracting parties

Government organizations outsource to three main types of parties: private firms, non-profit organizations and other government entities. Private sector organizations are distinctive in that they operate in an economic market, they seek to satisfy customers to generate revenues, and to a greater or lesser extent the profit incentive channels managerial effort toward the creation of private value (for example, profit maximization, customer satisfaction and shareholder returns) (Moore 2000). In the *theory* of contracting, private firms are assumed to be driven by the pursuit of profit, which provides high-powered incentives to deliver cheaper and/or better goods and services to attract customers and outwit competitors.

To the extent that profit does dominate the interests of private corporations, it is a two-edged sword. On the one hand, as will be discussed below, companies' urge to make a profit, spurred by competition and disciplined by contractual controls, is supposed to impel them to deliver better value for money and innovation, making them attractive to government purchasers. On the other, the drive to maximize profits is said to impel them to find ways to cut corners and skimp on quality (Brown *et al.* 2006: 327). The Western Australian prison breakout, discussed at the start of this chapter, was a telling example of quality suffering for the sake of reducing costs.

But while the profit motive is important to private companies, it is a little simplistic to say that it is their only concern. They are also concerned, in varying mixtures, about their reputation and to a greater or lesser degree about their social responsibilities (Fisse and Braithwaite 1983). As Ayres and Braithwaite put it: 'all corporate actors are bundles of contradictory commitments about economic rationality, law abidingness, and business responsibility' (1992: 19). These more complex concerns will attenuate the impact of the profit motive.

Likewise, non-profit organizations come in various forms, from small faith-based organizations, to large global advocacy groups and they differ from private firms in several ways.[13] For example, they *primarily* operate in donor markets, constantly seeking to attract donor resources (for example, volunteer effort or donations) and are focused on the achievement of social purposes rather than the generation of profits and shareholder returns (Moore 2000). They *usually* engage in different activities than for-profit firms, with heavy involvement in complex social services which are labour intensive and which have uncertain outcomes, and where labour productivity increases are rare or difficult, for example, mental health services, or service to vulnerable children. Working with non-profits is attractive to government organizations for several reasons. Proximity to clients, legitimacy with local communities, lower costs, programme innovation, the ability to raise funds and cross-subsidize programmes, and quick start-up times have all been seen as important advantages.[14] The lack of profit motive has prompted some to argue that monitoring costs should be lower as there may not be strong incentives to shirk or act opportunistically, and others have claimed that non-profits share similar missions to government (see Brown *et al.* 2006 on this point). It is true that non-profits are driven more by purposive and other motivations, which at least qualify the extent to which earning revenue is important. On the other hand, to the extent that revenue is important to the survival or expansion of socially useful programmes, non-profit leaders may seek to maximize it as a means to pursue purposive values. Indeed, the expansion of contractualism has recast these organizations somewhat as markets have developed for a range of social services. So whilst being responsive to the donor market, many non-profit organizations are now involved in large-scale activity through contracts with government and this changes their incentive structures which can, in the long-run create perverse incentives and undermine the very benefits that government have seen in these relationships (Van Slyke 2007).

Government organizations can also 'contract' with other parts of government (although not legally), and this has been seen in practice through the use of purchaser–provider models – quasi-contracts to create internal markets. These models can be within organizations, within or across a portfolio, or between levels of government. There may be some expectation that 'contracting' with another government organization will overcome some of the challenges of working with other parties, however this has been much more challenging in practice and, in the end, these relationships are subject to all the *potential* issues of any principal–agent relationship.[15]

When to contract out

In Chapter 2 we argued that services should be externalized when the benefits of doing so outweigh the costs, and this is no less true of contracting out. As with other types of externalization, there is a variety of types of benefits and costs. Most attention has been paid to the service benefits and costs, but often overlooked in assessments of the relative worth of contracting are the other types of benefits and costs: those to do with the relationship, and those to do with the strategic situation of the organization.

Relationship costs and benefits

The logic of contracting

To consider relationship costs, we need to understand the logic of contracting (see Figure 4.1). Its under-pinning assumption is that the provider seeks to make a profit. But as indicated above, this is not quite true, not only for non-profit organizations but also to some extent for private for-profit firms. For the purposes of analysis, however, we will first assume that is true in order to explain the orthodox logic, then acknowledge the more complex motivations. In its most straightforward form, with for-profit firms, contracting entails both harnessing the profit motive and enabling the particular expertise of the provider to deliver value for money, largely because the agent (or provider) seeks to make a profit.

The contract will have this effect if the provider can be subject to a sanction for inadequate performance (or a reward for good performance), and can be held accountable for how well it performs. The most powerful sanction in a contracting situation is termination of the contract, non-renewal or, where there is a competitive market, replacement with another provider. Holding the provider to account is best done by specifying the service in output terms in advance, and monitoring its delivery periodically after the fact. Specifying in output terms is preferable to specifying processes or inputs, firstly because it focuses on the *results* the purchaser wants, and secondly it gives the provider autonomy to determine *how* best to deliver these, and hopefully thereby to tap their specific expertise. It is also useful if the purchaser wishes to deploy incentives, which can be tied to measured performance against the specified outputs. At the same time, outputs are usually easier to measure than

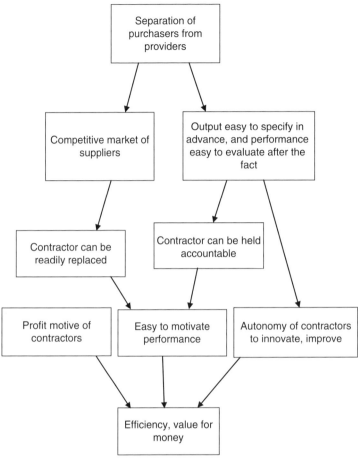

FIGURE 4.1 *The logic of contracting*

outcomes – even if the latter may be more relevant to purchasers' concerns.

Finally, to facilitate specification of services and to encourage competition, purchaser–provider separation is required (O'Flynn and Alford 2008; Bevir 2009). Thus the hope is that the provider's desire to make a profit can be channelled into inducing them to deliver value for money to the government purchaser. But this hope is founded on several assumptions which, on closer examination, appear to be problematic in the real world.

Specification and monitoring

First, it is not always easy to specify and monitor services, even though the clear articulation of what the principal wants the agent to do is at the core of contracting success. As Kettl puts it, public sector organizations must become 'smart buyers': 'Government must know what it wants to buy. It must know how to buy its goods and services. And it must be able to determine what it has bought' (1993: 17; see also Brown and Potoski 2003). In the Western Australian case, the Department of Justice sought the provision of court security and custodial services with the intention of 'creating an improved, integrated service that releases police and justice staff from non-core activities of court security and prison transport' (Department of Justice 2003: 50).

However, several factors make specification and monitoring difficult, particularly in terms of outputs (see Prager 1994; Hendry 2002; and Greve 2008). One reason is *uncertainty*: the fact that at the time of writing the contract, the precise work to be done may not be known. For instance, providing court security and custodial services might have some unforeseeable aspects such as prisoner escapes, calling for big redeployments of personnel at unpredictable times. This problem can be addressed in one of several ways, but each of them incurs costs. A contingent contract could be written, full of 'If . . . then . . . ' clauses, but it would take time and money to formulate, especially if the purchaser and provider bargain aggressively, and in any case it may not anticipate every eventuality. Alternatively, the parties could renegotiate the contract when unpredictable circumstances arise. However, in these circumstances, the purchaser is likely to be more dependent on the provider, who will therefore have a bargaining advantage and, if motivated by profit, might have incentives to exploit it. Another solution is to write a contract in outcome terms, but this shifts the risk to the provider, who will then seek a higher price. In the court security case, among the mandated outcomes were the maximum number of prisoner escapes (two per annum) and the number of prisoner deaths (zero per annum) (Department of Justice 2003: 22–3).

Another reason is *information-asymmetry*, that is, that providers have greater knowledge of what they can do and have done than the purchaser. The more this is the case, the more there are costs, first, in selecting the right providers, such as analysing tenders, interviewing, evaluating and ranking, and second, in monitoring performance (such as inspection, data-collection and so on). The latter problem might be addressed by enabling clients to act as monitors. But this is difficult where clients are unable to judge performance against the standards, if they know them at all, or where they are unable to express grievances, for example children or the elderly. This problem had dramatic consequences in the Western Australia Supreme Court example. It was either resource-intensive or inconvenient for the Department of Justice to keep tabs on the actions of the contractor's staff who allowed the break-out, such as propping doors open, putting both cell and perimeter keys on the same ring, and fielding insufficient guards – in all of which there was no occasion for Departmental personnel to be present in the holding cells. By the same token, if the Department had devoted staff to monitoring the contractor's day-to-day operations, it could reasonably be accused of interfering in processes, and not leaving the provider to find the best way to deliver the desired results. At the same time, failure to achieve these required results – which in this case was protecting public safety by minimizing prisoner escapes – has serious consequences, for which only partial success is not good enough.

A further issue is *interdependency*, either between the purchaser and provider, or between the provider and other parties. To the extent that it is difficult to distinguish the provider's contribution to performance from that of the purchaser or other parties, it is harder to assess performance and to apply appropriate incentives or sanctions. This is especially an issue in many areas of social policy where co-production with clients and coordinated effort between providers is common. Often this interdependency demands more collaborative relationships among providers, which, in practice are undermined by competitive tendering processes.

Of course, services will vary in how much they are prone to these problems. Where standard goods or services are the focus of government contracting, then classical contracting can be highly effective. But with more complex bundles of services, contracting out can be dysfunctional (see Bajari and Tadelis 2001; Entwistle *et al.* 2005). As Behn and Kant noted, 'contracting for social services is inherently more complicated than contracting for pencils' (1999: 458). Education is a classic example, where easy-to-measure indicators – test scores, attendance rates, and pledging alliance to the flag – do not actually capture all we expect or demand from schools (Donahue 1989).

Competition (or lack thereof)
Competition provides an essential discipline on providers and an absence of competition strips away many of the potential benefits: 'Most of the kick in privatization comes from the greater scope for rivalry when functions are contracted out, not from private provision *per se*' (Donahue 1989: 218). Competition, however, has been elusive in many areas of public sector activity. In more than a few public sector activities, there may be insufficient providers of a particular service to constitute a competitive market (deHoog 1990: 321). This may be addressed by pro-active attempts to develop markets, for example, through encouraging consortia or sub-contracting to enable groups of providers to assemble the required sets of capacities. But such practices are vulnerable to intra-consortium tensions and lengthened accountability chains. Alternatively, a department may disaggregate the service into elements for which there are competing providers, but this adds to tendering and contract management costs, and can undermine a holistic service experience for clients, for example. A related problem is asset-specificity, or the degree to which assets (human, physical, or site, for example) can be redeployed to other uses or other users without a related reduction in productive value.[16] Where these investments are made, bilateral dependence or forms of 'lock in' are likely, and the desire to subject the relationship to competition will reduce (Riordan and Williamson 1985). Higher levels of asset specificity increase switching costs for the principal. Thus, an incumbent provider may have a market advantage simply by already having the contract, which has enabled it to build up relationship- or contract-specific assets, knowledge or client relationships.

Separating purchasing from provision
Although separating purchasers and providers is a necessary precondition for governing the relationship in the terms described above, it can be difficult to implement in practice. It has been shown that the effectiveness of separation relies on the ability of the parties to draw a clear line between policy and implementation. Also, the making of policy often requires some input from those on the implementation side, which may not be forthcoming if the latter

have different interests to the former (Stewart 1996). It has also been the case that in some organizations, separation meant that the purchaser had little, if any, knowledge of what they wanted from providers, who were therefore in a position to exploit them (O'Flynn and Alford 2008).

Profit and other motives
All of these factors are problems in commercial contracting precisely because it relies on the fact that providers are profit-seekers. If there is a competitive market and services can be specified and monitored in output terms, the profit motive will drive them to perform well. But if competition is absent and it is hard to specify and monitor outputs, it will prompt them to take advantage of the purchasers, delivering poorer services at excessive cost. To guard against this possibility, the purchaser has to incur considerable costs, in structuring markets, specification and monitoring. In some circumstances, these costs may outweigh the benefits to government of outsourcing. Thus, the profit motive is a two-edged sword.

None of these factors is in itself a reason not to contract out. Rather the essential point is that they impose costs on the management of the relationship, and these need to be factored in when sizing up all the costs and benefits of this mode of operating.

However, the key assumption that all providers are profit-driven is not entirely true. As discussed above, some company executives, and to an even greater extent many non-profit leaders, take other factors besides material reward, such as their reputation or their commitment to the clients, to staff or to ethical standards, into account in the way they run their organizations. One way they assign the relative weight of these non-material motivations and material incentives is in their 'lexical ordering' of them, as discussed in Chapter 3: they feel that one must be satisfied before the other can be addressed. For instance, a nursing home proprietor may take the view that he should provide a minimum standard of care as a basic requirement and then pursue profit maximization over and above that.

To the extent that contractors are more broadly motivated, there is room for reliance on other motivations, such as intrinsic, social or normative ones, to help govern the relationship, potentially lessening the relationship costs – but at the same time weakening the high-powered nature of the profit incentive.

Strategic benefits and costs

A major strategic benefit for which outsourcing has been praised is that it impels organizations to be clearer about what their core business is – to assess carefully what they should be doing themselves and what they should be engaging others to do (see Osborne and Gaebler 1992; Quinn and Hilmer 1994; Domberger 1998). Delineating these core competences is, however, both tricky and high-risk. In particular, it is critical not to hand over to external parties those functions which affect organizations' future capacity to manage externalization. For example, if the IT division of a government department were to outsource the design of its system architecture, that could hamper its ability to hold providers to account in future (see Weill and Ross 2004).

Another problem relates to accountability: outsourcing removes the government organization's direct control over service performance, but it remains responsible for any serious mishaps:

> Despite the enthusiasm for entrepreneurial government and privatization, the most egregious tales of waste, fraud, and abuse in government programs have often involved greedy, corrupt, and often criminal activity by the government's private partners – and weak government management to detect and correct these problems. If reliance upon private markets is the answer to the government's problems, and the government has been expanding its partnerships with the private sector, why have such problems endured and, indeed, multiplied.
>
> (Kettl 1993: 5)

The Western Australian government learnt this in the case of the Supreme Court breakout, of course, and when a man died in custody while being transported by the same provider (Department of Justice 2003).[17] Scandals continued with this service, raising issues not just of cost and quality but of human rights and accountability. In 2007 the Western Australian Human Rights Commission found drivers transporting prisoners ignored the cries of men from the back of a scorching hot van; the air-conditioning was malfunctioning and the men became so severely dehydrated and distressed that one drank his own urine.[18] Soon after, an Indigenous elder died of heat stroke whilst being transported by the same company (Phillips 2010). Again, the air-conditioning in the van was not working, with temperatures soaring to 50 degrees Celsius. The van was so hot, the man received third-degree burns on his abdomen, and died of heat stroke during the four-hour journey. Whilst the coroner found that the company, the drivers, and the government shared blame, it was the Western Australian government who paid compensation of A\$3.2 million to his family; the company blamed the drivers for not following procedures, and then paid a fine of just A\$285,000 (although not until three years after the man's death). In the end the government took the lion's share of responsibility for the actions of other parties.

The contracting-accountability link is much debated, with advocates arguing that contracting clarifies these relationships, and detractors arguing that it undermines accountability. A more nuanced account by Mulgan (2000a) shows that there are *different* accountability structures and requirements and that this can, in part, explain why private firms are more efficient and therefore able to offer services at lower prices. Public organizations have much greater accountability for processes and how they go about making decisions, with public servants ultimately accountable to politicians. Private firms have a focus on returns and the bottom line, which tends to dominate concerns about process. The range of activities for which private managers are held to account is much narrower in Mulgan's analysis, than that for which public servants can be held to account. There is potential for an accountability-efficiency trade-off. This does not make contracting out inherently problematic *per se*, it just means that there will be more complex accountability structures and relationships in place.

Weighing up when to contract out

The decision as to whether to contract out is analogous to the 'make-or-buy' decision that any firm faces. As Donahue (1989: 38) put it:

> Once we have decided to pay collectively to accomplish some task, we have to decide on the form of the contract with people who will carry it out – will we hire employees and produce internally, or use contractors and use an external production model?

As discussed earlier in this book, this decision has tended to be made on a variety of grounds, such as ideological predilection or a desire to cut government spending, in some cases through government requirement based on these or other considerations. Here we take the position that whether to outsource is a contingent matter; it depends on the circumstances. This is not a matter of 'paint-by-numbers' precise calculation, but rather of public managers exercising judgement, using these concepts to organize their assessments. The foregoing discussion provides the ingredients for understanding these circumstances. Basically, deciding whether to contract out is a matter of weighing up the different kinds of benefits and costs (see Table 4.2), which can be unearthed by asking three key questions:

1 Are there no strategic reasons, such as maintaining core competences, for keeping the function 'in-house'? (the *strategic* question).
2 Can an external provider do the task better and/or cheaper? Are there potential gains in effectiveness or efficiency to be reaped from having an external provider? (the *service* question).
3 Are the costs of managing the relationship minimal? (the *relationship* question). Specifically: Is there a competitive market? Is it relatively easy to specify and monitor the service?

Where the answer to all of these three questions is 'yes', then external providers should take on the task and relatively 'classical' contracts can be used. But if, on the other hand, the answer to all of them is 'no', then the service should be produced by the government organization itself. Here the problem is not only that outsourcing will fail to achieve the expected benefits, but also that the private provider will be likely to take advantage of the situation to the extent that the government organization is actually worse off. As Van Slyke puts it: 'if the basic principal-agent problem and various market imperfections exist, and defining goals is difficult and elusive then privatization should not be seriously considered' (2005: 497).

However, it is more usual than not that the answers to these questions are mixed, and therefore benefits and costs need to be weighed up against each other, and sometimes alternative arrangements considered. For example, if the government organization can perform the task better or cheaper than any external provider, or indeed if there is no outside supplier at all, so that competition is absent, but the task is relatively easy to specify and monitor, then it may be worthwhile to establish an arm's length service-delivery

TABLE 4.2 *Weighing up costs and benefits of contracting out*

Contract type	Strategic factors present	Benefit achievable	Level of competition	Ease of specification and monitoring
In-house production	Yes or no	No outside provider can provide better or cheaper	No competitive market exists for supply of the service	Difficult to specify outputs and/or monitor performance
Service agency (quasi-contract)	Yes or no	No outside provider available	No competitive market exists for supply of the service	Easy to specify outputs and/or monitor performance
Relational contracting	No	Outside provider and governemt organization together can provide a better or cheaper service	No competitive market exists for supply of the service	Difficult to specify outputs and/or monitor performance
Classical contracting	No	Outside provider can provide better or cheaper service	Competitive market exists for supply of the service	Easy to specify outputs and/or monitor performance

agency to do it, as occurred for instance, with Australia's Centrelink or with the 'Next Steps' executive agencies in the UK.[19] If, by contrast, there is an external provider which can deliver the service well, but it is difficult to specify and monitor and competition is absent, then the possibilities for a collaborative relationship should be explored (this is dealt with in more detail in the next chapter).

Some of the trickiest judgements are posed when the service benefits are high and the transaction costs are low, but there is a significant strategic reason why the activity should be performed by government. For example, Donahue (1989) points to the risks inherent in privatizing prisons, because it involves handing over the right to exercise coercive power on behalf of the state to private companies and their staff. He observes that contracting out appears to be somewhat more manageable for low-security prisons than for high-security ones, for precisely this reason. Thus, even if private prisons can be run more cheaply and with better quality service than public ones, there may be good reason to avoid contracting high-security institutions to them.

Here we demonstrate these three questions using two examples. The first is the contracting out of court security and custodial services which opened the chapter, and the second is the provision of catering services for the Ministry of Finance in Turkey. The former has been explained throughout the chapter, and the second needs only a brief introduction.[20] In Turkey, a subsidized lunch is provided to civil servants when the number of employees exceeds fifty in any ministerial unit; when the service was contracted out this equated to some one million employees (out of 1.3 million). Each government organization had the option to contract out (although few did), and the Ministry of Finance Central Office decided to contract out provision of a four-course lunch in four different dining rooms (depending on the seniority of staff).

The strategic question

In the court security case, it could be argued that the core business of the court is the application of 'justice' (that is, what happens *inside* the courtroom) rather than court security or court custody; indeed this was the view of the Department of Justice which described these services as non-core.[21] Therefore, we could argue these functions are not core competences, but rather allied services, and handing such functions out to providers, many of them large multinationals that have developed expertise in these areas, should not represent any serious threat to the core competences of the Department of Justice. At first glance, then, we might answer this question by saying 'no', that is, there is no strategic reason to keep this in-house.

However, this case showed that we may only realize the broader strategic costs once a serious contractual problem occurs: a person dies a horrible, inhumane death being transported by the company; a group of prisoners overpower the unarmed guards and escape into the community. Accountability questions arise immediately: who is responsible when the actions of a contractor culminate in the death of a person in custody? Who 'pays' when a group of prisoners escape into the community? This raises broader strategic issues that may concern politicians or a government organization such as legitimacy, fairness and so on. In this case, the answer to the question is not 'no', but more likely 'maybe', once we consider these broader strategic costs.

In the Ministry of Finance case it is hard to imagine that retaining the production of meals in-house has any 'strategic' value. The core competences of a Ministry of Finance would be centred on the management of tax and financial affairs of the country, rather than catering. So the answer to this question is a straightforward 'no'; there are no compelling strategic reasons to keep it in-house.

The service question

In the Ministry of Finance case, it was shown that the external provider could provide the service better and cheaper. There was a well-developed supplier market, indeed the winner of the contract was an international firm. In such cases we can expect large multinationals to have developed organizational routines, and/or economies of scale, that enable them to deliver lower costs (provided there is a competitive market, which in this case there was). Labour costs were lower under the external provider model because they used fewer staff (75 compared to 110 for the same amount of meals),[22] employees were on different conditions (previously staff were covered by the Civil Service Personnel Act), and a series of rigidities that had developed over time were eliminated. And quality, as judged by consumers, increased. The answer here is a clear 'yes' – the external party could provide the service both cheaper and better.

The court security case is more complicated. The provider held the contract for several years (indeed the Department renewed it post-escape) and it was seen to 'present enormous challenges for the Department of Justice' (Director General, Department of Justice 2003: 2). Three years into the contract there were still major concerns about quality, and the contractor had not met the Department's objectives in any of these years: 'justice customers around the state express little enthusiasm for the levels of customer service' (2003: 2). There was little incentive for the contractor to deliver 'value for money' because of the incentive model used – indeed it took three years for the provider to deliver the service within budget forecasts and a departmental review found the service could be delivered for *at least* A\$1.5 million less. The Department also incurred considerable costs in working with the contractor to monitor resource use and business costs, so it could enhance its efficiency. This is not what is expected in the contracting ideal, and it means the answer to our questions is: 'maybe'.

The relationship question

In the case of catering for the Ministry of Finance, the catering market was well-developed, and six companies entered bids for the tender. It is also noteworthy that the contract was only for one year which, in incentive terms, can act as a fairly strong discipline on providers to satisfy their principal. Also the service was easy to specify – a four-course meal served in four different dining rooms – and monitor – a committee of consumers did this and reported regularly. Here, the answer to the question is 'yes': the costs of managing the service were minimal.

Relationship costs in the court security and custodial services contract, however, were more mixed, reflecting several factors. Three years into the contract, the Director General of the Department noted that 'relationships with the contractor have improved somewhat from a very low base ' (Department of Justice 2003: 2). For the first few years, the parties were engaged in protracted arbitration, senior provider managers did not engage with the Department in a cooperative way, and trust levels were low: 'the level of trust in senior AIMS management, which continued to transfer operational risk to the Department and take little responsibility for service issues, had deteriorated' (2003: 3).

Monitoring of the contractor's performance was clearly an issue. Whilst performance measures existed, worrying practices had emerged at the courthouse where the prisoners escaped, and transport drivers were not following procedures, both of which ultimately created major scandals. The performance standards were linked to a bonus/sanction scheme, which went to the specifics of the service. Each of the nineteen measures had a 'maximum allowable' number of incidents per annum before a penalty applied and this included escapes (two allowed per annum), and assaults on a member of public (two). Of course, the Department of Justice's ability to gather the data to monitor across these areas was reliant on its relationship with the provider which was described as 'turbulent' by the Department's Acting Director General five years into the contract (Department of Justice 2005). At various times the Department had to call in auditors to assess whether the costs charged reflected services provided (Department of Corrective Services 2010).

The level of competition in the 'justice' market is relatively low, making switching providers difficult. Whilst there are major multinational providers, there appears to be market concentration. The CEO of one of the big players, G4S, commented that 'There is only two or three major players, typically sometimes only two bidding ... in time we will become a winner in that market because there's lots of outsourcing opportunities and not many competitors' (Bernstein 2011).[23] In this case the answer to the question is likely, 'no' the costs are not minimal because of challenges in monitoring, and low levels of competition.

In the case of catering at the Ministry of Finance the recommendation is clear – contracting out should deliver benefits because we can answer 'yes' to the three critical questions. Classical contracting should work well in this environment. The case of court security and custodial services is, however, much more complicated. It appears that:

1 there are strategic costs involved, but ones that may or may not be decisive;
2 it is not clear the provider could do it 'better or cheaper'; and
3 competition was lacking, and there was potential for high monitoring costs, especially given the scandals observed over time.

In this case, the answers to our questions would seem to push us away from classical contracting toward relational contracting or in-house production.

Eliciting provider effort: structuring incentives

As previously discussed, the primary if not the only motivator, on which contracting relies, is material reward. This is obviously so for private firms, but only partially true of non-profit agencies; while their purpose is not to make a profit, they attach significance to the money they receive from government for contracts since it is important to their ongoing survival as organizations, and achievement of their social purpose. The salience of this motivation has been one of the topics of debate in discussion of the merits of contracting. On the one hand, monetary reward can be seen as a high-powered incentive, in that it can be applied to measurable actions, and thereby prompt the specific performance desired by the purchaser. On the other, the very fact that providers are motivated by monetary reward should make us wary about potential gaming behaviour, aimed at maximizing rewards whilst minimizing efforts. Monetary reward is thus a two-edged sword. This puts a premium on the intelligent structuring of incentives, to encourage optimal performance and to avoid opportunistic behaviour.

Incentives can be built into contracts in various ways. The most obvious is a *fixed-price* contract, where there is a set price to be paid in exchange for goods or services. In a tendering context this means 'the payment is simply the firm's bid' (McAfee and McMillan 1986: 326). This provides certainty for the government department in terms of cost, and should produce lower costs provided there is competition. The main challenge for public managers will be specifying the tasks as exactly as possible because variations will require negotiation and will likely incur additional costs.

The second common approach is a *cost-plus* contract, where government pays the full costs of production plus an additional fee which may be either fixed in advance or represent a proportion of costs. The cost-plus model was at the core of the court security and custodial services contract between AIMS and the Department of Justice in Western Australia. It was generally viewed as being a high-cost approach. Three years into the contract, the Director General of the Department stated:

> The services delivered under the . . . contract are *generally* meeting service level expectations, until recently, there had been little effort to drive efficiencies and the cost-plus contract structure means there is little incentive to do so.
>
> (Department of Justice 2003: 2, emphasis in original)

A third form is the *incentive* contract which involves payments for meeting specific targets in either delivery or performance levels. Combinations are also possible, for example a *cost-plus-incentive contract* would involve the government paying the full cost of production then making additional payments where performance targets are met or delivery is made early. This approach was used in the court security and custodial services contract – it required the Department of Justice to pay: (1) all direct and indirect costs actually and reasonably incurred by AIMS; (2) a margin of 1.5 per cent of (1); and (3) a performance-linked fee up to 4.5 per cent of (1).[24] The contractor frequently failed to meet the performance standards which meant that the performance-linked fee was lower than if it had met the measures; for example, in 2004–5 it had the potential to earn A\$898,852 in bonuses, but instead incurred penalties of A\$201,233; this included a A\$100,000 penalty following the death of a prisoner being transported. There is some argument, however, that this encourages gaming of deadlines or production targets. There has been some suggestion this model has created perverse incentives for Iraqi military contractors:

> Ultimately the company does not care how much it spends, because under its contracts, the military pay Halliburton for costs plus a small profit margin of one per cent. It addition to its direct costs, Halliburton can bill as cost a percentage of its overhead, all the way up to its Houston head office. Once the work is complete, a committee of military brass determines if Halliburton should get an additional performance bonus of up to 2 percent . . . Thus the more money the company spends, the more profit it can make.
>
> (Chatterjee 2004: 29)

If these models do encourage gaming of targets and deadlines, in the end, *total* costs (rather than production costs) might be higher than under fixed price contracts because there are additional fees to be paid where targets are exceeded. In reality, although monetary incentives are the official mechanism for eliciting performance from contractors, very few contracts function adequately without extra-contractual factors being in play; in particular, trust is an important ingredient in making contracts actually work in practice.

Conclusion

Contracting out is the most common type of externalization, and has been the subject of much debate, about its capacity to deliver value for money, the ethics of its operations, and its impacts on accountability and governance. We have shown that outsourcing is not as problematic as its critics charge, nor as virtuous as its advocates proclaim. Rather its appropriateness and effectiveness varies from one situation to another.

Whatever the case, the rush of largely ideologically driven enthusiasm for contracting out that surged in the late 1980s and 1990s has given way to a more measured approach, based on a recognition of its shortcomings as well as its merits. One result of this has been a willingness of governments to bring some services back in-house, for reasons of market success and market failure, but also, interestingly, when they are faced with substantial budgetary stress.[25] Part of this recalibration has also been increased attention to alternative forms of externalization, and different modes of coordination, especially partnering and collaboration, which are the subject of the next chapter.

Chapter 5

Partnering and Collaboration with Other Organizations

On Christmas Day 2009, a Nigerian man, Umar Farouk Abdulmutallab, tried to detonate a bomb hidden in his underwear while on board a Northwest Airlines flight from Amsterdam to Detroit. Fortunately, he had trouble setting the bomb off and was overpowered by fellow passengers and aircrew. If he had succeeded, the plane would have been blown apart, killing 290 passengers. Al-Qaeda claimed responsibility for the attempt.

The incident highlighted ongoing shortcomings in the United States' security arrangements. It quickly emerged that Abdulmutallab had been placed on a watch-list after his father had approached the US Embassy in Nigeria expressing concerns about his son's increasing radicalism and his associations with Yemen. Security agencies also had electronic intercepts indicating that an unnamed Nigerian was being groomed for an al-Qaeda mission around Christmas. Yet the two pieces of information were not collated by any agency, and nobody saw fit to stop Abdulmutallab boarding the plane. A frustrated President Obama demanded a full accounting into what he called 'systemic intelligence failures'; the CIA, the National Security Agency which conducts electronic eavesdropping and the State Department in particular were under a cloud. He demanded urgent reports from senior officials. They spelt out that the intelligence agencies had failed to share or highlight potentially relevant information. More generally, the agencies set up after 11 September, 2001 – the Department of Homeland Security and the National Counterterrorism Center – seem to have failed to play their proper coordinating role.

The episode highlights key issues in partnering and collaboration. First, it shows how important it can be for organizations to cooperate with each other in order for vital public purposes, such as protection from violent extremism, to be realized. In this case the organizations are public sector ones, but such cooperation can also be with private firms or non-profit organizations – or some mixture of all three; indeed there is a large, growing, private sector intelligence industry in the United States. The need for cooperation has been recognized increasingly by government organizations since the 1990s. They have commonly resorted to partnering, that is, to share the work of producing public services with external providers –public, private and non-profit. New governance and organizational arrangements, such as network governance, public-private partnerships, joined-up government, whole-of-government, strategic alliances, inter-organizational collaboration and cooperation have proliferated (see Klijn *et al.* 1995).

In part, this has been a reaction to some of the problems of contractualism discussed in Chapter 4. Outsourcing and contracting have been found not to be the panaceas that their exponents had hoped for (Flynn *et al.* 1996). Aside from the problems of structuring competition and of specifying and monitoring services, contractualism tended to fragment service systems, especially in social services such as health and welfare, and promoted a culture based on 'self-interested behaviour rather the public interest' (Ranade and Hudson 2003: 35). Contractualism had also 'hollowed out' the capacity of the state to coordinate service delivery (Sullivan and Skelcher 2002).

At the same time, governments were increasingly conscious of 'wicked problems' – complex, open-ended, intractable issues affected by multiple stakeholders whose cooperation was needed in order to address them, such as global warming, the drug trade, child protection and illegal immigration. Faced with these problems, government organizations are increasingly willing to tap the knowledge and commitment of interested parties through partnering arrangements (see Klijn *et al.* 1995; see also Roberts 2000; Bingham *et al.* 2005).

However, the second issue the 'underpants bomber' episode raises is that while partnering and collaboration are at times very necessary, they can also be very difficult. An array of structural and procedural factors can constitute obstacles to collaborative working between government organizations and their external providers. As long ago as 1990, President Bush senior had directed all the key national security agencies, including the CIA, the FBI, the Customs Service and the Drug Enforcement Agency, as well as the State Department and the Treasury, to collaborate with the Financial

Crime Enforcement Network (FINCEN), a new agency set up to monitor money laundering by drug syndicates as a means of building prosecutions against criminal activity. Even though the orders came directly from the President, FINCEN struggled to secure cooperation (Kennedy and Sparrow 1991). Twenty years on, as the Abdulmutallab incident demonstrates, the problem persists.

This chapter considers the nature of inter-organizational partnering and collaboration, and explores how they might be furthered in the public sector context. In particular, it explains how trust, a crucial element of collaboration, is developed, but also how some inherently governmental structures and processes can undermine efforts to build trust. In the main, this chapter will be confined to *dyadic* partnerships; multi-party networks will be taken up in Chapter 9.

The meaning of partnering and collaboration

Not surprisingly, the flourishing of collaborative arrangements has given rise to a proliferation of terms. Indeed, the terminological complexity of the field of external provision of services overall, discussed in Chapter 1, mainly lies in these developments in partnership and collaboration.

However, here we will contrast partnering as a role relationship with the outsourcing discussed in Chapter 4, and collaboration as a mode of coordination with contracting (see Table 5.1). Specifically, 'partnering' will here refer to any arrangement where the

TABLE 5.1   *Key dimensions of partnering and collaboration*

Distribution of roles	*Partnering*
Who decides?	Government organization and/or private firm and/or non-profit/voluntary agency and/or other government organization
Who produces?	Government organization and private firm and non-profit/voluntary agency and other government organization
Mode of coordination	Collaboration

government agency *shares* the producing role with one body (by contrast with outsourcing, wherein the external party performs the *whole* of the producing role). And 'collaboration' will refer to the *mode of coordination* based on more or less joint deliberation, involving shared commitment and trust (by contrast with contracting, which refers to the mode of coordination involving the use of specification and monitoring, incentives and penalties and competition). Three terms here merit elaboration.

Partners: range of parties involved

Partnerships can vary by the number and type of partners involved. This affects the dynamics of collaboration among the parties. A partnership between only two parties is likely to entail more intense communication and interaction between them than between any two among a partnership of, say, ten parties (see Chapter 9).

Arrangements can also vary according to whether they are intra-sectoral or cross-sectoral. In intra-sectoral partnerships, the government organization shares the work with one or more other government organizations. This can be differentiated further according to whether the organizations are within the same government or another, and in the latter case whether the other government is in the same tier (that is, federal, state/provincial, or local).

In cross-sectoral partnerships, the government organization may partner with organizations from the private or non-profit sector, or both. At their most complex, some partnerships involve multiple partners from all three sectors, including ones from different governments and levels of government (see Chapter 9). Some examples of types of partnerships are given below.

Collaboration

There can also be variation in the degree of collaboration as a mode of coordination. Here we are referring not to the contributions to production made by the respective parties, but rather to the communication and decision-making mechanisms through which the parties manage to act consistently with each other's requirements. Simply put, the more the parties empower each other, the greater the degree of collaboration.

Useful constructs for understanding this come from a longstanding literature canvassing public participation in decision making, starting with Arnstein's famous 'ladder of citizen participation' (Arnstein 1969; see also Thomas 1995). Similar constructs have applied in the area of employee participation (Walker 1977; Deery *et al.* 1997). A contemporary example is the 'Spectrum of Public Participation' put forward by the International Association for Public Participation (IAP2 2007). It posits a continuum of participation, ranging from a minimal position, where citizens' have the right to be provided with information about decisions, to the maximum position of 'empowerment', in which the agency undertakes to implement what the public decides. In between are 'consult', 'involve' and 'collaborate'.

This construct can be adapted to the field of partnership by taking into account the putatively *mutual* nature of the relationship. For the sake of simplicity, we mention three indicative points on the continuum (see Figure 5.1). The first is mutual access to information, where each party has the right to regular information from the other about matters of mutual relevance. The second is consultation, where each party provides opinions and feedback to the other about the latter's plans and actions, but final decision rests with the latter. The third is joint decision making, where the parties share the right to deliberate and determine issues in the relationship.

The greater the degree of jointness in deliberation, the more each party has knowledge about and influence over the options and decisions, and the greater the degree of mutual empowerment.

Of course, it is simply a fact of life that in the absence of such collaborative governance arrangements, the parties will have unequal power. Typically, the non-governmental party or parties will have less information, money, legislative authority and other power resources than the government agency. This may be even more true of non-profit/voluntary agencies than private sector firms.

FIGURE 5.1   *Continuum of collaboration*

The point is that collaboration between governmental and non-governmental organizations will usually require the public sector agency to cede some power to external providers. They need to do this not because collaboration is a nice idea, replete with friendly, harmonious overtones, but because in some circumstances it may be the only way to secure the benefits of externalization. Especially relevant here is the role of inter-organizational trust, to be discussed further below.

Collaboration life-cycles

The variations posited above can also have a temporal dimension – that is, partnerships and collaborations evolve through stages to a greater or lesser degree (Ring and Van de Ven 1994; Osborne and Murray 2000). Partnerships can develop from less to more blended sharing of productive contributions over time, as the exigencies of working together unearth potential improvements to be derived from rearranging tasks into more integrated processes. Collaboration can move from more modest power sharing, such as information exchange, to more full-blooded mutual empowerment in the form of joint decision making. Lowndes and Skelcher (1998; see also Sullivan and Skelcher 2002: 122–35) conducted a longitudinal study of partnerships in Britain and constructed a life-cycle model with four broad stages: (1) pre-partnership collaboration; (2) partnership creation and consolidation; (3) partnership programme delivery; and (4) partnership termination or succession. Each of these stages tended to have causal connections with differing modes of governance and relationships between stakeholders. One implication of this is that other dynamics of collaboration, such as the trust-building spiral, may be related to the stage of evolution of the partnership, as will be discussed below.

At the same time, it must also be acknowledged that partnerships can exhibit arrested development, becoming 'stuck' at some stage short of closure. This also has implications for trust building.

Key types of partnership

Although there are many kinds of partnerships, varying along many dimensions, a few types have been more common. Here we note three – one with private businesses, one with non-profits, and one with other government agencies.

Public-private partnerships (sometimes)

In Chapter 4 we observed that only some public-private partnerships (PPPs) in practice involve 'partnership' in the sense we
employ in this book. Instead, they most usually entail arrangements better described as 'outsourcing' in our terms (Klijn and
Teisman 2000). However, although most PPPs do not really fit
into a discussion of partnering, some PPPs (probably a minority)
do involve the sharing of the productive task between the government agency and the private firm. These are usually established in
situations where it is not possible to deliver the service without
both business and government contributing some effort. An important area where this occurs is in vocational or industrial training,
which requires both classroom education to be provided by government and on-the-job experience to be provided by business
employers (Gray 1996; Schaeffer and Loveridge 2002). Businesses
have an incentive to take part in such partnerships because training is a collective good for the business community (as well as
being a private good for workers), and the collective commitments
made in the partnership serve as something of a safeguard against
free-riding.

   Another interesting example comes from the Marlborough
wine-producing region of New Zealand, source of internationally
respected sauvignon blancs. Local grape-growers were encoun-
tering increasing difficulty in attracting sufficient labour during
seasonal peaks for harvesting and pruning, despite the fact that
New Zealand as a whole was experiencing relatively high levels of
unemployment. The Ministry of Social Development (MSD), which
was responsible for, *inter alia*, job matching and welfare benefits,
joined with local grape-growers and industry bodies to establish
a Viticulture Advisory Group, which proceeded to establish a seasonal coordination service, operated by the industry with support
from MSD (Schwass 2007).

   Moreover, even if PPPs don't involve partnering in terms of
productive roles, many of them do seek to fashion a collaborative relationship characterized by trust and mutual adjustment.
In other words, they pursue arrangements in which the role relationship is outsourcing by a purchaser to a provider, but the mode
of coordination is collaboration (Almqvist and Hogberg 2006).
The discussion below on collaboration and trust applies to both
'purchaser-provider' PPPs and to 'shared production' ones.

Community partnerships

As with the government-business partnerships described in the previous section, many of those between public and non-profit/voluntary organizations are not really partnerships in the sense used here (although some of them are, as discussed below). Instead, they have been of two types which differ from our notion of sharing the production. One is an arrangement in which the actual work is done by a government or quasi-government agency, while organizations in the two sectors share the task of deciding what to do (to a greater or more usually a lesser extent). In other words, the government agency consults (or claims to consult) with the voluntary sector about what that agency will do. In the terms we have employed here, there is collaboration but not partnership between the two sectors. An example of this is the Primary Care Trusts in Britain, which usually entail representation of local voluntary organizations in deliberative bodies, but the delivery of health services is by employed professional medical staff. These types of arrangements fall outside the scope of our discussion.

The other type is where government organizations engage in a purchaser-provider relationship with voluntary organizations, and moreover conduct that relationship through classical contracting. This model has been especially common in the United States. Federal, state and local governments have sought to capitalize on certain characteristics that they see as peculiar to non-profits. One is their legitimacy with local constituencies whom public sector agencies are trying to reach – for example, local ethnic communities. Another is their accumulated knowledge and experience of those constituencies. Still another is their capacity to innovate, unencumbered by bureaucratic constraints and processes. Finally, governments seek to reap cost advantages from the voluntary impulse that drives these organizations' staff, hoping to pay them less for services than they might to private profit-making businesses.

But the rhetorical nature of the partnership, exacerbated by the power differentials between the two sectors, has made the experience of collaboration with government an unhappy one for non-profits. They see government-sponsored consultation as deficient, non-profit contributions as devalued (Rawsthorne and Christian 2005; Lee 2010), and time-frames for capacity development as too short. They experience government using coercion to expand provider tasks, and 'punishing' those non-profits that may disagree with it or engage in advocacy activities that may not suit the state.

An extensive study of non-profits in the United States identified five government behaviours harming these relationships (National Council of Nonprofits 2010):

1 *Failure to pay the full costs of services and administration*: not updating service fees for many years, limiting or not paying at all for overheads, imposing unfunded mandates through contracts, requiring matching funds.
2 *Changing terms of contracts mid-stream*: cutting payments, cancelling contracts. Almost 60 per cent of non-profits report that government organizations changed terms during the contract.
3 *Late payment of funds*: More than 40 per cent of non-profits report that government organizations were late in making payments, often for services already delivered. In 2009 this equated to US$97,635 on *each* contract for the federal government; $117,679 for state governments, and $38,937 for local government.
4 *'Complexification' of contracting processes*: government parties don't understand the service being contracted and they freeze funding levels during contract extension (p. 20).
5 *'Complexification' of reporting requirements*: different government agencies use different budget categories, databases and reporting systems, all of which require duplication and additional effort from providers.

Interestingly, however, as Smith and Lipsky (1993) have shown, by engaging in these kinds of contracting methods with non-profit organizations, governments end up undermining the very qualities they seek from them. And the more tightly they engage in this kind of contracting, the more they undermine them. Thus, to the extent that they bind the non-profit contractors to specific behaviours, they reduce their legitimacy in the eyes of their constituencies. This in turn tends to cut the non-profits 'out of the loop' of the community, and thereby reduces their access to information and knowledge. Similarly, to the extent that they impose detailed process requirements on the non-profits, they discourage innovation. And by skimping on expenditure and therefore the salaries of non-profits' staff, they make it difficult for non-profits to maintain or upgrade professional standards, and prompt high staff turnover – both of which undermine legitimacy, knowledge and innovation. In effect, the 'contract culture' has perverse effects (Sullivan and Skelcher 2002).

In response to these problems, some government organizations have sought to adopt more genuinely collaborative approaches to working with non-profits. As with public-private partnerships, some of these approaches are not partnerships in the sense employed in this book. But many of them do constitute service-delivery partnerships, in which government organizations and non-profit/voluntary organizations share the work of achieving some agreed social purpose. The precise mixture of public and non-profit in governance, funding and service-delivery in these partnerships varies considerably, meaning that they take many forms (Sullivan and Skelcher 2002). However, it is noteworthy, and not surprising, that they tend to be local or regional in nature.

One well-known illustrative example in several countries is Neighbourhood Watch, in which police work with local groups to reduce crime and enhance community safety.[1] The contribution of community members is to keep their premises secure, mark their property for easier detection in the event of theft, be vigilant about possible offences and report them to police. The role of the police is to respond to calls and enforce the law.[2]

Another interesting example, from the United Kingdom, is Sure Start, aimed at increasing children's life-chances by focusing services on their early years. Its involvement of clients as co-producers is discussed at length in Chapter 8, but here note that it also entails extensive partnerships with non-profits (Melhuish *et al.* 2010; NHSA 2011; http://www.oeyc.ca).

Joined-up government

A third category of partnerships comprises those between government organizations. They can be either within a particular government, or between public sector organizations in different governments, either vertically (for example, national government departments and local government agencies) or horizontally (for example, between government organizations in different states or provinces). As noted in Chapter 1, it is harder for agencies in different jurisdictions to have recourse to higher authorities to decide responsibilities and issues between them. But it is almost as difficult for organizations within the same jurisdiction, usually because the lowest level official with authority to do so is the President, Prime Minister, Governor or Premier, who simply doesn't have the time to intervene in all but the most significant issues.

Since the 1990s, inter-agency collaboration has been subsumed under the rubric of 'joined-up government', first coined in Britain but taken up in many other countries. Pollitt (2003: 35) defines joined-up government as 'the aspiration to achieve horizontally and vertically coordinated thinking' (see Ling 2002; Hood 2005). Some writers (for example, Ling 2002) take the term to embrace 'joining up' between government and non-government agencies, but here we shall limit its application to relationships among government organizations.

Joined-up working serves various purposes (Pollitt 2003; Mulgan 2005). One is to eliminate duplication between different programmes, notably where both federal and state/provincial governments are involved in the same policy area (as occurs for instance with respect to programmes for indigenous people in Australia). Another is to tackle contradictions between programmes, for example in drugs strategy, where a 'supply-interdiction' approach by the police, involving arrests of users in concerted crackdowns in a locality, forcing addicts to either lie low or move to another jurisdiction, may be at odds with the 'harm-minimization' approach of health authorities sponsoring safe injection houses and needle exchanges. A further purpose is to provide seamless services to clients, for instance by establishing 'one-stop shops' to enable access to a plurality of services under one roof. Providing integrated services has particular significance with citizens with multiple needs – for example, a homeless person with a drug habit and health problems. Finally, joined-up working may encourage the cross-fertilization of ideas between different actors in a policy area.

One risk arising from the fact that the 'joining-up' agencies are in the same sector, or especially within the same jurisdiction, is that more powerful agencies or levels of government may seek to dominate the relationship, preferring what they may refer to as 'coordination' rather than collaboration. In some governments, central agencies such as the prime ministers department or the Treasury may be prone to this type of behaviour. In these circumstances, the deliberative forums governing joined up arrangements can take the form of ritualized consultation.

Partnering as an alternative to outsourcing

Chapter 4 explained that outsourcing requires particular conditions, namely, that external providers can deliver the service more cheaply or effectively than in-house producers; there is a competitive market of potential suppliers; and it is relatively easy to specify and monitor the service. Without all of these conditions, there is a risk not only that outsourcing will fail to be beneficial, but also that it might actually be worse than in-house production, because of the leeway it allows for opportunistic, profit-seeking providers to game the process. In these circumstances, the organization might find it more effective or efficient to provide the service itself.

But to choose between outsourcing and in-house production in this manner, taking the benefits and costs into account, may end up with a sub-optimal arrangement. This is because it does not take account of a third possibility: that in some situations the contribution of *both* the governmental organization and one or more external providers is necessary to achieve cost savings or service effectiveness. Here the unit of analysis is the *partnership*, rather than either party on its own. The benefits derive not so much from the competency of the provider, but rather from the fact that the two (or more) organizations are in a partnership.

Chapter 2 canvassed the ways in which a partnership might be better than either producing the service in-house or outsourcing it. Both of those options entail the whole of the production being carried out by one provider, which in particular circumstances has little or no capability to perform well by comparison with a partnership. One of these circumstances is *complementarity*: where the government agency and the external provider each have specialized capability or competence, which is different from that of the other but the achievement of the task at hand requires the exercise of *both* sets of capabilities in an inter-dependent fashion. The other circumstance is where a partnership can *promote innovation and learning*, by cross-fertilizing innovations and opportunities for performance improvement and fostering their sharing between partners (Lundvall 1993: 59–60; Selsky and Parker 2005). Neither of these types of benefits could be achieved as readily by either party acting on its own.

Given these conditions, it is not surprising that the kinds of activities for which partnerships are likely to be preferred are those entailing complex and evolving bundles of services, rather than simple, static and discrete ones (Teisman and Klijn 2002: 199). This has significant implications for the management of partnerships, to be discussed later.

Collaboration as an alternative to contracting

Thus, our external provider might satisfy the first of our three conditions either by performing the whole of the task on an outsourced basis or by sharing it with the organization, as a partner. But what if the other two conditions don't hold? What if an external provider or a partnership is more able than the government agency to produce at lower cost and/or to provide better service, but the market of providers is not competitive and the service is hard to specify and monitor? In these circumstances, although the external provider or partnership may be *capable* of outperforming the government agency, it could be argued that the provider or partner may not be *willing* to do so, because the lack of competition or of meaningful performance monitoring enables it to perform sub-optimally without much fear of discovery or sanction by the government agency. That agency would then need to make judgements about whether the expenditure savings or service enhancements outweigh the costs of creating competition and/or of specifying and monitoring services.

However, it is precisely in these mixed situations that collaboration may be relevant as an alternative mode of coordination to contracting. Partnering can be coordinated through either contracting or collaboration (or for that matter, most of the other modes of coordination discussed in Chapter 2). But in the same way that outsourcing sits more comfortably with contracting, so too does partnering sit more comfortably with collaboration. The reason is that the reciprocity between the partners does not involve a monetary price for services, but instead an exchange of behaviours and services in kind. It therefore tends to be more diffuse and less strictly defined than the exchange between a purchaser and a contractor, where quantification of the values being exchanged is more practicable. This vitiates the efficacy of the contracting mechanisms of specification and monitoring and the competition they enable. Exchanging behaviours and services in kind also tends to entail greater uncertainty, which further complicates specification and monitoring.

In the face of these problems, collaboration has special advantages as a mode of coordination. Because it involves trust between the purchaser and the provider, it can obviate or at least mitigate the transaction costs of outsourcing that arise from lack of competition or specification and monitoring difficulties. In order to understand why, we need to look more closely at the concept of trust.

The meaning of trust

The literature on trust contains a myriad of definitions of the term (see Hardin 1993; Bardach 1998; Blois 1999; Korczynski 2000). A number of writers also distinguish between different types of trust (Lewicki and Bunker 1995; Child and Faulkner 1998; Hudson 2004). To distil the commonalities among the definitions, but also to take account of different types, we have encapsulated the largely common elements in the following:

> To trust someone is to be confident that in a situation where you are vulnerable to that person's behaviour, she will be disposed to act in a manner consistent with your interests.

Several aspects of this definition deserve elucidation for the present analysis (see also Edelenbos and Klijn 2007: 29). First, trust is only important in a situation where you are *vulnerable*. Vulnerability is where the situation is uncertain or risky, and you are dependent on the actions of the other. Your willingness to remain in this vulnerable situation (which may be a pre-requisite for gaining any potential benefits from the relationship) is greater to the extent that you trust the other to act benignly toward you despite her having the opportunity to take advantage of it. Where you are not vulnerable – for example, where there is no uncertainty or risk – it is irrelevant whether you trust the other person or not.

It is important, however, to recognize that there are different types of risk (Sheppard and Sherman 1998; Hudson 2004). We can distinguish between risks of *action* – that is, the risk of the trustee doing the wrong thing, such as being indiscrete about the trustor's affairs to a third party, or taking advantage of information-asymmetry to cheat the trustor – and risks of *inaction*, that is, of the trustee failing to do the right thing, such as delivering on time, or anticipating the changed needs of the trustor as circumstances change. These can vary in the amount of thinking or effort they demand of the trustee, which will in return be related to either his level of commitment and/or his level of competence. Risks can also vary in magnitude, depending on such factors as the number of people affected, the economic consequences, the possible political damage that could result, and so on.

This means, second, that the behaviours expected of the trusted party can vary. A minimalist version of trust entails an expectation of a non-negative: a reliance that the other to whom you are vulnerable will not act adversely towards you. For example, Baier (1986: 235) sees trust as 'accepted vulnerability to another's possible but not expected ill will (or lack of goodwill) towards one'. But this form of trust is unlikely to be useful to the trustor in unexpected circumstances, which require the other party not only to abstain from doing anything negative, but also to conceive and execute a positive response to the unpredicted contingency – in other words, to 'go the extra mile'. In these circumstances trust 'involves the expectation, not just of a lack of ill will, but of an element of goodwill from the other party' (Blois 1999, 204; see also Hosmer 1995: 238). Both these conceptions are allowed for in our formulation that the trustee will be disposed to 'act in a manner consistent with your interests'.

Closely related to this is that the other party is perceived to have a *disposition* to act in a trustworthy fashion. She does not simply do it because she has to. To expect that someone will act consistently with your interests because, for instance, she is legally or contractually obliged to is not to trust her. It is merely to observe that she has a compelling reason to do so.

Fourth, trust has both a *cognitive* and an *affective* component, both of which are encompassed – perhaps inadequately – by the term 'confidence'. You trust in part because what you know about the other party and her situation leads you to believe she will act in a particular fashion. But in the most fully developed trust relationship, you trust because you empathize to some degree with the other's identity; you feel an affinity with her needs, preferences, behaviour patterns, and so on. This more emotive element entails identification with 'traits of character such as uprightness, honesty, integrity, and sincerity' (Bardach 1998: 263). The cognitive component has been described by Lewicki and

Bunker as 'knowledge-based trust', and the affective component as 'identification-based trust' (1995: 121–2).

Finally, trust exists between *people* rather than organizations. Put another way, the trustworthiness of an organization is derived from that of the people who comprise it – and the interests and characters of those people will be different both from the organization and from each other. True, an organization can seek to influence its members to act in a more trustworthy fashion, and may gain a better reputation as a result. One accounting firm, for instance, may be more trustworthy than another. But the reputation derives from its people; trust does not exist between organization charts.

Trust and relationship costs

The sponsoring of trust-based collaborations between partners can mitigate the transaction costs of outsourcing in a number of ways. First, the building of trust provides a motivational mechanism which is an alternative or supplement to the profit motive that competition relies upon. Competition is a spur to elicit good performance to the extent that suppliers are self-interested profit seekers; they fear losing the contract to competitors because that will mean a loss of profits. But collaboration involves a wider array of concerns. As discussed previously, in the real world, people have more complex motivations than economic self-interest. These motivations include normative purposes, which are likely to be significant when the provider is a non-profit organization. They also include solidary rewards, which are especially significant for this analysis. To the extent that people value solidary incentives, they are more likely to value the partnership *in itself* – in addition to whatever outcomes they may hope to derive from it. Moreover, the more collaborative the relationship, the more these solidary motivations will be fostered. Enhancing these alternative motivations also makes it easier to encourage collaborations *among* providers, which is useful when competitive markets are absent (Edelenbos and Klijn 2007: 32).

Second, the trust underpinning a collaboration makes it easier for the parties to vary services when unpredictable circumstances arise. Each party is more confident that the other will adjust what it does or, in the best case, 'go the extra mile' to overcome difficulties presented by unexpected contingencies. In turn, the other feels less nervous about varying its side of the arrangement. Consequently, there is less need to refer to the specific terms of the contract, which may constrict the possibilities for creative solutions to new contingencies. And there is less need to specify every conceivable eventuality in rigid detail. As Luhmann puts it, trust functions to reduce complexity (1979: 24). This is especially significant in facilitating learning and development, in that each party is more inclined to invest time and effort in innovation and improvement, in the knowledge that the other is likely to reciprocate (Klijn and Teisman 2000: 92).

Third, a collaborative relationship is one which both necessitates and encourages information-sharing, thereby mitigating information-asymmetry. Information sharing is necessary to a partnership because, without it, the parties will find it harder to discover ways of mutually adjusting their processes to accommodate unexpected contingencies (Lax and Sebenius 1986: 113). At the same time, a cooperative relationship encourages the sharing of information, since each party feels more able to trust the other not to withhold information or use it opportunistically.

Finally, trust turns inter-dependency into an advantage rather than a contractual problem. The enhanced information-sharing that comes from greater trust means that it is easier to get an honest picture of how much the performance (good or bad) of the provider or partner is due to their own efforts rather than other factors. And the heightened trustworthiness of the other party means that they are less likely to take advantage of claimed interdependence to engage in opportunistic behaviour.

In summary, a collaborative partnership has the potential to mitigate the problems that arise from lack of competition or difficulties in specification and monitoring. At the same time, it enables the involvement of an external provider. It is therefore a suitable alternative to either in-house production or contracting out in situations where external providers can deliver some or all of the service cheaper or better, but the transaction costs of engaging them are high. As suggested above, it may be particularly suited to the provision of complex packages of services.

However, partnerships cannot realize these benefits unless there is significant trust between the parties. Without it, there is a risk that providers or partners will take advantage of the relative lack of competitive discipline, access to privileged information, and attenuated accountability that partnerships embody. The development of trust is therefore essential for government organizations seeking to establish and maintain collaborative relationships with providers. This brings us to the question of what fosters trust in a relationship.

Developing trust

What makes one person (the trustee) trustworthy in the eyes of another (the trustor)? This question has two aspects. First, by what means does someone learn about whether another person is trustworthy? Second, what can that other person do to persuade the first person that she is trustworthy?

Whether we trust someone depends on what we know of her. Bardach (1998: 254–60) suggests a number of data sources a person might draw on in assessing someone else's trustworthiness (see also Dasgupta 1988: 53; Coleman 1990: 102–3; Hardin 1993: 505). One is the trustee's *reputation* – for honesty, competence, commitment to a particular cause, or whatever is important in the context. Another source is *categorical knowledge*: generalizations about the classes of people (occupational, national, religious, regional, and so on) with which she is identified. For instance, her trustworthiness might be perceived differently if she was a social worker than if she were a real estate agent. Another is the trustor's *prior personal experience* of the person – for example, if they had developed a close personal relationship when they worked together in a previous situation or in a shared social network (Lambright *et al.* 2010). Also relevant may be the overall *political and organizational environment* in which the parties are operating – for instance, the level of trust among directors and screenwriters in Hollywood was probably lower during the McCarthy era than at other times.

All of these sources can give a part of the picture about someone's trustworthiness, but in newly formed relationships the information they impart can be relatively limited, whereas in already longstanding ones it can also be prone to bias, over-simplification, attribution, or over-generalization. Most importantly, the information may not be very applicable to how much one can trust someone else in respect of whatever issues are important in the present relationship. The most significant source of information about a person's trustworthiness, therefore, is one's *current experience* of her – that is, how she is behaving in the current relationship. This brings us to the other aspect of the question: what can a person do to persuade another that she is trustworthy?

At the most basic level, she can exhibit characteristics and behaviours in the relationship which demonstrate that she is likely to act benignly towards another even when that person is vulnerable. Any of the attributes we associate with trustworthiness in everyday discourse might figure here: honesty, openness, integrity, consistency, thoughtfulness, and so on (Butler 1991). From observing these characteristics, the trustor will probably form the view that the person at least has a propensity to act in a trustworthy manner. Certainly the display of the reverse of these characteristics (for example, competitiveness, secretiveness, and so on) will make the formation of trust impossible.

But perceiving someone as likely to act in a trustworthy manner is not the same thing as actually trusting her. The development of a deeper level of trust is a more dynamic process, in which both parties play a role. Drawing on exchange theory, we can see this process as one of *reciprocal gift-giving* (Blau 1964; Ekeh 1974). (By 'gifts', we do not mean things wrapped in shiny paper – nor especially in brown paper envelopes! – but rather anything tangible or intangible that the recipient values. The term comes from a major strand of social science, including numerous anthropological studies and the work of Titmuss, discussed in Chapter 3.) Gift-giving is a diffuse process with non-linear intervals between gifts, but conceptually we can distinguish discrete stages.

The first step is where one gives a 'gift' to another. The gift can be anything which the other party values – tangible or intangible, economic or non-economic – such as performing unsolicited favours, sharing information, bending (but not breaking) rules, making the other feel welcome, showing concern or respect, taking on part of the other's workload in an emergency, or not taking advantage of unpredictable circumstances. In the case of the intelligence community discussed at the start of the chapter, a trust-building move may be to give another agency a piece of information which is helpful in an ongoing investigation.

According to what Gouldner (1960) famously termed the 'norm of reciprocity' which prevails in most human societies, the most likely response of the other person to one's gift is to reciprocate at some point thereafter, by giving a gift to the other. Seeing this response, the original giver is likely to bestow further gifts on the other, and vice versa. Each positive response is likely to enhance the predisposition of each party to trust the other (Zand 1997: 95–6). It is more likely to have this effect if it is perceived as valuable by the recipient, and as entailing some sacrifice by the donor. This ongoing process can be seen as a 'high-trust spiral', in which each instance of goodwill by the one party prompts reciprocal acts by the other (Fox 1974: 114). The reciprocity is not necessarily immediate, but may be deferred to some suitable opportunity for response. Nor does the value of each gift have to precisely match that of the other's. Rather, there is a rough equivalence of value over time, and the reciprocity can therefore be described as diffuse.

But as Gouldner points out, while reciprocity is the most likely response, it is not a certain one (1960: 177). The recipient may simply take the initial gift, for example, and not reciprocate. By giving that gift, the original donor therefore makes herself vulnerable to opportunistic behaviour by the other (for example, by disclosing personal information, or by being open to humiliation). This will almost certainly be true in our intelligence agencies example. In fact, gifts are more likely to promote trust if they also render the giver more vulnerable. Conversely, less valuable gifts reduce the donor's vulnerability, but they are also less likely to generate trust.

What is it about these kinds of gifts that engenders trust in the other? The fact that the gifts (1) are valuable to the recipient and (2) entail some sacrifice or vulnerability is a signal that the donor gives some weight to the recipients' interests relative to her own. The more valuable the gift and the larger the sacrifice, the greater the perceived weight. This perception will be enhanced if the gift is ungrudgingly given, with no expectation of reciprocation apparent at the time, nor any immediate calculation of benefit. Paradoxically, therefore, gifts are more likely to inspire trust when they do not seem as though they are intended to do so.

Just as trust can be built, it can also be diminished. In a 'low-trust spiral', one party engages in a breach of trust by either reneging on a commitment (for example, by failing to deliver on a promise, or by misusing confidential information) or by acting opportunistically (for example, by taking advantage of the other's vulnerability, or by showing disrespect) and the other responds with a retaliatory breach, and so on (Fox 1974: 102–3; Morrison and Robinson 1997: 233–4). From the point of view of one, it is largely irrelevant whether the reneging is because of the other's unwillingness to uphold the commitment, or his inability due to factors outside her control. Either way, the other's trustworthiness is diminished. Thus, promises need to be both attractive and credible.

These mechanisms have practical implications for how public servants representing government agencies should behave in partnerships with non-government organizations if they are to build trust. At a minimum, it would be important that they did not renege on undertakings made to providers, about such things as funding, process requirements, agreed purposes, or programme continuation.

Just as significantly, they would need to be able to offer and receive 'gifts', in the sense we have been using that term here. At the outset of a partnership, this might include allowing the provider to share in the formulation of the objectives and outcomes of programme or project, rather than imposing some required outputs and leaving the supplier autonomy only in deciding how to deliver them. It would also mean not imposing rigid monitoring requirements, which effectively signal a lack of trust – as President Reagan did memorably in arms-reduction talks with the Soviets when he declared: 'Trust, but verify.'

During the partnership, it would involve taking steps out of the ordinary when unpredicted contingencies arose – for example, cutting the provider some slack or bending the rules when it didn't deliver as required for reasons out of its control. It would also mean taking steps to help the provider, with information, assistance, training, infrastructure, and so on. Crucially, all of these processes would take time – more probably measured in years rather than months, given the relatively lengthy feedback loops they typically entail.

Building trust would also entail emphasizing elements of shared identity – fostering commonalities of occupation, background or purpose. It would be aimed at promoting a strong sense of identification between the public servant and the people acting for the partner, tending toward the point where they each attached as much significance to the partnership, and invested as much emotional weight to it, as they did to their home organization. This means that the public servant would have a dual identification, with both her government agency and the partnership.

All of this would necessitate a high level of autonomy on the part of the public servant interacting with the partner. She would need to have considerable discretion to set and adapt the terms of the relationship as circumstances unfold. To the extent that the partnership is a learning process, she would also need to have room to make honest mistakes and learn from them without fear of reprimand or retribution from her superiors.

The delegate's dilemma

There are contradictions and tensions, however, between the role a public servant plays in a partnership and the role she plays acting on behalf of a government organization. Precisely because she is a *public* servant, the behaviours required of her in the partnership, especially those directed towards building trust, are rendered problematic, or may be obstructed, by some of the structural and operational imperatives inherent in the workings of government (Hardy *et al.* 1992). Because they are also relevant to other forms of externalization, these factors are discussed more comprehensively in Chapter 11, but insofar as they relate to trust-building, some essential points can be made here.

First, government is prone to turbulence – changes in policies, strategies, resource commitments, structures and personnel, manifested most significantly in elections, but also in daily politics and bureaucratic reorganizations – which can necessitate reneging on undertakings, as well as difficulty in developing a relationship over time. Second, there are often cross-cutting responsibilities between government activities, generated by the complexity of their roles. This can result in organizations sending mixed messages to partners, and consequently undermining their trustworthiness. Third, government agencies are subject to accountability obligations in respect of such things as financial reporting, public service employment, expenditure delegations, and purchasing rules, which constrain the scope for gift giving and for adjusting to changing circumstances. Moreover, if monitoring is rigid, it conveys a message of mistrust and may foster an ongoing low-trust spiral. Finally, there may be mismatches between the organizational cultures of the respective partners. This is reinforced by the fact that public sector organizations employ many types of professional specialists, who subscribe to occupationally specific beliefs and values which may diverge from those of partner organizations. It is also heightened by the fact that government staff tend to have imbibed a 'public service ethic' which may be at odds with the norms animating partners.

These issues are all mediated by the fact that the activity of engaging in the partnership is usually performed by someone who is representing the government organization rather than exercising direction over it. Turbulence, complexity and accountability all constitute ways in which the organization pulls the front-line delegate away from a collaborative relationship. The greater the impact of these factors, the less likely is trust to be developed and sustained with the partner.

One way the delegate might deal with this problem is to make some degree of common cause with the partner against the constraints imposed by the organization or the government. At a minimum, this might involve simply expressing sympathy about the constraints, or being critical of them to the partner. But if the constraints mean that the organization is effectively reneging on undertakings, this will be small comfort to the partner, and the delegate's protestations will lack credibility.

A more substantial approach might be to advocate on behalf of the partnership to the organization or government, criticizing the constraints or making constructive proposals to alleviate them. This would send a stronger signal to the partner of the delegate's commitment to the relationship. But it also distances the representative from her organization, a situation which has its own risks. If the delegate's advocacy of the partnership is sufficiently strong and sustained, it may cross a line beyond which the organization begins to question her loyalty.[3] In response, the organization may start to treat the partnership with suspicion – for example, by withholding information – and potentially set in motion a low-trust spiral.

Thus, where turbulence, complexity and accountability are serious obstacles, the representative faces a dilemma. She can seek to maintain closeness with the partner, but risk losing credibility with her organization, or she can maintain an identification with the organization, but jeopardize the trust she enjoys with the partner. She has to walk a fine line between the two.

To a greater or lesser degree, therefore, partnering is vulnerable to some of the ways in which public management is different from private sector management. Because they are inherent characteristics of government, they are likely to be resistant to measures to eliminate them. But there may be ways the organization can attempt to ameliorate them, at least to the extent where the relative benefits and costs of partnering compare favourably with those of alternative arrangements such as classical contracting or in-house production. These are discussed further in Chapter 11.

Conclusion

Both partnering (the sharing of production) and collaboration (as a mode of coordination) have proliferated in the age of what has been termed 'network governance' (Rhodes 1997). Indeed, the label 'partnership' has become so popular that it has been applied to phenomena such as public-private partnerships which do not really merit the term.

Fuelling this approval is widespread enthusiasm for collaborative modes of governance and inter-organizational coordination. Partnering and collaboration have come to be seen as inherently worthwhile, as the preferred way to do things. Consequently, enormous time and effort has gone in to their establishment and maintenance.

Here we take a more contingent position. Just as outsourcing and contracting make sense in certain circumstances, so too do partnering and collaboration in others. Specifically, *partnering* should be adopted when two conditions are present. The first is that production by the government organization and the external provider(s) acting together can create more value than each on its own. In some cases, this may be a strong imperative, in that an important public purpose – such as protection from terrorism – simply cannot be realized without such partnering. In others, it might be preferable but less essential.

The second condition is that the government partner has some means of inducing the external provider(s) to act in a manner that contributes to the realization of the value sought. Of the modes of coordination discussed in Chapter 1, two are especially relevant here: contracting and collaboration (although the others could conceivably be applied, especially negotiation). Partnering can be coordinated through contracting, but to a more limited extent than in outsourcing. The reason is that the very fact of it being a partnership reduces the salience of the two essential features of contracting as a mode of coordination: competition, and specification and monitoring. On the one hand, partnerships typically form through methods other than competition, with its attendant possibility of replacing the external provider in the event of poor performance. They may come into being through less formal processes such as introduction through networks, or through approaches by the providers. Even where the external partner is selected through a tender process, it is quite likely that a key selection criterion is its complementarity with the government organization, which imparts to the partner the advantage of a degree of asset-specificity. However, this does not mean that the government organization is without means of inducing the partners to perform. Specifically, it can apply incentives and sanctions, for example bonus payments or penalties.

On the other hand, the fact of a partnership is likely to complicate the other key contracting device which is essential to the application of incentives and sanctions: the specification and monitoring of services. Engaging in joint productive activity with the partners is likely to entail considerable inter-dependence. Indeed the more integrated the partners' productive processes, the greater the inter-dependence. This will make it more difficult to assign responsibility for good or bad performance, which is a pre-requisite for applying bonuses and penalties.

Thus, it makes more sense for the government organization to employ contracting as a mode of coordination for a partnership when there is less inter-dependence between the partners' work, and inducements other than replacing the external provider are available as means of discouraging poor performance.

This raises the other mode of coordination: *collaboration*. As discussed at length above, the crucial lubricant of collaboration is trust. Consequently, collaboration should only be adopted when it is judged that a reasonable level of trust between the partners is either already present or can be built within the relevant time period. This judgement can be informed by two sets of factors. One is the trustworthiness of the external partner(s), which can be weighed up by considering their reputation, prior performance, context, and so on. The other is the capacity of the government organization to demonstrate trustworthiness in return. Most directly, this will depend on the ability of the public sector agency to give 'gifts' and to avoid reneging on undertakings. This will require the agency's delegate(s) to have sufficient time and autonomy to build a spiral of increasing trust, which in turn will be a function of the accountability regime, turbulence, complexity and cultural difference besetting the organization and its representatives. Thus, while trust is extremely valuable in a relationship between a government purchaser and a non-government provider, it is important to be realistic about how hard it can be to foster.

Partnering is therefore most appropriate when partners acting together can create more value than when they act alone, and it is possible to employ either contracting or collaboration as a mode of coordination. However, these circumstances may be only partially present. Specifically, one common situation is where the partners can jointly create more value than separately, but neither contracting nor collaboration is easy, either because it is difficult to specify and monitor services or because trust between the partners is difficult to establish (or revive). In these circumstances, more complex assessments of costs and benefits have to be made. The relative importance of the public purposes at stake needs to be weighed against the intricacies of coordinating with external partners. The more significant the value in question, the more worthwhile it is to devote effort and resources to dealing with the difficulties of contracting or collaboration.

Chapter 6

Calling on Volunteers

At a certain point in their ageing, many elderly people find it difficult to do the shopping and cooking they need in order to eat proper meals. At the same time, they are not so frail that they need to be in nursing home care, and can otherwise cope in their homes. In these situations, a local council service called Meals on Wheels fills the gap, providing home-delivered meals to the frail housebound elderly, for a modest charge.

Meals on Wheels is a well-known example of the use of volunteers in delivering public services. Originating in Britain in the Second World War, the service was established in Australia, the United States and Canada from the 1950s. Whereas preparation of the meals is usually done at a central kitchen run by a council or a private contractor, the actual delivery is typically by volunteers. Officially, they perform two important daily functions. One is to provide recipients with vital regular nourishment; the other is to check on their well-being, and if necessary report any perceived problems to council staff for follow-up. However, they also perform another role, less explicit but just as important: they offer, even if only episodically, some human contact or even companionship to their elderly clients, who are often isolated and lonely. Significantly, how well the volunteers perform this role is a function of their personal empathy and commitment.

This service is valuable, not only for the elderly clients and their families, but also for the society at large. It upholds the important public value of equity, in that those who are vulnerable are looked after to the extent of the programme. More instrumentally, it helps obviate the necessity of placing the elderly in nursing care, which is much more expensive for either their families or the taxpayer, depending on the health funding system.

137

At first sight, the advantage to councils – or indeed to other public sector organizations – of using volunteers seems obvious: as an Australian study put it, the contribution made by volunteers 'significantly reduces labour costs' (Meals Victoria 2008: viii). However, this does not account for the fact that some councils use paid staff for delivering meals. Nor does the evidence indicate that this is the primary advantage of volunteers more generally. Moreover, as will be explored below, the research indicates that other factors in addition to costs are important in public sector utilization of volunteers. It suggests the need to think carefully before taking the step of transferring tasks from paid staff to volunteers.

Until recently, one factor driving the increasing use of paid staff was a growing shortage of volunteers. For about three-quarters of the councils covered in the Australian study, this was a recruitment problem; it was becoming increasingly difficult to attract volunteers (Meals Victoria 2008: 99). The same was true for many other public sector and non-profit organizations which made use of volunteers (Brudney and Meijs 2009: 565). But the research also showed that the *retention* of existing volunteers was a growing challenge, as turnover rates increased (Jamison 2003; Hustinx 2010). However, the onset of the global economic downturn from 2008 has complicated this picture as people, retrenched from their jobs, offer their services as volunteers.

This chapter primarily considers the phenomenon of volunteering for public services, since the book as a whole is about externalization by government organizations. But we also recognize that public services can be produced by non-profit organizations as well. We therefore focus mainly on public sector volunteering, but also refer to volunteering more generally – not least because much of the research applies equally to both. First, we sketch the nature and dimensions of volunteering, then we delineate the benefits and costs to government organizations and their publics. Finally, we explore what motivates people to volunteer for such services, and in light of that how public sector agencies might attract and retain their contributions.

The nature and scope of public sector volunteering

Volunteering to public sector organizations is a sub-set of volunteering more generally, of which the largest part is in the non-profit sector. Surveys consistently show that about a quarter of the population in developed countries performs some voluntary work, with a smaller proportion in developing and former socialist bloc countries (Anheier and Salamon 2000). Moreover, the voluntary sector relies heavily on volunteer labour: about two-thirds of its imputed philanthropic income is in the form of labour input by volunteers, with the remainder in the form of cash donations, which together with government contracts and other income, funds work by employed staff. Volunteer labour accounts for an average of 2.5 per cent of non-agricultural employment (ranging from 0.2 per cent in Mexico to 8.0 per cent in Sweden) (Salamon and Sokolowski 2001).

The research about public sector volunteering is not as extensive as that for volunteering more generally, but it suggests that volunteers constitute an important source of productive capacity for government, and that their significance may be growing. In the United States, regular surveys show that about a quarter of all volunteering time is directed towards government organizations (Hodgkinson *et al.* 1996: 105; Brudney 2000: 112–13). This constituted about 9 per cent of total government employment in the US (Hodgkinson *et al.* 1996: 28–9), most of this effort directed toward local government (Brudney 2000: 113; see also Brown 1999). In Australia, volunteering to public sector activities was 14.5 per cent of total volunteering in 2006 (ABS 2006: 29). In the UK, 23 per cent of volunteering is in the public sector. (GHK 2010: 85). Elsewhere in Europe, 16 per cent of volunteering in Denmark is in the public sector, with a similar proportion in the Netherlands (GHK 2010: 85).

This volunteering covers a wide variety of services, but a few predominate. In the voluntary sector, volunteers are most commonly used in human services – education, health and welfare – in culture and the arts, and in recreation services. Volunteers in public services are also concentrated in these areas, as well as in emergency services such as local fire brigades and ambulance services. Among the specific areas of involvement are homeless shelters and food programmes, drug and alcohol treatment, child welfare, veterans' administration, libraries, and specialist education support.[1] In short, volunteers are an important and widely used feature of public sector work. Table 6.1 sets out the key dimensions of calling on volunteers.

TABLE 6.1   *Key dimensions of calling on volunteers*

Distribution of roles	*Contribution by volunteers*
Who decides?	Government organization and/or non-profit organization
Who produces?	Volunteer
Mode of coordination	Quasi-employment relationship

Benefits and costs of using volunteers in government work

Utilizing volunteers offers government organizations a particular combination of benefits and costs in terms not only of the service itself but also of the relationship with the provider and of the strategic implications for the public agency.

Service benefits and costs

At first sight, the main service benefit from volunteering seems obvious: volunteer labour is free. There is a tangible benefit at no cost to the government organization, as the Meals on Wheels case makes clear. This is indeed an important factor for many agencies using them. Their services are reliant on volunteer labour to be viable, and it would be difficult to run them without that contribution.

One possible inference from this is that public sector organizations should transfer activities currently performed by paid staff to volunteers, in order to reduce their costs. But this is problematic, for a number of reasons, underscored by the fact that very few agencies have done so in practice.

First, it is not actually true that using volunteers is cost-free. Running an effective volunteer programme has inevitable costs attached to it (Brudney 1990). Some of these costs relate to the management of the relationship, and are discussed further below, but some can be seen as indirect service costs. They include office space, utilities, insurance, corporate services such as computer systems, and out-of-pocket expenses – for example recompensing Meals on Wheels volunteers for the cost of petrol.

Second, replacing paid staff with volunteers is likely to generate trenchant resistance by staff in the organization more generally, whose attitude to volunteers, as we will explore below, is one of the critical factors in managing them (Levine 1984). This resistance may be all the more difficult to deal with if the staff are unionized. Moreover, the volunteers themselves may be averse to taking the jobs of paid staff. As Brudney (1999: 34) points out, this is a strong element of the ethos of volunteering. People volunteer in order to help others or further a cause, not to bail out the finances of a public agency.

Finally, many public sector jobs entail specialist qualifications, training and experience. In these cases, volunteers simply will not have the requisite knowledge and skills, nor will they be able to acquire them readily.

A more robust rationale for using volunteers in the public sector is not cost-saving but *cost-effectiveness*. According to Brudney, 'their true value lies in supplementing and broadening the services provided to clients by regular staff' (1990: 36), an observation borne out by a substantial body of research. Far from substituting for paid staff, they offer what Ellis (1996: 25) describes as 'leverage money' funding services considerably more valuable than the initial outlay. They do this in three ways.

First, some of them have specialized skills or capacities which are important to the work of the organization. These capabilities can derive either from previous training and experience or from the volunteers' structural situation. One example of the former is the Service Corps of Retired Executives (SCORE) whose members work for the US Small Business Administration to provide counselling and training on business management to the agency's clients (Brudney 1990a: 40–1). In this work they bring to bear their accumulated wisdom and experience in management. An example of the latter is where members of a particular ethnic community volunteer to assist crime prevention activities, which they are able to do more effectively because of their knowledge of, and legitimacy within, the community. Thus the value emanating from these types of capabilities can be said to derive from specialization by the provider, and/or complementarity of the provider's capabilities with those of the organization. Whether that value is generated depends on how well the providers' capacities square with the requirements of the job.

The second way in which volunteers leverage public services is by contributing to the effectiveness of paid staff. They can allow paid staff to focus on their areas of expertise, and thereby add to overall productivity. This is not uncommon in law enforcement, where volunteers assist not only with support activities such as telephone answering and record keeping, but also with specialist activities such auxiliary units, bilingual interpretation, or conducting community meetings on crime prevention (Gaston and Alexander 2001; Ayling *et al.* 2006). In Crown and Magistrates courts in England, for example, Witness Service volunteers provide information and support for people attending the court (Volunteering England 2010). This bridges a gap in the court system by helping witnesses prepare to participate in the justice system, and enables paid staff to focus more squarely on core tasks. In New York, the building of a wilderness trail on Bear Mountain (Applebome 2010), comprising 800 steps made of 1,000-pound slabs of granite was largely carried out by 700 volunteers doing low-tech rock and quarry work (rock splitting and shaping) alongside paid employees of the National Parks Service.[2] The extent to which volunteers can complement the overall service and work with paid staff is, of course, improved by effective supervision.

A variation on this process is where volunteer staff, less subject to the large and sometimes intractable systems of the public sector, are able to focus on a specifically tailored service that obviates the need for clients to access broader services. Thus, Meals on Wheels meets the particular needs of its clients in a way which would otherwise have to be met by placing them in an aged care facility.

Finally, a significant benefit of using volunteers is what Brudney (1990: 66) calls the 'volunteer intangible'. This derives from the fact that people volunteer because, as will be discussed below, they have a normative, social or intrinsic commitment to the purposes of the government programme in question. This means they are more likely to 'go the extra mile' in support of the purpose. They are more likely to show empathy and care about the concerns of clients. To the extent that they have an interest in the cause served by the programme, they are more likely to be knowledgeable about it, or understanding of clients' needs.

Strategic benefits and costs

There is also a mixture of advantages and risks to the organization in strategic terms. On the positive side, where significant numbers of volunteers are used, their commitment to the agency's purpose is likely to translate into a more aware and more supportive political constituency. In a 1990 survey in the American state of Georgia, local public managers reported increased public support for programmes as a significant advantage they perceived in involving volunteers in their agencies. This factor increased in significance in a follow-up survey in 2003 (Gazley and Brudney 2005).

On the other side of the ledger, and probably looming larger, are two related strategic risks, both of them arising, paradoxically, from the fact that volunteers are motivated by moral conviction or intrinsic rewards. One is what we might call 'mission rigidity'; volunteers may be resistant to changes to the organization's purposes or methods – necessitated by a changing environment or resource constraints – because those changes embrace different purposes or methods to the ones which motivated them to volunteer in the first place.

The second arises from the fact that volunteers do not receive any salary for their work. This is of course a great advantage of using them, but it also means that the organization has consequently less leverage over them. Whereas the threat of dismissal of paid staff has some potency in inducing them to comply with work requirements because it means that they might lose vital income, it has comparatively less impact on volunteers, because they do not rely on their voluntary work for income. Even more importantly, it means that volunteers are more readily able to withhold their labour, either individually or collectively, than paid staff, who must think twice about taking industrial action if it means they will lose pay. If the organization depends on volunteer contributions, it is more vulnerable to withholding of effort. Combined with mission rigidity, it can pose a challenge for agency managers seeking to institute necessary change. It requires them to appeal to volunteers' non-material motivations to persuade them to go along with the organization's direction. Concomitantly, it necessitates engagement and dialogue, underpinned by mutual respect, in working through the rationale for change.

Relationship benefits and costs

Managing the organization's *relationship* with volunteers has particular costs. First, there are the costs of recruiting, selecting and orienting them, which of course are harder in economic downturns or for some government organizations, such as zoos, museums or art galleries, where there is a surplus of volunteers. But in boom times, where volunteers are in short supply, agencies must engage in activities such as advertising, publicity or recruitment information sessions to encourage people to contribute their time. Even where there are plenty of volunteers, the agency needs to screen them and select the most suitable. This can be akin to a selection process for paid staff, and many organizations make use of it, with selection criteria, applications, interviews and reference checks. In some areas, such as child welfare or security work, there are extra checks to ensure applicants are suitable to work with children or do not have a criminal record. A balance between formality and flexibility in the recruitment process is important. A study of volunteer management in England found many organizations have no formal process at all (as reported in Gaskin 2003), and at the other end of the spectrum where processes are too formal, bureaucratic or not tailored to individual, volunteers are put off from working with the organization.[3]

Once recruited, volunteers need to be inducted into the organization so they understand policies and procedures and are given an idea of what will be expected of them. They also need some training which, depending on the role they will take on, can be basic or more complex. Volunteers in a police support programme in England were required to do weekend training for three months, so they could understand everything from race relations to answering the telephone (Gaskin 2003). All of these activities have costs.

Another set of costs attaches to the ongoing process of managing volunteers. For many organizations, this takes the form of employing a manager or supervisor with specific responsibility for leading and organizing the volunteer effort. In addition, whether the agencies have supervisors of volunteering or not, some portion of the time of paid staff is taken up with dealing with volunteers – explaining the tasks, correcting mistakes, coordinating schedules, giving day-to-day directions. Even where the agency or its paid staff give only minimal attention to these responsibilities, some portion of their salaries is necessarily attributable to the costs of managing the relationship. Where the agency adopts a conscious and strategic approach to managing this relationship – for example by providing development opportunities, involving volunteers in organizational deliberations, or staging 'recognition events' to reward good performance – these costs will be greater.

Unfortunately, some organizations using volunteers perform these relationship management tasks poorly. The net effect of neglecting them is typically not to save money but rather to incur additional costs in volunteer turnover, as dissatisfied volunteers quit and recruitment processes have to be set in train again. At least as significantly, the quality or effectiveness of the service is compromised by uncommitted or less than fully competent volunteers. By the same token, an overly formal and bureaucratic management model can be just as problematic. Finding the middle path which works for the organization is important to ensuring volunteer satisfaction, motivation, and retention (Zimmeck 2001).

On the other hand, the relationship benefits of using volunteers, while not to be ignored, can be hard to pin down. Because volunteers tend, by comparison with other providers, to have more moral commitment to the programme purposes, this may translate into goodwill to the organization itself, and by extension to its management and staff. Thus there may be solidary benefits arising from the 'volunteer intangible'. This benefit, like the others considered above, basically depends on how positively volunteers perceive the mission and style of the organization, which are in turn functions of how it is led and managed – a topic to which we now turn.

Attracting and retaining volunteers

Motivations

The relationship between volunteers and organizations that use them (public or non-profit) is distinctive. On the one hand, it is like an employment relationship, in that volunteers are subject to directive supervision much as an employee of a company or a department is. In this sense, volunteers become part of the organization, and the relationship is functionally close. On the other hand, however, it is quite unlike an employment relationship in that volunteers do not get paid by the organization for their work. This means that the organization lacks a managerial lever that is normal in respect of paid staff: the option of curtailing the workers' income by removing them from the job. They can of course dismiss them – and may well do so, for example, if their work is dysfunctional – but this does not have the sanction attached to it of cutting off the workers' livelihood. The fact that they are volunteering implies they already have some other source of income (such as a salary, a pension, or a personal fortune) to sustain them.

Consequently, enlisting work by volunteers calls for mechanisms appealing to different motivations than material self-interest. Not surprisingly, non-material motivations loom large among the reasons why people volunteer their services. Intuitively, normative values and their associated moral convictions constitute the most important of these motivations, and the research shows that they are indeed very significant factors influencing people to donate their time and effort. Drawing on Gallup Organization data, Sundeen (1990) reported that wanting 'to do something useful, help others, [or] do good deeds for others' was clearly the most significant reason, with intrinsic motivations, such as interest in and enjoyment of the activity, next most important, but by a considerable margin. Much less important were having a child, relative or friend who might benefit from it, or the desire for work experience to help in getting a job. An occasional survey since 1988 for Independent Sector, the peak body for voluntary organizations in America, has shown consistently that the main motive impelling people to volunteer is a desire to do something useful to help others (Brudney 1990a: 93). In the most recent, conducted in 2001 (Toppe *et al.* 2002), the three most significant reasons, each given by more than 90 per cent of volunteers surveyed, were: feeling compassion toward people in need; giving back to the community; and helping those with less. The next three most important reasons, but some way behind the first three, related to social affiliation: the activity was important to people whom respondents respect (83.2 per cent); someone close was involved or benefited; and to meet new people.

Surveys by Clary *et al* (1996, 1998) found six types of motivations, of which the most important was 'values', in which people volunteer in order to express humanitarian values or altruistic concerns. Next in importance, equally, were intrinsic and solidary motivations: 'enhancement' of volunteer's psychological development and self-esteem; the opportunity to increase knowledge and skills; and 'social' motivation, in which volunteering helps people to fit in and get along with social groups important to them. Least important were motivations closer to self-interest such as career enhancement (Clary *et al.* 1996; see also Hodgkinson and Weitzman 1988; Janoski *et al.* 1998; Stukas *et al.* 2009).

The limited available data indicates similar motivations outside the United States. In Britain, a survey for the Cabinet Office (2008) found that the most important reason for volunteering, cited by 53 per cent of the volunteers interviewed, was a desire to improve things or help people. Next most important were: a belief that the cause was important (41 per cent) or having time to spare (41 per cent) (multiple answers possible). Much less important were to 'help get on in my career' (7 per cent) or to 'get a recognised qualification' (2 per cent).[4]

These data concern all types of volunteering, not just volunteering in the public sector. In the latter case research is more limited, but what there is suggests that moral values are also the most important motivations, but not to the same extent as in the non-profit/voluntary sector. The study by Sundeen (1990) cited above found that whereas the desire 'to do something useful, help others, [or] do good deeds for others' was cited by 63 per cent of non-government volunteers surveyed, it was only cited by 39 per cent of volunteers to local governments, just 4 per cent more than the next most cited reason.

If moral/normative values are as important as the research indicates, this suggests that mission alignment – the extent to which the perceived purpose of the organization or programme fits with potential volunteers' purposive values – is the mechanism of central significance to the organization's efforts to attract them. As will be discussed further below, this is true, but it is not the whole story. Both research evidence and practitioner experience show that the mechanisms most likely to *attract* volunteers are different from those likely to *retain* them: the issue is not so much the recruiting of volunteers as retaining them once recruited (Brudney and Meijs 2009).

What happens is that once people join as volunteers, the inner workings of the organization and their relationships with other participants become more salient. As a result, they attach greater weight to friendships and social interaction, and to their experience of the job itself – in short, to intrinsic and solidary rewards (Brudney 1990a).

According to Sundeen (1990), this motivational shift is even more true of volunteering for public sector agencies. Whereas the continued involvement of volunteers in *non*-government agencies was associated not only with greater intrinsic and solidary motivations but also greater moral conviction, for those in *government* agencies their continued involvement saw a 5 per cent decline in those motivated by a desire to help but a sharp increase in intrinsic and solidary motivations. Sundeen speculates that this could indicate that public agency volunteers have more of a 'consuming' orientation (that is, one in which they seek to gain from volunteering) than a 'giving' one. But this motivational shift could just as likely reflect how well (or badly) the agency organizes the work or manages its volunteers.

The latter explanation was more consistent at the time with the widely reported problem encountered by agencies (public or nonprofit) utilizing volunteers: high levels of turnover, characterized by episodic or 'revolving door' involvement (Putnam 1995; Jamison 2003; Hustinx 2010) – a problem which metamorphosed into one of excess supply of volunteers with the onset of the global economic crisis at the end of the 2000s. But before then, volunteers might still be initially signing on in sustained numbers, driven by enthusiasm for agency missions, but increasingly they were choosing not to stay (Glass and Hastings 1992; Lindhorst and Mancoske 1993; Jamison 2003). The reason appears to be dissatisfaction with a mixture of factors besides mission alignment, such as work conditions, interpersonal relationships with supervisors and peers, and the challenge and interest of the work itself (Brudney 1990b; Jamison 2003). A study in England of older volunteers found that several factors are critical to volunteer retention, including: being kept busy and active; flexibility in time commitments; changes in contribution over time to match experience; real responsibility and autonomy; opportunities to be involved in policy making; learning and skill development opportunities; and a feeling that their contribution was valued (Rochester *et al.* 2002.). Whereas mission alignment is an alternative motivator to monetary remuneration, these other factors resonate with the fact that volunteers have something like an employment relationship with the agency.

Motivators

Mission alignment remains, of course, a key consideration for organizations – including government ones – seeking to attract volunteers. People will volunteer their services to an organization if they see it as embodying a cause to which they have a strong attachment. This means firstly, that an organization needs to create awareness among potential volunteers of the virtue and importance of its work, through positive media publicity, testimonials by celebrities, celebratory events, appeals for help during crises and even positive 'word of mouth'. But it also means that it must actually have a mission that potential donors of time and effort see as worthwhile. The fact that people are volunteering provides tangible proof of the appeal of its current mission, which can be reinforced by volunteer induction processes and periodic training. But where this issue becomes difficult is when an agency seeks to *change* its mission, either explicitly – by amending its charter – or implicitly, by adopting or dropping an activity, a sponsor or a constituency that recasts the definition of its business in a way that volunteers find problematic. One example is of a service offered to mothers in the first year following childbirth, referred to as Healthy Start (a pseudonym) in a study by Minahan and Inglis (2008). Widely recognized as an important contributor to the well-being of new mothers, Healthy Start had attracted more than 200,000 paying members at its peak and many volunteers who ran local chapters. However when membership started to decline, the management committee changed the organization's stated aim from providing support to mothers to promoting its services to health professionals to gain more grants. The decision caused considerable conflict between the management committee and volunteers, many of whom withdrew their time and effort, even though they were committed to its values.

In these circumstances, the organization has two broad options. One is to try to reshape the mission in such a way that it still fits with the value-orientation of its volunteers. This need not be a matter of capitulation to volunteers' preferences. It could entail framing the mission at a level of generality where there is ambiguity about the contested issues, although this is unlikely to be sustainable for long. A more fruitful course would be to seek to unbundle the issues of volunteers and of the agency, and through that discern purposes which constitute 'win-wins', in that they meet or partially meet the respective concerns of the different parties. Discovering these differential interests would be facilitated by the organization sponsoring open consultative processes. The other option open to the organization is to seek to persuade volunteers to accept the alteration to the mission, through information and education of one kind or another, such as internal newsletters, briefings or consultative processes.

Another way organizations can foster an alignment between its mission and the values of its volunteers is to pay attention to their recruitment and selection. The normal human resource practices in respect of paid staff – such as asking for CVs, personal interviews and reference checks – can assist, if not guarantee, the recruitment of volunteers who have some affinity with the purposes of the agency, as well as the necessary skills and knowledge (Clary *et al.* 1992; Fisher and Cole 1993; Ellis 1996).

But while mission alignment is fundamental to the initial involvement of volunteers, and of underlying importance to their continued involvement, it is supplemented or even outweighed by other motivators once volunteers have joined the organization. Some of these resonate with intrinsic motivation, specifically, those steps the agency takes to make the work more satisfying for the volunteer. One significant measure in this respect is job design (Brudney 1990b; Fisher and Cole 1993). Organizations which assign volunteers to mundane or monotonous tasks should not be surprised if they turn over frequently. Research by Gaskin (2003) found that while volunteers will tolerate 'boring' roles for a while, without change they will exit. By contrast, agencies making good use of volunteers put some thought into the characteristics of the work, which make it more interesting, and also signal respect for the competence of the volunteer. This does not mean that volunteers need to be assigned to the complex technical work that the organization's paid employees have been trained and selected for, merely that the support or special niche roles that they are given should be ones which sustain their interest and acknowledge the particular skills they do have.

Also important to intrinsic motivation is recognition and feedback. Many successful volunteer programmes have periodic 'recognition events', in which well-performing volunteers are given awards or acknowledged publicly (Fisher and Cole 1993). More specifically, some organizations measure volunteers' performance and provide them with feedback. This can, of course, be a double-edged sword. To the extent that performance measurement is seen as underpinning sanctions or rewards – for example through rankings of volunteers' performance – it can crowd out intrinsic motivation, as discussed in Chapter 3. But where it is used for the purposes of developing volunteers' capacities, it can resonate positively with those motivations.

Another organizational practice resonating with intrinsic motivation is training and development, which not only acknowledges volunteers' existing sense of their own competence but also enhances it, as they acquire new skills and knowledge (Brudney

1990a; Ellis 1996). One example is that of volunteer ambulance officers (VAOs), often the front line for medical emergencies in rural and remote areas of Australia (Fahey *et al.* 2002). A survey of VAOs in the state of Tasmania found that training was highly sought after and critical to building individual competency and confidence. Volunteers feared a lack of training would impede them in responding to medical emergencies, thus undermining confidence, and flowing through to retention issues.

Finally, intrinsic motivation is also tapped by bestowing a measure of autonomy on volunteers – in how they work given the outcomes expected of them and the orientation and training they have undergone. This is where the 'volunteer intangible' can come into play: volunteers can draw on their own experience, empathy and insight to fashion responses to individual clients' needs and circumstances. Respecting this autonomy in appropriate circumstances not only enhances the service but also reinforces volunteers' sense of personal competence. Interestingly, one way of respecting volunteers' autonomy and enhancing their sense of personal competence is to involve them in deliberation and decision making about organizational purposes and/or processes. Thus, the sponsoring of consultative or participatory processes to foster mission alignment, preferred to above, also has positive effects on intrinsic motivation.

Another set of motivators important in encouraging volunteers to continue their service are those resonating with sociality. Organizations can pay attention to three kinds of interactions experienced by volunteers: with their fellow volunteers; with clients; and with paid staff. In general, social interaction is in itself a motivator; as far as possible, tasks should be designed so that they do not entail volunteers working in an isolated fashion. This can occur, *inter alia*, by organizing work on some sort of team basis, so that volunteers interact with their fellows in the course of their work, or by enabling volunteer contact with the organization's clients, which also, as discussed above, resonates with normative motivations.

A final set of motivators consists of what Herzberg (1959) calls 'hygiene factors' – conditions and pre-requisites for doing the work. Most volunteer programmes provide basic facilities such as offices or equipment where this is necessary to the work. Most ensure that their volunteers are not out of pocket for expenses, such as petrol, telephone calls or job-related apparel. All are expected to provide legally mandated necessities such as workplace insurance and health and safety compliance (Brudney 1990b).

One hygiene factor of distinctive importance is the work schedule. Volunteers often work part-time, and have particular scheduling requirements dictated by the demands of their paid work or their family circumstances. Good practice in volunteer programme is to facilitate flexible scheduling in ways which optimize the needs of both the organization and the volunteer (Brudney and Meijs 2009; Hustinx 2010).

Thus, while volunteers are not employees, eliciting useful contributions from them calls for the same level of attention as to paid staff – and if anything more so, since they do not get paid. Whilst this has some costs attached to it, these costs can be substantially outweighed by the benefits.

Staff resistance

Perhaps the most pervasive and perennial problem in managing volunteers is the attitude of paid employees toward them. Sometimes, this can be supportive and encouraging, but in other cases, it can be negative, even hostile, or at least mixed.[5] There are several reasons for this kind of hostility, each capable of being ameliorated (Brudney 1990a).

First and foremost, employees view volunteers with suspicion because they see them as potentially stealing their jobs. This can be especially pronounced in highly unionized settings where trade unions express concerns about job substitution, assigning volunteers to inappropriate roles and poor working relations between volunteer and paid staff (Volunteering England 2010). Public sector volunteers in Gaskin's study in England recounted their experience:

> We never felt welcome, They were hostile really . . . they thought we were after their jobs ... when you go to an organisation with paid employees they see you as a bit of a threat . . . there's often a difference between the upper echelons and the people who are doing the day to day work. The bosses have the big ideas – 'let's get volunteers in' – but they don't tell people lower down, so there is hostility.
>
> (2003:20)

Indeed, where agencies seek to replace paid staff with volunteers, this perception is validated for those who lose their jobs and exacerbated for those who are left on the payroll. In these circumstances, paid staff will be resistant to helping train volunteers, for fear they are giving away vital skills and knowledge. This is a significant reason why it is usually unwise, as discussed previously, to use volunteers as a means of cutting payrolls. This fear can be mitigated by being clear about the rationale for utilizing volunteers, and encouraging employees to understand that rationale, through communication and more potently through involving them in deliberations about why and how volunteers may be engaged. Where public sector unions have a strong presence, this will also involve seeking to negotiate an understanding with them about the use of volunteers.

Second, paid employees often perceive volunteers as being unreliable: because they don't get paid, they may not feel the need to turn up on time, or they may fail to follow-through on agreed tasks. These kinds of issues concern the way volunteers are managed. Good practice in this respect is to have a clear job description for the volunteer role, and if possible an explicit understanding of work and attendance expectations such as a contract. The aforementioned flexible scheduling may also facilitate reliable attendance.

Third, paid staff tend to see volunteers as inexpert or incompetent, since they lack the requisite training, skills or experience. A volunteer working in an English school recounted: 'The teachers, it's like "what right do you have to be here? What experience do you have?"' (Gaskin 2003: 19). Where experience is lacking, the consequence is that employees have to devote some of their working time to showing volunteers how to do tasks, or to rectifying problems caused by incompetent volunteer work. This is not so true of volunteers who are engaged for their specialist skills (for example, accountants providing pro bono advice to poor people on how to complete their tax returns), but it can be a problem for volunteers engaged in organization-specific tasks they have not encountered previously. The obvious solution is to provide for or improve the orientation and training of volunteers. It is also helpful to design the work so that it is not beyond the capacities of people of normal intelligence.

Related to this is that volunteers are perceived in some organizations as requiring excessive supervisory time. Such a perception, actually, is more likely to signal a shortcoming in the management of the organization than in the volunteers. It is likely to rest on an assumption that volunteers simply need to be pointed to their task and then left to their own devices. But just as paid employees need some supervision, so too do volunteers. Some organizations employ coordinators or directors of volunteering. Some also pay attention to educating employees in how they can better relate to and work with volunteers.

All of these problems of employee perception can also be mitigated by following good practice in recruitment and selection, to ensure that volunteers have the appropriate skills and attitudes to the work. And all of the suggested solutions are likely to be facilitated by involving not only volunteers but also employees in deliberative and consultative processes about organizational purposes and methods, and ensuring that the rationale for engaging volunteers is clear to all parties. Creating an environment where paid staff and volunteers can work productively together depends in part on encouraging paid staff to create a friendly and welcoming atmosphere where volunteers can feel part of a team, and will be therefore more likely to stay with the organization (Gaskin 2003).

Conclusion

The genesis of these problems lies in the unique status of volunteers. On the one hand, they are embedded within the organization in that they are performing tasks alongside paid employees and subject to its supervisory hierarchy. In this sense they are close to the organization, and more particularly, can jostle up against the paid employees. But on the other hand, they are distant from the organization in that they do not have the same remunerative stake in it that employees have. They can leave at any time without financial consequence, and therefore easily be cast as external parties. Finding ways to validate and dovetail both groups' respective stakes in the organizational mission is the key to making the best use of volunteers.

Chapter 7

Regulatees as Contributors to Social Outcomes

Regulatees – the people or organizations subject to obligations imposed by government authorities – seem at first sight to be unlikely candidates for external providers of services. Take the restaurateurs who are regulated by the Dutch Food and Consumer Product Safety Authority, whose job includes protecting human and animal health (Mascini and Van Wijk 2009). Far from being contributors to the Authority's purposes, at least some of them seem more like obstacles. They have to be compelled either to do things they find inconvenient or costly to do, such as to keep foodstuffs cooled to a particular temperature, or to refrain from doing things they want to do, such as hanging Peking roast ducks in their windows (which the Authority's scientific research has found to be unhygienic). A sizeable proportion of restaurateurs are seen by the Authority's inspectors as reluctant to meet their obligations, seeking to hide from or find ways around the law by exploiting loopholes.[1] Indeed, to the extent that they break the law or avoid their obligations, these regulatees are quite the opposite of contributors to Authority purposes. Far from serving those purposes, they detract from or undermine them, and therefore have to be compelled to comply.

But these perspectives start from a particular way of thinking about regulation – namely, as the exercise of compulsion over those who are being regulated. It is seen as applying sanctions against those who break the law, or more usually wielding the threat of sanctions against those who might do so. In this view, typical regulatory activities include detecting breaches, prosecuting offenders, and applying penalties, in the hope of deterring others from similar malfeasance.

These enforcement activities do indeed constitute important aspects of regulation, but they are not the only aspects. The important thing about regulation is not the process (compulsion) but rather the *outcome*: compliance. It is true that the term 'compliance' is sometimes used in a narrow sense. Regulatory agency staff, for instance, are sometimes said to have a 'compliance mentality', usually meaning they are sticklers for the rules and don't care about whether they make sense in a particular situation.[2]

But there is a broader way to look at compliance: it entails people or organizations acting in a manner consistent with the public purposes the regulatory agency serves. The critical point here is that people act in this way for a variety of reasons, *only one of which is compulsion*. They may comply because they agree with the purposes of the rules being imposed, or because they firmly hold the view that the law should be obeyed. They may comply because they do not want to incur the shame that might come with being publicly blamed for non-compliance. They may comply because there is some material incentive or reward for doing so, or because it is relatively easy to do so. In other words, their compliance may be more or less voluntary, and not simply a result of fear of punishment.

Whether regulatees comply willingly or grudgingly, they are contributors in a more profound sense: by complying, they further the achievement of desired social outcomes. The legal obligations that the regulatory agency is imposing have typically been promulgated to advance some aspect of the common good. The regulatee usually suffers a detriment so that the public at large may benefit – for instance, he has to devote extra labour to scrubbing and disinfecting surfaces and utensils so that the 'externality' of food-borne disease does not afflict the public. Thus, in complying, the regulatee is simultaneously contributing to the achievement of social outcomes. And, as we shall see, the more voluntary this compliance, the more useful it is to the agency and the public.

This chapter considers regulatees in this light (see Table 7.1). We begin with a consideration of the meaning of regulation, and then identify how voluntary compliance might contribute to social outcomes. We go on to explore ways in which a government organization might elicit contributions from regulatees, while not allowing recalcitrants to avoid their responsibilities. We then consider when it is valuable for a government organization to enlist contributions from them, taking into account the trade-offs involved in doing so.

TABLE 7.1   *Key dimensions of using regulatees as contributors to outcomes*

Distribution of roles	*Regulation*
Who decides?	Government organization
Who produces?	Regulatee (government organization, private firm, non-profit/voluntary agency and/or individual)
Mode of coordination	Compulsion and negotiation/collaboration

None of this is meant to imply that people's rights and responsibilities as citizens are in any way diminished – merely that, as will be explained further in Chapter 8, they have additional roles besides that of citizen, including those of client and regulatee. Where these roles are in conflict – as they often can be – that of citizen should, in the end, trump the other roles. Moreover, in canvassing the various motivators and facilitators of compliance, we are not suggesting that regulatees (or indeed clients) are Pavlovian reactors to government-applied stimuli. Their propensity to contribute time and effort to social outcomes is mediated by the judgements and choices they make in the context of various motivators and facilitators affecting them. In the end, it is still open to people do things for their own good reasons.

The meaning of regulation

Simply put, regulation is the imposition of obligations on individuals or organizations to comply with rules promulgated by the state in order to promote the achievement of some public purpose (see Hood 1986; Baldwin and Cave 1999; Freiberg 2010). It usually entails those who are regulated being disadvantaged for the benefit of the wider community.

Regulation can apply either to individuals or to organizations – in the latter case, especially private companies, but not excluding non-profits and government organizations. This is important because the motivational mechanisms are different in the case of organizations than they are with individuals. It is true that only individuals can be said to have motivations, but those of individuals within organizations affect compliance differently, because they are structured and mediated by organizational imperatives and processes, as we discussed in Chapter 3.

It also needs to be recognized that regulation is an activity undertaken by a wide range of organizations within the public sector, not only by those we see primarily as 'regulatory authorities'. For this broader set of organizations, the imposition of obligations is important to their primary role of implementing policy or delivering services. For example, mental health authorities provide clinical, counselling and other support services to people with mental health problems, but also on occasion need to have those clients committed to institutional care. Social security agencies provide income support benefits to welfare recipients, but also enforce conditions attached to them such as requirements to report changes in income, address or family status. Both public and private schools provide education to students, but also are licensed to discipline their behaviour *in loco parentis*. In these and other cases, service-delivery agencies are also partly in the business of imposing obligations, just as regulatory agencies are.

Regulation takes different forms (Baldwin and Cave 1999). One common way of understanding these forms is to consider different approaches to regulation on a continuum, from 'hard' to 'soft' types. At the 'hard' end is what is typically described as 'command-and-control' regulation, in which the regulator monitors compliance with the rules, which might include detailed process requirements, detects breaches and penalizes or prosecutes offenders – just as some of our Dutch food inspectors did as a first response where restaurateurs hung Peking ducks in their windows. At the 'soft' end is self-regulation, in which an industry association promulgates a set of rules, monitors the behaviour of its members and induces them to act in conformity with those rules, an approach considered, but ultimately not recommended for private funds (that is, hedge and private equity funds) in the United States in 2011 (United States Government Accountability Office 2011). In between these two extremes are hybrid forms such as 'enforced self-regulation' (sometimes known as 'co-regulation'), where a self-regulation scheme is subject to some form of governmental oversight. Its logic is generally to allow an industry to regulate itself, with the authority able to intervene when the regulatory practice is seen to be inadequate. Social housing in Britain is based on this approach.[3]

Another alternative is incentive-based regulation, which seeks to encourage compliant behaviour by applying taxes or subsidies, or more radically, introducing tradeable permits, such as cap-and-trade regimes for carbon emissions. There is a wide variety of other regulatory mechanisms, such as mandatory disclosure rules (requiring producers to inform consumers of key facts about their products, such as their fat or salt content) or technical compulsion (subjecting regulatees to technologies which give them little choice but to comply, for example, installing speed humps on roads to force motorists to slow down).

Of increasing prominence among the various approaches is responsive regulation (Ayres and Braithwaite 1992), which involves 'combining punishment and persuasion' to 'tailor the enforcement style to the propensity and capacity of regulatees to comply' (Mascini and van Wijk 2009). Significantly for the present analysis, its focus is on the motives and actions of those being regulated. We discuss this approach at length below.

These approaches differ in the extent to which they seek to encourage voluntary compliance, and by corollary, in their respective contributions to achieving social outcomes.

How voluntary compliance contributes to social outcomes

Voluntary compliance is considerably more useful to regulatory authorities, for two reasons. One is that it is generally less costly. Consider police officers arresting a drunkard on the streets at night. If the arrestee is resistant, it usually takes more than one officer to apprehend him. There is more likely to be violence, which may result in injury to either the drunkard or the officer. In this case either the arrestee might subsequently lodge a complaint of police violence, which will then take up costly police or perhaps court time. Or the injured police officer may require medical attention, with costs of health services, or at least of police time off work and later workers' compensation claims. In a violent scuffle, officers' uniforms may be damaged, necessitating expenditure on replacement apparel. Once at the police station, it is likely that the offender will have to be put in a cell overnight rather than bailed, with additional costs. By contrast, an arrestee who comes along relatively peaceably requires fewer officers, generates less violence, chews up less police time with complaints, and incurs less costs for medical services, uniforms and workers' compensation claims. In short, it is cheaper for the police if arrestees comply voluntarily than if they resist.[4]

The second reason why voluntary compliance is more useful is that it is generally of higher quality, especially if the obligations are complex. The more complicated the obligations, or the harder they are to specify precisely in advance, then the more the regulator relies on regulatees to exercise discretion, consciously plan their actions, and take positive and sometimes intricate steps. In these situations grudging compliance, where regulatees only obey the letter of the law rather than its spirit, is rarely adequate. Consider, for instance, an occupational health and safety agency, responsible for inducing companies to adopt safe and healthy practices with the aim of reducing workplace accidents and diseases. If the companies' stance is one of reluctant compliance with rules, they will not achieve the desired outcome of minimizing injuries and work-related diseases. This is because each company's operations and circumstances are different to at least some degree, and optimal health and safety systems have to be tailored to their specific situations. It is not possible for the agency to specify and apply a set of rules which will encompass the uncertainty and complexity of each company's situation. In the face of company indifference or resistance, all the agency will generate is low-level compliance, with the result that injuries and diseases will not be minimized.

By contrast, a company committed to health and safety at work is likely to perform better on this score, because it invests the thought and effort necessary to analyse the specific requirements and put in place means for addressing them. This kind of company can therefore be said to exhibit compliance of higher quality than its more reluctant counterparts.

Thus, if it is possible to elicit willing contributions from regulatees, the public as a whole will benefit, since individuals will be behaving in a manner more consistent with public purposes. In this sense, then, regulatees can be seen as contributors not only to agency functioning but also to social outcomes. It is true that some regulatees will comply only if they are compelled, but as we shall see, many will do so voluntarily. The important issue is whether the focus is on the process of applying coercion or on the achievement of publicly valued outcomes. The latter focus directs our attention to *why* regulation is applied, and encompasses a wider array of means for getting regulatees to comply, each of which has particular advantages and disadvantages.[5] These means differ in their mixes of motivational appeals to regulatees. Thus in order to delineate when it is useful for a government agency to enlist regulatees as contributors, we need first to understand the ways in which those contributions might be elicited.

Eliciting regulatees' contributions

The problem with sanctions

A substantial body of theory has evolved to explain what makes regulatees comply with regulatory obligations and thus contribute to the achievement of its purposes. A traditional view of regulation holds that the state intervenes and sets out 'forbidden behaviour' which, if then engaged in, will attract punishments such as fines, prison or social contempt (Fuhr and Bizer 2007). This view, reflected in the original charters of many regulatory agencies, has translated into the notion that strong sanctions are needed to ensure compliance (Erlich and Posner 1974; see also Wilson 1984; Sigler and Murphy 1988). As Kagan and Scholz (1984: 69–70) portray it for private companies:

> Today's most widely accepted model of corporate criminality portrays the business firm as an amoral, profit-seeking organization whose actions are motivated wholly by rational calculation of costs and opportunities. In this Hobbesian view . . . businessmen, driven by the norms and pressures of the marketplace, will break the law unless the anticipated legal penalties . . . exceed the additional profits the firm could make by evading the law.[6]

But as most regulatory officials have long been aware, securing compliance is a more complex matter than the expected utility model encompasses.[7] For a start, the model does not distinguish between people and organizations. While people can be said to have motivations, corporations cannot. Instead, their behavior is driven by the motivations of the people who comprise it. This recalls two complexities in the expected utility model, discussed in Chapter 3. One is that people have varying motivations; it is unlikely that those who comprise the company will all feel the same way about its legal obligations, in part because they have differing interests, in part because their personal values vary. The other is that within the corporation, people have differing levels of power. The preferences of some, such as its senior managers and in particular its chief executive officer, or its key professionals, will be much more likely to prevail than those of shop-floor staff. Moreover, the CEO and senior executives are answerable to the corporation's directors and shareholders, and subject to the imperatives not only of the marketplace but also, somewhat transversely, of the law and of public opinion. Thus, how a company might respond to one or other regulatory instrument depends on the interplay of these several factors.

Another problem with the expected utility model is that sanctions can, in important respects, be counter-productive as instruments of regulation. First, as discussed in Chapter 3, material self-interest is not the sole driver of people's behaviour – and not all company executives are motivated solely by profit.[8] Contrary to the profit-seeking stereotype, many company managers, while keeping a basic concern with economic return, also give weight to moral and legal responsibilities.[9] In particular, as regulators themselves often see, some corporate executives exhibit a principled concern to obey the law for its own sake (Robens 1972; Kagan and Scholz 1984; Grabosky and Braithwaite 1986; Sigler and Murphy 1988; Sparrow 1994). Thus, while it would be naïve to underestimate the significance of economic calculation among business regulatees, it would also be short-sighted to fail to see that many of them have moral concerns as well. As Ayres and Braithwaite (1992: 19) put it:

> Some corporate actors will only comply with the law if it is economically rational for them to do so; most corporate actors will comply with the law most of the time simply because it is the law; all corporate actors are bundles of contradictory commitments to values about economic rationality, law abidingness, and business responsibility.

The dilemma for regulators is that if company managers who are inclined to obey the law see the way regulations are applied as unjust or rigid, they will feel resentment towards the agency and/or the law (Bardach and Kagan 1982; Braithwaite 1985; Grabosky 1995b). Our food inspection example shows this commonly happens in regulatory encounters, especially where different teams of inspectors interpret and apply the rules differentially (Mascini and Van Wijk 2009), or where heavy handed approaches are taken (Todd 2008).

The second reason why sanctions have been found inadequate is that it is very difficult to formulate regulations to take sufficient account of all the activities being regulated (Diver 1980; Bardach and Kagan 1982; Kagan 1984; Peacock 1984; Scholz 1984; Hood 1986; Breyer 1993; Grabosky 1995b). For example, what might be valid for one restaurant may make little sense for another; what was valid for the technology of ten years ago may be out-of-date now.[10] Consequently, any regulation is bound to seem excessively costly, unfair or illegitimate to at least some of the actors to whom it is applied. In those cases, regulatees will be able to point to other ways of reaching the same result for the public with less harm to their firms. But if the regulatory agency insists on applying the same rule to everyone, regardless of their particular circumstances, they will experience it as an arbitrary imposition.

These two factors mean that enforcement directed towards punishment is very likely to generate at least some resentment on the part of those being regulated. At least some of this resentment engenders reduced willingness to comply, manifested in various ways. At the very least, it takes the shape of minimal compliance, that is, conforming with the letter of the law and not its spirit (Bardach and Kagan 1982: 107). This may be sufficient when the required behaviour is simple, but is more problematic when it calls for interpretation or adaptation of complex obligations.[11] More seriously, reduced compliance can take the form of cutting off cooperation and withholding of necessary information, making it more difficult and more costly for the regulatory agency to carry out its work (Diver 1980; Kelman 1981; Leone 1986; Makkai and Braithwaite 1994; Grabosky 1995b). Most seriously, it can entail active resistance, either by individual firms or their industry lobbies, bolstered by the aggressive use of legal devices (Bardach and Kagan 1982: 112–16).

This problem is aggravated by the same regulatory complexity which sets it off. Regulatees may seek to take advantage of the indeterminacy or ambiguity the complexity allows, whereupon agencies will draw the rules in more stringent detail and apply them more strictly, which the regulatee in turn experiences as even more arbitrary red tape, and so on, in a downward spiral of increasing mutual suspicion (Diver 1980; Bardach and Kagan 1982). One consequence is that the agency must employ more enforcement resources for such companies.

Thus, sanctions can be counterproductive as regulatory instruments, by reducing willingness to comply, and engendering non-cooperation and resistance, while also adding to the costs of regulation. But at the same time, no serious regulator would advocate the elimination of sanctions from the regulatory process. The reason, as indicated above, is that at least some regulatees can be expected to act opportunistically and break the law if they can get away with it. If they do, others who are more compliant will be less inclined to meet their obligations, partly because they become more aware of opportunities for non-compliance, and partly because they feel like 'suckers' for complying when others do not. The implications of this for regulators are taken up later in this chapter.

Eliciting voluntary compliance

Given that sanctions are problematic, how can government organizations elicit voluntarily compliance from regulatees? To answer this question we need to consider regulatees' propensity to comply which, broadly, has two dimensions: willingness and ability.

A range of factors affect the *willingness* of regulatees to comply (Bardach and Kagan 1982; Kagan and Scholz 1984; Roth *et al.* 1989; Ayres and Braithwaite 1992), which is partly a function of the pre-existing disposition of regulatees, which stems from their social and moral values as well as their perceived self-interest. But it is also partly a function of what the agency offers them to seek to influence their dispositions in a more compliant direction. These include not only *material* incentives, such as simplifying or speeding up agency responses to regulatees' needs, thereby providing a material benefit in time saved (Slemrod 1989), or providing penalty reductions if a future non-compliance event does occur (Parker 2000), but also some of the less tangible ones discussed in Chapter 3.

Thus, showing respect for regulatees' privacy or competence resonates with *intrinsic* motivations for autonomy or self-esteem, as does providing information or advice (Deci 1975). *Social* affiliation or belonging is appealed to by an agency showing empathy with the regulatee's needs (Cialdini 1989; Grabosky 1995b). For some regulatees the notion of becoming known as 'compliance leaders' – for example, through greater than required emissions reductions – can also be reputation building (Parker 2000).[12] Conversely, government organizations name and shame those who fail to comply; this is increasingly used in the restaurant trade, for example, to identify those who breach food safety regulations.[13]

Finally, people's *normative* concerns affect their propensity to comply. Etzioni (2008) has gone so far as to argue that a 'good society' will seek to use moral suasion rather than power to manage the tension between individuals (and their rights) and the common good (and social responsibilities). But more modest in scope is that fair application of rules appeals to people's attachment to procedural justice (Fisse and Braithwaite 1983; Hawkins 1984; Kagan and Scholz 1984; Cialdini 1989; Tyler 1990); people will obey laws which disadvantage them personally, if they feel they are applied fairly (Tyler 1990: 25), and also in cases where they have a moral commitment to their purpose (Grasmick and Green 1980; Tittle 1980; Klepper and Nagin 1989: 144; Scholz 1994). Conversely, people are less likely to show a positive disposition to comply voluntarily if they feel laws have been applied unfairly or arbitrarily. The uneven application of food inspection rules in the Netherlands demonstrated this point (Mascini and Van Wijk 2009). In the Peking duck case, for example, restaurateurs routinely asked what inspection team inspectors were from because they knew that the rules were applied differently and perhaps arbitrarily, creating considerable antagonism.

How do these offerings by the regulatory agency foster voluntary compliance? One way of understanding this is through social exchange theory, as discussed earlier in this book. Each offering by the agency constitutes a gift of something valued by the regulatee – not necessarily a tangible one of calculable worth, but typically one broader in nature, resonating with the latter's intrinsic, social or normative motivations. As with the trust spiral described in Chapter 5, to the extent that these offerings generate a positive disposition on the part of the regulatee, they usually (but not always) prompt reciprocity, in the form of compliant behaviour.[14]

The other factor in the propensity of regulatees to comply is their *ability*. Compliance is less likely if the obligations themselves are hard to deal with – for example, if they are inconvenient, complex, or inaccessible. In the Dutch case of food safety inspections, language differences were a barrier to the effective adoption of regulations (Mascini and Van Wijk 2009). In one example, a Chinese restaurateur believed he had been fined in relation to the *temperature* of oil, when the fine related to *toxins* in the oil; lengthy exchanges between the inspector and the restaurateur did nothing to solve this.[15] In such situations, authorities need to simplify the requirements or enhance their accessibility. Or instead, they could work to enhance the capacity of the regulatee to engage, through means such as information or training (Alm *et al.* 1992a; Hutter 1997: 207–9; Braithwaite 2003), or the provision of materials in multiple languages or the hiring of multi-lingual staff.

The problem of recalcitrance

But there is a fundamental problem with the social exchange model set out above: its theory of human motivation and behaviour is not valid for some regulatees. In any set of regulatees, people will have varying 'compliance postures' (Braithwaite 1995). This idea originated with Chester Bowles, head of the US Office of Prices Administration during the Second World War, when he said that 20 per cent of the population would automatically comply with any regulation, 5 per cent would attempt to evade it, and the remaining 75 per cent would comply so long as the 5 per cent were caught and punished (Hood 1986: 56). Kagan and Scholz (1984) theorized it by drawing on interviews with regulators in a various agencies, to identify three types of regulated companies: *amoral calculators*, who disobey the law when they calculate it is profitable to do so; *political citizens*, who are ordinarily obey the law; and *organizational incompetents*, who are inclined to obey the law but prone to incapacities which make them unable to comply. Building on this work in an analysis of nursing home managers and regulators, Braithwaite *et al.* empirically derived four 'compliance postures': *resistance*, which saw regulators as the problem and resisted their intervention; *disengagement*, which involved mistrust of government and the view that 'it is not our fault if things are wrong'; *accommodation*, which was cooperative and where the proprietor accepted responsibility for implementation; and *capture*, which was highly cooperative and in which regulatees closely identified with the regulators (1994: 379–80; see also Braithwaite 2003).

In short, any set of regulatees is likely to comprise a range of compliance postures, from very compliant to very non-compliant.[16] This has important consequences for regulatory strategy.

At one extreme will always be some proportion of *voluntarily compliant* regulatees, motivated in part by intrinsic, social or normative values, and disposed to obey the law on principle. To the extent they don't comply, it is because it is too difficult or they lack capacity to do so. The problem is that if legal obligations are enforced in a manner that treats everyone as recalcitrants, this group feels their efforts to 'do the right thing' are being disrespected. Consequently, they are antagonized, take a more jaundiced view of the law and its enforcers, and are less likely to comply. One team in the Dutch food inspection case treated business owners in this negative way from the outset, and as a result generated more grudging compliance (Mascini and Van Wijk 2009).

At the other extreme are the *opportunistic non-compliers*, who avoid their obligations every chance they get. They comply only as much as they feel likely to be detected in malfeasance, and calculate the likely sanctions to outweigh what they may gain from non-compliance. If the agency neglects sanctions and enforcement, and chooses strategies to appeal to intrinsic, social or expressive motivations, the risk is that the recalcitrants will exploit the 'softer' regime, and not comply.

In between these two extremes are more mixed postures, which tend to be open to influence from regulators. For instance, some of them will be willing to comply provided they feel the system is fair: how they are treated compared to others. Partly this is a function of how they are treated personally – the level of procedural fairness and respect shown to them as individuals. But also important is whether they see opportunistic rule-breaking left unpunished, and therefore feel disadvantaged by comparison.

Thus the dilemma for the regulator is that more use of enforcement and sanctions tends to diminish voluntary and contingent compliance, while relying on appeals to intrinsic, social and normative motivations (with less emphasis on applying sanctions) tends to allow more non-compliance. Optimizing compliance means treating different parts of the regulatee population differently, but it is hard to know in advance which parts will be compliant and which will not. Furthermore, it is legally dubious to treat them differently, since the law is supposed to be impartial. In this context, how can punishment and persuasion effectively be combined (Braithwaite 1985)?

Combining punishment and persuasion: responsive regulation

An approach which enables regulators to use a mix of techniques is 'responsive regulation' (Ayres and Braithwaite 1992), based on 'Tit-for-Tat' (TFT) strategies (Axelrod 1984). Scholz (1984: 393) has adapted TFT to encompass the work of a regulatory agency:

> The agency sets a minimum level of compliance, and uses its less rigorous co-operative enforcement routines against any firm that met the minimum compliance level in the previous period. The more rigorous deterrence routines are used against any firm not meeting minimal compliance levels in the previous round.

In responsive regulation, this strategy is formulated as a hierarchy of regulatory tools, backed up by the possibility of heavy sanctions in the background, in which firms segment themselves by the way they respond to the agency's treatment of them. Such an approach recognizes that not only do 'segments' of the regulatory population have different motivational bases, but that individual regulatees will often have multiple motivations (Ayres and Braithewaite 1992; Nielsen and Parker 2009). The hierarchy is illustrated with the Dutch food safety example in Figure 7.1. The relative space in the

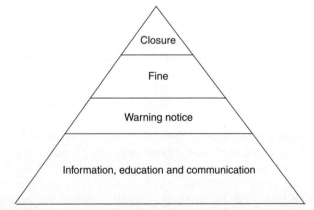

FIGURE 7.1   *Hierarchy of regulatory enforcement options in Dutch food safety*

Source: Adapted from Ayres and Braithwaite 1992, drawing on Mascini and van Wijk 2009.

diagram for each tool suggests the weight which the agency should give to it (Ayres and Braithwaite 1992: 35).

Specifically, the Authority's initial approach is to act helpfully, applying information, persuasion, education and fair treatment to regulatees. For firms responding well to this, cooperation continues. For those who try to take advantage by not meeting their obligations, the Authority switches to a more directive approach, by issuing a warning. If as a result the regulatee complies, the Authority reverts to information and persuasion. If, however, the regulatee continues to break the rules, the inspector moves to the more stringent sanction of issuing a fine. In the case of continued non-compliance, the inspector was entitled to temporarily close the business until the problem was remedied (Mascini and van Wijk 2009: 31).

Thus the agency employs different strategies with different regulatees, treating compliant actors as good citizens, to whom it applies persuasion, and the non-compliant as criminals, to whom it applies punishment.[17] And the 'Tit-for-Tat' logic of the strategy means it can work well without prior knowledge of who is compliant and who is not. So non-compliant firms select themselves for stringent treatment. It is also consistent with an impartial application of the law, since the varying treatment of different categories is based on their degree of compliance after the fact.[18]

Lest we think this approach applies only to private firms, it is important to realize that these ideas have also been applied to a range of social policy areas as well, including child welfare (Adams and Chandler 2004). Escalation up the layers of the regulatory pyramid are a response to failure to comply, and approaches may begin with jointly and cooperatively working with families at risk to ensure child safety through education and communication, then into development of family agreements, and could then escalate up to forceful removal of children or the termination of parental rights – quite different, of course, to the imposition of fines or bans on products.[19]

Alternative perspectives

Responsive regulation has spawned a huge literature. Some of it seeks to elaborate the concept. Examples include: 'smart regulation' (Gunningham and Grabosky 1998), focusing on the interaction of different instruments; and 'really responsive regulation'

(Baldwin and Black 2008), which considers not only the inter-play of enforcement instruments and external stakeholders, but also agencies' internal dynamics. Ayres and Braithwaite themselves recognize potential shortcomings in responsive regulation in their warning, for example, of the risk of 'regulatory capture' or even corruption in situations where inspectors have a lot of discretion as well as ongoing close interaction with particular regulatees (1992: 57–60).

Despite (or perhaps because of) the widespread adoption of the responsive regulation model by practical regulators, it has also attracted extensive critique from some scholars (for a survey, see Freiberg 2010). Some of these criticisms are about what Baldwin and Black call 'policy' issues. One is that 'in some circumstances step by step escalation up the pyramid may not be appropriate. For example, where potentially catastrophic risks are being controlled' (2008: 62). Another is that it can be less easy for the regulator to move down the pyramid than up it, because wielding sanctions can, as we have seen, impair the relationship between the regulator and regulatee. Moreover, while the steps in the pyramid have their own specific calibration, these might not square with the size of the wrongs committed by regulatees in a particular instance. Furthermore, although responsive regulation may work well in a binary regulator–regulatee relationship, communication can be difficult in more complex regimes.

Other criticisms concern practical matters. An important one observed in the Dutch Food Safety Authority is that regulators' staff may lack the requisite flexibility because they are wedded to a particular compliance approach by virtue of organizational resources, structure, practices or culture. Another is that an agency may lack the requisite support in the political, judicial or business environment. Further, in some industries 'there might be insufficient repeat interactions between regulator and regulated to allow a pyramidal strategy to be operated' (Freiberg 2010: 100).

More generally, the fact that regulation entails the exercise of the law means that issues such as fairness and consistency come into play. The very term 'responsive' suggests the law is somehow open to serving particularist ends, instead of being 'majestic in its impartiality'. As we have discussed, the theory of responsive regulation can answer that charge, but nevertheless it evokes a little anxiety among those committed to the formalism of the law.

When regulatees' contributions are useful

The question of when it makes sense for a government agency to seek to enlist regulatees as contributors to agency purposes is actually two questions. The first is: given a public policy rationale for government involvement, such as market failure or equity, when should an agency *regulate* an activity rather than utilize some other tool of government, such as undertaking the activity itself, or engaging a contractor to do it? This is a staple question in policy analysis, addressed in many public policy primers (see for example, Stokey and Zeckhauser 1974; Parsons 1995; Bardach 2000; Weimer and Vining 2004; Scott and Baehler 2010). Suffice to say here that regulation is the most relevant tool when the activity being regulated is secondary to, or a by-product of, the regulatee's primary activity. For instance, an environmental protection agency is best served by regulating pollution emissions from a petrochemical plant rather than operating the plant itself.

The second question is: when should an agency seek to encourage voluntary compliance by regulatees (and by implication, when should they not do so, instead relying on coercion to get compliance)? Part of the relevant rationale has already been discussed in this chapter. Voluntary compliance obviates or at least mitigates the costs associated with applying coercion, and improves the quality of regulatees' cooperation with agency purposes.[20] However, voluntary compliance is not without other types of cost, which need to be offset against its benefits. In terms of the categories outlined in Chapter 2, the regulatory agency does not buy units of compliance from the regulatee, so there is no purchase price to consider. However, the other two categories of cost are relevant: relationship costs and strategic costs.

The relationship costs associated with voluntary compliance are those the agency incurs in prompting regulatees to be more inclined to conform with their obligations. As with volunteers and clients, two factors are important. One is encouraging greater *willingness* to comply; the other is enhancing the *ability* to comply. As discussed earlier in this chapter, voluntary compliance is basically prompted by positive motivators, which foster goodwill and commitment from regulatees, and enablers, which make it easier for them to comply. The essential point is that these motivators and enablers can entail costs, broadly speaking. For instance, fair processes can entail the dissemination of information about rights or the establishment and operation of appeal processes. Assisting regulatees can necessitate the employment of extra staff at counters or call centres, or the provision of translators or materials in multiple languages. In deciding whether to place greater emphasis on encouraging voluntary compliance, these types of costs need to be weighed against the benefits (such as reduced coercion costs or more thoughtful compliance).

Beyond relationship costs are also strategic ones – those affecting the future of the organization or its strategic situation. One factor here is the effect on core competences, which applies especially to approaches at the self-regulation end of the continuum. Simply put, if a regulatory agency divests itself of expertise in its particular regulatory role, it will find it difficult to resume a tougher role should that become necessary – in the event, say, of scandalous breaches of the rules in an industry, prompting strong public calls for the agency to step in. Cases as diverse as the regulation of financial products, or lack thereof, in the lead up to the global financial crisis of 2008, to genetically modified (GM) crops, to the sale of rancid meat have shown the broader costs of a loss of regulatory capabilities and capacity (Bratspies 2003; Avgouleas 2009; Crotty 2009; Goodman 2010; Lodge *et al.* 2010). In some cases this is due to the complexity of the product/service which means regulators may not have the technical expertise to understand the 'thing' being regulated (for example, derivatives, petrochemicals, pharmaceuticals or genetically modified seeds) and in other cases, a lack of capacity/resources to monitor compliance in a more 'self-regulatory' environment.[21] The broader repercussions can be profound. This was the case when GM crops, not approved for human consumption, found their way into the food chain in the United States in the StarLink corn fiasco: 'One company, with one GM crop, managed to contaminate food for millions of households and brought an international commodities market to a standstill' (Bratspies 2003: 595). In the case of global financial crisis at the end of the 2000s, as economies went into meltdown the resounding question was, 'where were the regulators'?

But perhaps more important is the effect of emphasizing voluntary compliance on the organization's reputation and political standing. This involves countervailing factors. On the one hand, an over-emphasis on voluntary compliance may result in an agency gaining a reputation for being a soft touch that industry players can largely ignore. As a result, citizens with legitimate complaints about corporate behaviour may simply give up trying to do something about it. Their willingness to provide information to assist the agency in its work will atrophy, to the detriment of the agency's effectiveness. Even worse, it may gain a reputation, deserved or otherwise, for being corrupt, further demoralizing those citizens who might assist it.

On the other hand, a judicious level of emphasis on voluntary compliance may enhance an agency's reputation for reasonableness or for being citizen-centred, thereby augmenting its political capital with the government of the day, but also contributing to a greater level of trust in government among the citizenry more generally.

Conclusion

Regulatees contribute to public purposes simply by complying with the obligations to which the law subjects them. They contribute even more when they do so voluntarily. Securing this voluntary compliance is the essential challenge for regulatory authorities and indeed for other agencies which impose obligations as part of their service-delivery work. Emerging theory and practice indicates that providing assistance and information, and appealing to a variety of social and normative values, are key ingredients in eliciting that compliance. However, strategies incorporating these positive appeals can be vulnerable to opportunistic behaviour by a (usually small) proportion of regulatees. One increasingly widely used device for tackling this dilemma is 'responsive regulation', which combines punishment and persuasion in a manner tailored to the given context. Whether the practical benefits of such an approach can outweigh the governance risks they pose is for future experience to reveal.

Chapter 8

Clients as Co-producers*

Children's ability to cope and succeed in school and later in life is affected by their development in their first four years. This happens through several mechanisms, including their diet (affecting obesity), their learning, and the affection they receive from their parents – all of which are in turn affected by the socio-economic circumstances of the family. Put simply, children in poverty fare worse on these and other factors, which thereby act as transmitters of disadvantage. They are 'at risk of doing poorly at school, having trouble with peers and agents of authority (that is, parents, teachers), and ultimately experiencing compromised life chances (for example, early school leaving, unemployment, limited longevity)' (DfE 2010).

Sure Start was introduced by the UK Labour government to improve 'the development trajectories of children at risk of compromised development'.[1] One important element was the Sure Start Local Programmes (SSLPs), which were situated in areas of high deprivation, and integrated all relevant policies, including early education, child care, health and family support in ways tailored to local circumstances. One of these programmes was set up in the northern English industrial town of Gateshead in 2001 (Bovaird 2007).

Like all the SSLPs, the Gateshead Sure Start initiative involved a partnership, including government and voluntary sector agencies and professionals, not unlike the collaborative ventures discussed in Chapters 5 and 9. But the SSLP also included another type of partner, especially relevant to this chapter: the parents. What makes the parents distinctive is that they were the *clients* of Sure Start, along with their children. At the same time, they were *co-producers* of the

---

* Parts of this chapter have been adapted from Alford (2011).

SSLP. For example, about 50 mothers in Gateshead were trained in counselling on breastfeeding, an important aspect of the programme. Their role was to make the initial contact by visiting all new mothers in hospital maternity wards. There are further visits after 20 weeks, and support groups which are accessed by mothers an average of once a month. This co-productive activity has valuable consequences, as Bovaird (2007: 852) notes:

> The greatest advantage of this peer support approach is that new mothers are much more willing to talk to other mothers who have had similar problems rather than professional midwives or health visitors. These regular contacts at an early stage in motherhood have also convinced mothers to use local child-oriented services, bringing much higher take up.

At first glance, clients seem to fit awkwardly into the category of external providers. Whereas private contractors, non-profit organizations, other government agencies and volunteers are more analogous to *suppliers* of services to a public sector organization or to a partnership, clients are more like consumers, who *receive* services from it. The idea that they are also suppliers of co-productive effort is therefore counter-intuitive.

But many government functions entail clients doing some of the work required to deliver the service or, more broadly, to realize a public agency's purposes. In order to perform their important role of collecting garbage, municipal authorities or their contracted providers rely on householders to place their domestic waste in bins or bags at the front of their residences for garbage-collection crews to pick up on designated days. In health services, hospitals rely on patients to take their medicines or undergo physical therapy. More generally, medical services seek to prevent diseases as well as cure them, and this requires their 'clients' to undertake regular exercise, eat healthy diets and pursue balanced lifestyles. In schools, education is not just a matter of teachers teaching; the students also have an active role, taking notes, contributing to class discussion, reading texts, doing experiments, writing papers and hopefully reflecting critically on the knowledge and ideas to which they are exposed. Part of the teacher's role therefore is to encourage these activities by students.

In these and a raft of other activities, government organizations need ordinary people, who in many cases are their clients, to act

TABLE 8.1   *Key dimensions of client co-production*

Distribution of roles	Client co-production
Decider	Government organization Client
Producer	Government organization Client
Mode of coordination	Collaboration (mainly) Incentives and/or sanctions (sometimes)

in ways that contribute to the achievement of their purposes, in a process we call client *co-production*. Managers of those organizations who ignore their clients will miss out on potentially significant capabilities and resources.

This chapter explores client co-production (see Table 8.1). It distinguishes the role of clients, illustrates the necessity of client co-production in many public services, and its potential desirability in some others, then provides guidance on how client co-production can be encouraged and managed.

Defining public sector clients

What constitutes a 'client' in the public sector is contentious, complicated by the fact that many terms deal with the same phenomena, mostly derived from the private sector, such as buyers, customers, users or consumers, each with many contending definitions. In this chapter, we use the term 'clients' to describe those people who receive private value at the agency's 'business end' (Moore 1995). There is no ideal term to describe these individuals and others could just as well be employed, but 'clients' seems to have the benefit of referring to people who receive services with less of a private sector connotation. What matters is not the exact term but rather its substantive content as defined here. Insofar as they have the *role* of clients, they receive private value from the agency's service, that is, benefits that are consumed individually. Insofar as they have the role of citizens, they receive public value, which they 'consume' jointly with their fellow citizens.

The role of client is therefore different. Citizens' relationships to each other and to government are not the same as consumers' relationships to each other and to producers (Stewart and Ranson 1988; Alford 2002). In a democracy, citizens develop and express aspirations collectively, through processes of deliberation such as voting, policy debate and other forms of political participation. Clients, on the other hand, signal their preferences as individuals to government organizations through surrogates such as client surveys, complaint departments or appeal processes rather than direct demands.

To the extent that they receive private value, clients seem analogous to private sector customers, but they are quite dissimilar in important ways, which we can show by explaining different client roles (Alford 2002). Some of them may pay money in direct exchange for the services they receive, just like *paying customers* of the private sector, for goods and services such as electricity, or internet access provided by government. But most of them – for example social security recipients or pupils at government schools – either do not pay any money, or only pay part of the actual cost of the service. They may pay taxes which fund these services, but unlike the private customer exchange, there is no direct nexus in that case between the money and the service. In this capacity, they play the role of *beneficiary*.

Further, many of them are unwilling clients: they are compelled to 'receive' the service provided to them – for example, prisoners, taxpayers, and others subject to regulatory or other obligations. In this capacity, they play the role of *obligatee* (Moore 1995), who can be seen as similar to regulatees (Alford 2002) – subject to some degree of compulsion by the agency with which they are dealing. But they differ in that the obligations imposed on the regulatee are more central to the purposes of the agency in question. For regulatory agencies, the central task is to bring about compliance by regulatees. For service delivery agencies, it is an adjunct to the central task of providing value to either the individual client or the collective public. The question might reasonably be posed as to where the line between obligatees and regulatees lies. The answer is that there is no line; the difference is a matter of degree rather than absolute, which makes the discussion here also relevant to that in Chapter 7.

Typically, an individual client embodies some mixture of these roles, in addition to being a citizen. Although different from the private sector customer, the public sector client is similar in one important and perhaps surprising respect: that she is engaged in an exchange with the organization. Each party receives something directly or indirectly from the other, and what she receives is linked to some degree with what she gives to the other. However, in the public sector, the types of things being exchanged, the process by which it occurs and ultimately the range of parties involved are of a quite different character to what happens in an exchange between a customer and a firm. This is a *social* exchange, which entails more diffuse and more deferred reciprocity, with less precise and longer term obligations, than the immediate *quid pro quo* transactions that occur between buyers and sellers.

Seen through this lens, the exchange between the public organization and the client is one in which the client 'pays' not with money but with *behaviours*, and does so at least in part to reciprocate the tangible or intangible 'gifts' he or she receives from the organization or from others prompted by the organization. The organization's aim is (or should be) to elicit behaviours from the clients which co-produce value for the public. This is much more likely to happen where public managers understand and respect client needs.

The necessity of client co-production

In some cases, client co-production is a *substitute* for production by internal staff. The issue for managers in these situations is whether the organization or the client will better perform the task. To inform these decisions, managers weigh up the relative cost-effectiveness of the two options, something akin to decisions about whether to contract public services out. They must try to determine, for instance, whether the co-producers have the requisite capabilities, and what it would cost to induce them to play that role usefully.[2] The breast-feeding counsellors in the Gateshead Sure Start programme, for instance, carried out work for which professional staff would otherwise have had to be appointed. Another example is the 'fix my street' website in England which enables people to report local problems such as graffiti, broken street lights, or potholes in the road which are then transmitted to the relevant local council to address (visit www.fixmystreet.com). This not only conserves resources at the local council because there is a lower cost of inspecting, but also can reduce calls to the council because the site displays all the recent reports.

In the City of San Francisco, in the United States, individuals and groups work with the San Francisco Neighbourhood Parks Councils to monitor the conditions of public parks in a scheme known as ParkScan (OECD 2011). Clients use mobile technology to survey the park and then report on a set of uniform park conditions using digital cameras and handheld computers. These activities help the government agency to maintain parks and determine where improvements are needed. Individual citizens, rather than those participating as 'monitors' can also report comments via the ParkScan website and the agency provides 'before and after' photos on the site to demonstrate where issues have been addressed. Such a programme could not have been adopted if the agency had to hire professionals to carry out the work.[3]

In the UK, some 80,000 participants have completed the six-week Expert Patient programme which teaches people with chronic illnesses such as arthritis, diabetes, multiple sclerosis, and asthma, how to self-manage their health. The programme has both reduced costs and produced better outcomes.[4] This is done through the provision of training courses, which increase knowledge about the specific illness, but also aim to improve confidence, well-being, and reduce depression, whilst teaching patients how to work better with health practitioners to manage their health (Shaw and Baker 2004). Cost savings have been achieved through reduced visits to General Practitioners (7 per cent) and fewer visits to Accident and Emergency (16 per cent) reaping savings of between £27 and £58 per consultation avoided. Some patients reduced their hospital visits by half and reported significantly lower severity of symptoms following completion of the course (Boyle and Harris 2009; see also Shaw and Baker 2004).

On many public housing estates (or 'projects' in the US) residents join together to manage a range of issues including monitoring and prevention of petty crime and vandalism. Of course, this could be done at considerable expense by security firms who could patrol the estates, but with costs – both financial and in feeling repressed. Effective models of tenant management can not only reduce these direct costs, but the development of behavioural norms which discourage anti-social acts will produce greater respect and reciprocity amongst the community, and further reduce costs. In one of the toughest estates in Cardiff, Wales, the Taff Housing scheme rewarded tenants for participating in management of the estate including attending meetings and focus groups, writing articles for the estate newsletter, and arranging events. This reduced public costs through tapping co-productive activity of tenants, built community capacity and social networks (OECD 2011).

In these and many other cases, while it may be possible for the organization to produce value without clients' involvement, it may nevertheless be able to do so better or at less cost if it does enlist client co-production. This is the situation where the respective contributions of the organization and the clients are substitutes for each other, and the latter is able to do the task better.

But there is another circumstance where it is not really a matter of choice as to whether client co-production should be utilized. This is where organizational and client co-production are *interdependent*; the task cannot actually be performed without some contribution from both parties. The issue for organizations is not whether to utilize client co-production, but how best to do so.

Consider unemployed people, who are, in many countries, clients of public employment agencies or of their contracted providers. At first sight we might think of these individuals as consumers of services, such as job referrals. However, a closer examination shows us that if the purpose of the agency is to help the unemployed get work, as opposed to getting them off the welfare rolls, these clients are also necessarily co-producers. They must secure jobs, even if the agency plays a role in matching or referring them, and to do this they need to make a good impression on the employer, largely a function of their knowledge, capabilities and attitudes. To get to this point, the unemployed person may need to acquire generic or specific skills and knowledge, and they might also need to learn interview techniques, for example. The agency may play a role in this by providing access to courses, skills training, or job search training, but unless the client engages with these programmes, he will not likely gain much from them. The agency depends on the client contributing some time and effort into becoming 'job-ready' and into securing jobs.

The task becomes even more complex if we focus on the *long-term* unemployed, who have often become profoundly demotivated by their experiences of failing to find work over long periods of time, typically instilling a sense of hopelessness and resignation, and fuelling a desire to avoid yet another rejection from a possible employer. The challenge for the agency in these cases is not just to find a job for these clients, but also to assist them in 'job-readiness', and to prompt 'job-willingness'. Here, clearly efforts from both parties will be required to deliver the desired outcome.

As the ranks of the long-term unemployed have swelled in many nations, governments have come under pressure to develop new ways to tackle this problem. In many of them, the answer has been 'mutual obligation', whereby an explicit link is made between the receipt of welfare benefits and giving back something in return (Mead 1986).[5] Under this model, jobless people must genuinely seek work, or undertake valid substitutes for it, such as education, training, work experience, and in some cases, 'work for the dole' programmes.[6] Accompanying this shift has been a range of changes in service offerings and operations, which has continued to evolve.

First, connections between benefits assessment and payment and job search have been strengthened, in some cases through the restructuring of social security systems, or the creation of 'interface' organizations such as Centrelink in Australia (Husock and Scott 1999) or Jobcentre Plus in Britain. Second, new labour market programmes (LMPs) have been introduced to wrap job search, job readiness, and job willingness aspects around clients including job matching, job-search training, skills training, work experience, basic education, and supports such as child care and transport assistance. These have varied in approach across countries. In the US, for example, there has been increasing emphasis on what are called 'work first' (as opposed to 'education first') programmes, in which the focus has been on getting the unemployed into some kind of job (usually a casual, short-term one) as soon as possible, the theory being that this provides experience and confidence to progress to more stable employment (see Bloom 1997). Third, sanctions have been introduced for clients who fail to meet either their 'activity' obligations (requirements to search for work) or their administrative obligations (for example, requirements to attend agency interviews or notify changes of circumstances). Penalties can include a reduction or suspension of benefits for a prescribed period, with subsequent 'breaches' incurring more severe penalties. This regime has been tightened under the UK Coalition government since 2010, with its 'Work Programme' (DWP 2010), and has remained strict in the US.

These changes formalize a co-productive relationship between clients and employment agencies. However, in most cases the relationship is characterized by economic rather than social exchange, and backed by sanctions. Its success at its officially stated purpose – getting the unemployed into work – has been mixed. But its success at another purpose – getting unemployed people off benefits – has been considerable (Grogger *et al.* 2002).

These examples could be generalized to many areas of public sector work, such as education, health, environmental protection, policing, tax administration or community welfare. In all these cases, there is a degree of interdependency between organizational production and client co-production. This gives public managers good reason to take account of the role of their clients: they are necessarily contributors to the creation of value.

Whilst these examples show how co-production can reduce costs, it is more typically the case that where it is substitutable for organizational production, client co-production is *less* cost-effective, as government organizations tend to have advantages such as scale and expertise that enable them to do the work better or cheaper.

The implication of this analysis is that client co-production is not just a 'nice idea' for public sector organizations. Rather, for many of them, it is a hard-nosed imperative; they simply cannot produce public value without enlisting clients as co-producers. The question, therefore, is how they can better elicit that contribution.

What induces clients to co-produce?

The two factors affecting whether clients will contribute time and effort to co-production are similar to those eliciting voluntary compliance from regulatees, although differing in the details of their mechanisms. One is their *willingness* to do so, prompted by a complex mix of motivators, which we will consider in three groupings: (1) sanctions; (2) material rewards; and (3) non-material motivators. The other factor is clients' *ability* to co-produce, which is a function both of the relative complexity of the task and of their own capacities.

Willingness: sanctions

The evidence from our examples indicates that, as with regulatees, both sanctions and material rewards are problematic motivators of client co-production. At best, sanctions are inadequate as motivators of client willingness, and at worst they tend to generate perverse behaviour, while material rewards only seem to have a motivational effect where the co-productive task is relatively simple.

The essential reason why sanctions are problematic is that they are not good generators of complex *positive* actions, which lie at the heart of client co-production. To act co-productively, as opposed to refraining from something prohibited, is to move from an inertial to an active state. This calls for 'consummate cooperation' rather than grudging compliance, one where judgement, forethought and discretion are required: to recall or compile an information input, to gain new skills or attributes, utilize an organizational output. By contrast, sanctions do not connect with these impulses, and indeed tend to demotivate clients.[7]

Further, sanctions tend to be applied to the most disadvantaged of clients. In the USA, Australia and the UK, those jobseekers who are least literate, drug addicts, those with health problems or criminal records and those lacking social skills tend to bear the brunt of sanctioning (Vincent 1998; ACOSS 2001; MDRC 2002). This suggests that penalties fall more heavily on the very group which is least able to respond positively to them, or least able to understand how to comply, than on those individuals who are wilful non-compliers (Klerman *et al.* 2000). Further, 'aggressive enforcement of sanctions may be counterproductive' (MDRC 2002) producing unexpected or mixed outcomes with wide variation in responses from clients including non-compliant behaviour, the exact opposite of what is sought.[8]

In the UK, experiments with programmes for 'chaotic' families – those who exhibit complex combinations of issues such as mental health problems, behavioural disorders, substance abuse, homelessness, educational under-performance, exclusion from school, unemployment, criminal convictions, and anti-social behaviour – have included stiff sanctions as part of the mix, but they also show how hard it is to determine the effects of sanctions alone (White *et al.* 2008a). The Family Intervention Projects are a 'whole of family' approach which brings together intensive outreach service with a dedicated key worker, temporary in community accommodation or 24-hour support in residential care, and underpinned by a behavioural contract which includes sanctions such as eviction or removal of children, which can be invoked where goals are not met (see White *et al.* 2008a; Horne and Shirley 2009). The model has produced cost savings, mainly through reduced demand for other services, especially as the majority of families involved reduce or cease anti-social behaviour. Whether it was the threat of sanctions, the relationship with dedicated caseworkers (that is, a 'Hawthorne effect'), the intensive approach, or the combination, is not clear. Notably, the motto of the programme was 'sanctions with support'. In the end, lower levels of anti-social behaviour were recorded for the families involved (White *et al.* 2008a).

This raises a practical problem, already observed in our discussion of regulatees. If organizations apply sanctions to *all* their clients, some of them will be demotivated from co-producing. On the other hand, if they refrain from applying sanctions to *any* of their clients, some may take advantage of the lax regime and withhold co-production. In the case of the Family Intervention Projects it has been argued that the threat of sanctions for those families who were unwilling participants at least got them engaged initially, whilst for those who willingly participated, the threat of sanctions were seen as effective in bringing about an acknowledgement that behaviour change was needed (White *et al.* 2008b).

Sanctions are deficient as motivators of positive behaviour by individuals for two reasons. One is that they signal that the required behaviour (co-productive work) is something unpleasant to be avoided, as discussed in our exploration of motivations in Chapter 3. For example, long-term jobless people may find intrinsic pleasure in the acquisition of skills in labour market programmes, but if they are told they must do these things, this intrinsic pleasure evaporates – a classic case of motivational crowding. The other reason is that to apply enforcement – that is, to limit people's choices, monitor their behaviour, and threaten sanctions – is to imply that they are selfish, and not to be trusted. Confronted with this message, the clients' likely response may not be one of increased willingness but of grudging compliance. Their behaviour may change in the short term, but not their long-term internalized attitudes (Bandura 1986; Ayres and Braithwaite 1992; Frey 1997a). Instead of being willing to contribute, clients who are subject to sanctions are likely to engage in opportunistic behaviour to minimize their contributions of time and effort. This can set up a spiral which is increasingly destructive of clients' voluntary impulse to contribute, as clients find loopholes and the organization imposes more stringent rules to close the loopholes. The end result is that clients experience the organization's enforcement as arbitrary and rule-bound, and the organization finds it increasingly costly to secure compliance (Bardach and Kagan 1982; Braithwaite 1985).

But if sanctions have these limitations, why do organizations such as employment agencies use them, and persist in doing so? The main reason is that clients differ in their propensity to comply. In particular, some – usually a minority– may be wilfully non-compliant, and will respond only to a firm hand (Kagan and Scholz 1984; Braithwaite *et al.* 1994). This poses a problem for the agency, alluded to earlier in this chapter: treating all clients as if they deserve to be trusted will enable the non-compliant to take advantage of an 'easier' regime, which in the longer term may undermine the compliance of others who see this as unfair. But on the other hand, treating them all as if they are non-compliant will prompt resentment on the part of the compliant. Here the 'responsive regulation' or 'tit-for-tat' strategy, discussed in respect of regulatees in Chapter 7, is a useful approach to dealing with this problem (Scholz 1984; Ayres and Braithwaite 1992) – an example of how 'responsive regulation' might spread beyond the world of regulation.

In summary, sanctions generally do not mobilize material self-interest to generate client willingness to co-produce. They are ineffective and sometimes counter-productive in stimulating the requisite voluntary impulse. To elicit voluntary impulses to contribute, organizations need to offer more positive rewards.

Willingness: material rewards

The most obvious of these within the contractualist framework are material rewards, the basic idea being that if people are offered rewards proportionate to their performance then they will be motivated to perform better. But interestingly, to use Herzberg's terms, they turn out to be more like 'hygiene factors' (that is, basic preconditions or enablers) than motivators (Herzberg *et al.* 1993). They are only motivators to the extent that the task is relatively simple.

Material rewards are now commonly used to encourage people to co-produce. Patients are now recompensed for engaging in actions that improve their own health in many countries. In England, the *Paying the Patient* report (Jochelson 2007) cited a range of practices from around the world where material rewards were used to encourage individuals to adopt simple health practices. This ranged from offering drug users cash to comply with cessation programmes, to lottery tickets to attend antenatal classes. These do not always work, but there is evidence of success in some areas. For example, in the US, 86 per cent of patients with depression attended appointments when they were given $10 compared to 69 per cent where no incentive was offered. In Russia, Latin America and some East European states, the provision of fruit baskets, transport vouchers and financial payment increased successful courses of treatment for tuberculosis. In England, there has been consideration given to offering financial incentives for adults to lose weight in an attempt to prevent a wide range of associated health problems, in part because of successful programmes in other parts of the world (Jochelson 2007; Boseley 2008). In Brazil, the Mayor of Curitiba rewarded residents of the *favelas* (local slums) with credits for the transport system for assisting in the removal of waste. Rubbish mounted up in the *favelas* causing health problems for locals, but the streets were too narrow for garbage trucks, prompting the Mayor to enlist the support of locals to address the problem (Boyle *et al.* 2006).

In the case of unemployed people, material rewards have loomed large in both the literature and practice, starting with a recognition that, at least for some people (for example, those with large families), the level of income to be derived from working in a paid job is not much greater than that from unemployment benefits. Aside from being part of the rationale for applying sanctions, this has been one of the justifications for the introduction of time limits for benefits, introduced under the Temporary Aid for Needy Families (TANF) legislation in the US in 1996.[9] A more positive response, by contrast, has been to introduce some form of income supplement for long-term unemployed people who get a job, available either continuously or for some initial period of being employed – for instance the Earned Income Tax Credit in the US or the Working Families Tax Credit in the UK (Bloom and Michalopoulos 2001; Finn 2002). This has the effect not so much of adding an incentive to find work, but of removing a disincentive.

However, where people are *long-term* unemployed, the prospect of additional income alone is not sufficient to prompt active job search, because of their deep demoralization in the face of repeated rejections from employers. Instead it must be combined with the provision of positive assistance (for example, job search training) to tap non-material motivations (Bloom and Michalopoulos 2001; Finn 2002; Grogger *et al.* 2002).

More significantly, material rewards entail economic exchange, which as we saw in Chapter 7 spells out the precise value of what is exchanged, rather than the more diffuse and deferred obligations of social exchange. The very diffuseness of social exchange, the lack of specifically defined reciprocity, 'requires trusting others to discharge their obligations'. Thus social exchange fuels a spiral of rising trust: 'By discharging their obligations for services rendered, . . . individuals demonstrate their trustworthiness, and the gradual expansion of mutual service is accompanied by a parallel growth of mutual trust' (Blau 1964: 94, 315).

By contrast, economic exchange engenders a spirit of vigilance, 'with each party watching the other for infractions; jealously guarding concessions; and refusing any request for *extra-contractual favours* unless precisely defined reciprocation is guaranteed' (Fox 1974: 72, emphasis added). This is unlikely to be a problem where the task is simple to prescribe and check, such as entering postcodes on letters (Alford 2009). But where the task calls for 'extra-contractual favours', involving the exercise of discretion, tacit knowledge, or additional enthusiasm by the client, such as the long-term unemployed, the requisite level and intensity of willingness will not be elicited by precise calculation of reciprocity.

Thus eliciting contributions from clients requires more than the wielding of carrots and sticks. The more complex the task, the more it is likely to call for active engagement rather than merely going through the motions. This in turn calls for appeals to more complex, diffuse, non-material motivations.

Willingness: non-material motivators

Where co-production activities are complex, the same three types of motivators as we saw with regulatees may play a role. One is intrinsic motivation (Deci 1975). In the Sure Start case, the training they received would have been an important motivator for the counselling mothers, boosting their sense of efficacy. In programmes for the unemployed, to the extent that assistance is tailored to individuals' needs – as evidenced by client 'diagnostic' interviews and individualized intensive activity packages – it shows respect for them as human beings, and enhances their sense of self-efficacy. A synthesis study of best practice in US programmes found 'personalised client attention' had a powerful impact on employment outcomes (Bloom *et al.* 2001: 40).

Moreover, programme assistance which increases unemployed peoples' confidence, sense of competence and autonomy is more likely to motivate them to search actively for work. Interestingly, the debate about whether clients should be directed to 'work first' or 'education first' says little about this issue. It seems likely that both approaches can connect with clients' intrinsic motivations – 'work first' because it gives jobseekers renewed experience and a sense of competence in the world of work (Gottschalk 2005), and 'education first' because it enhances their skills. Indeed, one study found that the most successful programmes were those which offered a mix of both types of options (Bloom and Michalopoulos 2001).

Another motivator is sociality. This was a powerful factor in the Sure Start case, in that nursing mothers felt more affinity with the trained counsellors than with the professional staff. Further, to the extent that peers' approval of cooperative behaviour or disapproval of non-cooperative behaviour affects clients, it makes sense for agencies to seek to influence these peers or to establish collective interactions. 'Job Clubs', in which groups of the unemployed jointly acquire and apply job search skills, is one example.

Finally, clients' propensity to co-produce is affected by their norms and commitments about moral and social issues,. To some degree, people encounter these issues more as citizens rather than as clients. But in cases where clients 'consume' public value, these norms and commitments can be important. One example is where people enjoy recreational use of national parks, while at the same time having a strong commitment to their conservation because of a deep attachment to maintaining the integrity of the environment. This is the animating spirit behind many 'Friends of the National Park' organizations in various countries, wherein park users donate time and effort to park maintenance and revegetation while also personally enjoying the experience of spending time in the park.[10]

Clients' willingness to co-produce is affected by a complex mix of factors. Moreover, different segments of clients are motivated by different factors. The efficacy of most non-material rewards is less immediate and targeted than the 'high-powered incentives' (Frant 1996) of managerialism, but significant nonetheless. If public organizations want to elicit co-productive activity, they must pay heed to these motivational complexities. They must 'give' their clients things they value – often non-material values – if they expect their clients to 'give' them co-productive effort.

Ability

Of course, clients may be willing to co-produce, but may lack the *ability* to do so. One way of fostering this ability is to make the task easier, as exemplified by the way many road licensing authorities have taken steps to simplify the process of renewing one's driver's licence or vehicle registration. In these cases, the use of technology seems to have been an important factor in reducing the complexity of the co-productive work. Providing mobile technology devices to those monitoring neighbourhood in parks in San Francisco is a good example of how technology has made co-production easier, and in this case, for both parties.

The other method is to enhance the client's own capacities to perform it, for example by providing information, advice or training. The training of counsellors in the Sure Start example increased the probability that they could play a useful co-productive role. In the unemployment case, clients' lack of job search skills has been addressed through job-search training, and their lack of job-readiness through skills training and work experience. And in the San Francisco monitoring case, training was provided to enhance capacities to perform, including formulating 'uniform standards' against which parks would be assessed.

Client focus

Underpinning all these instruments is the nature of the relationship between the government agency and the client. Front-line government workers, such as welfare, employment or tax counter staff are the key decision makers in the offering of various forms of positive assistance and in the application of sanctions, both in the initial encounter stage and in ongoing dealings. How they act shapes the clients' perceptions of the service they receive, and hence their levels of willingness to cooperate. Three inter-related aspects of client service are important motivators:

- *Bilateralism* refers to the degree to which the client has a meaningful say in shaping the relationship with the agency. At least, it means that the front-line worker needs to ascertain the clients' real needs and incorporate them into programme offerings, rather than presume what they might be. This is most salient in the initial encounters, for instance, the intensive interview or the activity agreement with the employment client. Whether the interview and agreement constitute meaningful motivators of work search depends on the degree of bilateralism, in which the client has some say in what goes into the back-to-work plan. Bilateralism also enhances trust between the public servant and the client, which is acknowledged in most casework practice as being very important, since it facilitates the further development of the relationship, but also very difficult to foster (Anderson 2001: 168). Where clients feel they are involved in negotiating the terms they are more likely to be positive about their obligations. By contrast, where they feel that the process of formulating their obligations was imposed on them, they have less commitment to them.[11] By reducing clients' sense of autonomy, imposed obligations diminish their motivation to cooperate actively. The activities identified become external impositions rather than internalized aspirations.

- *Helpfulness* affects the clients' sense of the competence as well as of the positive intentions of the agency's staff. Clients are more inclined to invest time and effort in attending the agency if they feel that its staff know what they are doing and are disposed to be of assistance.
- *Individualization* refers to the degree to which staff tailor activities to the particular needs of the client in question, rather than offering 'one-size-fits-all' services. Where used in services to the unemployed, this tends to have positive effects on employment outcomes.[12] In the case of Family Intervention Projects in Britain, individualization of services by a dedicated caseworker is part of how these chaotic families reduced their anti-social behaviours. (White *et al.* 2008a, 2008b.)

However, the unfortunate truth is that government organizations have historically been deficient in focusing on clients and their needs. One reason, of course, is the perennial culprit of lack of resources – often true, but sometimes an excuse. Another possible reason is offered by Osborne and Gaebler:

> Most American governments are customer-blind, while McDonald's and Frito-Lay are customer-driven... Why is it this way? Simple. *Most public agencies don't get their funds from their customers.* Businesses do. If a business pleases its customers, sales increase; if someone else pleases its customers

more, sales decline. So businesses in competitive environments learn to pay enormous attention to their customers.

(1992: 166–7, emphasis in original)

But as this chapter shows, there is a very compelling reason for public managers to pay attention to clients: they are potential – and often very necessary – contributors of time and effort towards the achievement of organizational purposes. Where co-production is necessary, understanding clients' needs can be vital for organizational performance.

A third possible reason for poor client focus in public agencies is the fact that they serve multiple types of clients, who may demand differing things of the agency. In addition to serving individual clients as we have defined them, a government organization will always need to give a prominent, indeed usually a pre-eminent place to the will of the citizenry as a whole. As discussed earlier in this book, a citizen's view of what quality and quantity of service should be provided to, say, a criminal, an unemployed person or an asylum-seeker is likely to be at odds with the views of those clients themselves. And because the main claim to represent the will of the citizenry as a whole typically comes from politicians, because they have been elected via the democratic political process, it is likely to over-ride the claims of the clients, in decisions about policy, rules, service levels and resources.

However, this need not be a zero-sum game, where in order for clients to be well-served, citizens must lose, or vice versa. Instead, smart managers can find ways to enhance service quality for one while at least not reducing value for the other (what we might call a 'win–neutral' outcome) – or even on occasion 'win/win' solutions, where client service is enhanced, for example, through a simplification of the rules that consequently cost less to administer.

Conclusion

This analysis has posited a type of exchange between public sector organizations and their clients, and suggested how it might be optimized. At first sight, given the power imbalance between organizations and clients, this may seem an unrealistic, even naïve idea. But this imbalance is no greater than that which exists between a private sector firm and its customers. In both the public and private cases, while the individual client/customer has little power, collectively clients can have significant power, because the organization needs certain things from them. Contrary to Osborne and Gaebler (1992), public agencies often 'earn' something very valuable from their clients: their contribution to the achievement of the organization's outputs or outcomes. This will be all the more valuable to the extent the organization cannot function without this contribution, as our examples illustrate. And as the examples also show, eliciting this contribution will entail offering some tangible or intangible benefits to clients. Thus, the process of delivering private value to clients has the effect of creating public value for the citizenry.

Chapter 9

Managing in Multiparty Networks of Providers

Despite being the world's leading superpower, the United States has a surprisingly mediocre level of performance in infant health: its infant mortality rate ranks 30th in the world, and 28,000 American children die each year before their first birthday (Bornstein 2011a). One important cause is that some mothers – especially those of low income or minorities and without health insurance – lack easy access to doctors and other sources of information about childbirth and infant health. Thus, they are unaware of the risk to their babies before birth of such factors as poor nutrition, or smoking or drinking too much, or high blood pressure or diabetes. And after birth, they are poorly informed about breast-feeding, getting immunized, safe sleeping positions and the need to make regular doctor visits. Moreover they are without internet access from which they might learn these things, whereas over 90 per cent of Americans have a mobile phone.

Text4baby is a free service that sends text messages containing useful health advice to pregnant women or new mothers. Managed by the National Healthy Mothers, Healthy Babies Coalition (HMHB), it provides 800-numbers through which women can find out about where to access local doctors, breastfeeding, buying a crib or giving up smoking. Mothers register with the service via a simple text message, are prompted for the child's due date or birth date, and thereafter receive three messages a week containing practical information relevant to the stage of pregnancy or the child's age. The messages are concise and friendly and delivered straight to mobile phone in-boxes.

What makes this innovation especially interesting is that it is delivered by a massive partnership of hundreds of providers: government organizations, private health providers, non-profit community groups, wireless carriers, and many others, each playing particular roles. In short, it is a network, and raises issues for government organizations engaged with them, which are over and above those already explored so far in this book.

First, networks are far less subject to the control or influence of government. As Klijn and Koppenjan put it: 'government is actually not the cockpit from which society is governed' (2000: 136). Typically they are formed out of the interaction and mutual exploration of multiple parties, among whom the public sector agency may be a latecomer to the table. The task, scope, resourcing, and even the membership can be a subject of negotiation or joint determination. Consequently, 'it is impossible, or at least precarious, to ignore the existence of networks. The network context of policy projects renders top-down management inadequate. Policy networks require a different method of governing' (Klijn *et al.* 1995: 438–9). This can pose a dilemma for the government. On the one hand, it has a 'special position, which in most cases cannot be filled by others', including such assets as budgets and personnel, special powers, media access, legal power and democratic legitimacy (Klijn and Koppenjan 2000: 151). On the other, inherently governmental factors limit the extent to which it can capitalize on its uniqueness.

Second, the preceding five chapters have, mainly for analytical purposes, considered dyadic relationships, that is, relationships between a government agency and an external party – either a private firm, a non-profit/voluntary agency, another government department, a volunteer, a regulatee or a client. But the reality is that many instances of externalization involve multiple parties. These can be networks within the same sector as the government organization, made up of two or more other public sector agencies, or they can involve providers from other sectors. At their most elaborate, they can involve multiple parties from across multiple sectors. (Note that the focus here is on *service-delivery* networks, not deliberative networks.) The dimensions of networks are set out in Table 9.1.

This chapter explores these types of arrangements, and considers the challenges and the opportunities they raise. The next section outlines how networks differ from other types of arrangements, and the management challenges they raise. In light of those challenges, subsequent sections look at when it is useful to engage in networks and at how best to encourage productive contributions from them, in the process unearthing some opportunities arising from having multiple parties involved.

TABLE 9.1   *Key dimensions of multi-party networks*

Distribution of roles	Working in multi-party networks
Who decides?	Government organization and/or multiple private firms and/or multiple non-profit/voluntary agency and/or multiple other government organization
Who produces?	Government organization and/or multiple private firms and/or multiple non-profit/voluntary agency and/or multiple other government organization
Mode of coordination	Mainly collaboration, but with elements of other modes such as classical contracting etc.

How networks differ from one-to-one relationships

The obvious fact about networks is that they involve more parties than one-to-one relationships do. In the simple form of this arrangement, the government organization might have a separate dyadic relationship with each external provider. The involvement of each extra provider has an incremental effect, in that it adds one more relationship to be managed. But in its more complex (and more typical) form, not only does the government organization have a separate relationship with each provider, but some or all of the providers also have relationships with each other. This means not an additive but an exponential increase in complexity. By way of illustration, one dyadic pair has one relationship; a trio has three relationships among them; a quartet has six relationships; a quintet has 10 relationships; a sextet has 14 relationships; and so on.

Of course, the relationships within actual networks will be more variegated in practice. Some external parties will be linked only to the principal government organization, whereas others will have links to other external parties as well as to the government organization. Some will act as intermediaries (or 'bridging organizations', see Brown 1991) between government and other organizations, in some cases in chains of interaction comprising multiple links. Some will be embedded as denser clusters of interaction within a wider network, and a number will be members of different but overlapping networks. But whatever the variations, the more inter-related parties there are in a network, the greater the complexity of the set of interactions among them, which engenders problems by comparison with dyadic relationships.

First, there are more likely to be differing interests among the parties. In Chapter 5 we saw how this poses challenges for government organizations. The challenge lies, of course, in the fact that sometimes these differences amount to the public sector agency being at odds with the external party, and some reso-lution of the conflict needs to be negotiated. These factors are magnified in multiparty networks. Having more parties involved increases the likelihood that there will be differing interests in play, and hence more potential for conflict among them. (How-ever, there are also opportunities in this situation, which are discussed below.) One example is reported in a study of a Bosnian peacekeeping mission, described by Ramarajan *et al.* (2011) as a complex, multi-organizational setting. A peacekeeper described the conflicting interests between different parties involved in the network:

> I was stationed in a small town in Bosnia. There were rumors of bad treatment of prisoners in the local police station. From our UN-IPTF team we were trying to build a relationship of trust and confidence with the chief of this local police station. An NGO concerned with human rights came and demanded we should investigate these rumors immediately, passing by the local commander. This would violate our relationship, and we refused. The NGO made threats to report and bring this into the media.
> (Ramarajan *et al.* 2011: 982)

A related but distinct point is that there are more likely to be dif-fering types of motivations among the parties, placing a premium on deliberation and negotiation at a group level rather than the offering of incentives to external parties by government organiza-tions. For example, offering monetary incentives in order to induce some parties to contribute may undermine the social or normative motivations of others who are also important.

Third, communication processes are more complex in a multiparty network. This follows from the larger number of relationships among multiple parties, which translate into more communication channels. But the variegation among relationships is also an issue, since it leads to variegation in communication. Thus some parties may have more 'inside' knowledge, whereas others may feel 'out of the loop', eroding their sense of belonging to the network and hence willingness to contribute productive effort. Extreme examples of the communication challenge have been provided by various incidents in the Iraq War, including cases where private contractors shot at the Iraqi police, Iraqi security forces, American troops and other contractors – all members of a complex web of providers waging a 'war on terror' on-the-ground (Glanz and Lehren 2010).

Fourth, having a multiplicity of parties reinforces the complexity of an issue that is already present in dyadic relationships: inequality of power. In Chapter 5 we noted that power inequality between the government organization and the external party complicates collaborative partnerships. It reduces the self-perceived capacity of less powerful parties to influence the relationship, and hence their sense of efficacy in contributing time and effort. It also makes the building of trust more difficult. Less powerful parties in partnerships are less likely to trust more powerful parties (Korpi 1974). Although the latter may be behaving in a trustworthy manner, the mere fact that it is capable of adversely affecting the other's interests engenders apprehension on the part of the less powerful. This means that the more powerful party has to make an extra effort to reassure the other of his or her trustworthiness. Having multiple parties involved aggravates these problems in two respects. One is that it increases the likelihood that there will be a variety of different levels of power among those involved, thereby reinforcing the inequality of self-efficacy and the potential barrier to trustbuilding. The other is that a likely response of a less powerful party to their lack of power is to form alliances with other parties having similar or at least reconcilable interests. This has the potential to foster factionalism, which may become difficult for the network.

Finally, a multiplicity of parties is more likely to exhibit differing *levels* of knowledge and capability among its members. This may result in inconsistency of productive outcomes from the network, and more ominously in differing mutual appraisals among the parties as to who is or is not contributing adequately to the achievement of those outcomes. This could provoke negative judgements or even recrimination among the network members.

All of these differences add up to challenges for the governance of networks. They mean that it is wrongheaded for the government organization to presume to direct the network. This complicates the ability to co-ordinate the productive contributions of the external providers. We have seen how externalization calls for the practice of indirect management in dyadic relationships. In networks, co-ordination is embedded in more diffuse and layered relationships, and more importantly there are multiple loci of power among the participants. But at the same time, the multiparty nature of networks also offers opportunities less available in one-to-one relationships. These are considered in the next section.

When networks are useful for service delivery

As with all the other service-delivery arrangements, the issue of whether to take part in a multiparty network should be determined through weighing up the benefits and costs – not only of the service itself but also those of taking part in the relationships and more broadly those impacting on the government organization's strategic situation.

The most significant *service* benefit derives from the very same factor that we noted as problematic in the previous section: the differences among the parties. Foremost among these is the variation in types of knowledge and capabilities among the network members. Whereas differences in *levels* of knowledge and capabilities can be problematic, differences in their *types* offer value-creating opportunities to network members. These opportunities arise from specialization and complementarity. On the one hand, a plurality of parties offers a wider array of different capabilities to bring to bear on the production of a given outcome. On the other hand, the fact that they are in the same network holds out the possibility of the parties agreeing to arrange them so that their contributions are complementary. Consequently, the whole becomes greater than the sum of its parts.

Text4baby is a clear example of this (Bornstein 2011a). Each of the different types of partners has made a distinctive contribution to the setting up and operation of the initiative. A company called

Voxiva set up the IT platform that manages the text messages. A non-profit group (CTIA-The Wireless Association) managed to persuade wireless carriers to send messages free of charge. The Centres for Disease Control quality-assure the messages. A private healthcare group manages the marketing of the service. Major funding comes from Johnson and Johnson, the multinational private firm. The White House mobilized support from the Department of Health and Human Services and the Department of Agriculture, which oversees a programme providing nutritional assistance for pregnant women. These and many other contributions, each based on the specialist capacities of the provider in question, added up to a whole service that offers value to mothers and their babies.

Another example is the Central American Handwashing Initiative, which began in 1996 and has been used in Guatemala, Costa Rica, El Salvador, Honduras and Nicaragua, to reduce morbidity and mortality in children less than five years of age, by developing a coordinated campaign to promote hand washing with soap in order to prevent diarrheal disease (Saadé *et al.* 2001). The initiative involved NGOs (for example, BASICS), private companies who manufactured soap (for example, Colgate-Palmolive, Unisola/Unilever), along with public sector organizations (mainly health ministries), and other parties (such as television stations, the World Bank, UNICEF), and enabled all of them to pursue their own goals, and broader social ones through the partnership. For example, the soap companies increased sales, and the health ministries could reduce mortality for young children, whilst BASICS would make a contribution to the achievement of the Millennium Development Goals.

Similar networks have developed in areas such as welfare-to-work programmes, environmental protection, land conservation, bio-diversity, combating domestic violence, and many others (see Clark *et al.* 1996 on domestic violence; Jahiel 1998 or Betsill and Bulkeley 2004 on environmental protection networks; McCarthy 2000 on conservation and biodiversity; and Stone 2000 on welfare-to-work). In each case, we would expect the parties involved to work together to achieve more towards programme or project purposes than they can acting alone or in smaller networks. They would seek to capitalize on the dovetailing of inter-dependent specializations. In service terms, they weigh up the perceived benefit of the combined contributions of the other parties against the costs – in money, time or other considerations – of making their own contribution of effort. Of course, these aspirations are not always realized.

Another possible service benefit from multiparty collaboration is the sharing of risk, with a plurality of parties to shoulder the burden if things go wrong. However, it has to be said that the sharing of risk may be more difficult where the network seeks to capitalize on the complementarity between different specializations. The reason is that each party, by bringing a different specialization to the table, is identified with a particular aspect of the network, and thereby assumes at least tacit responsibility if a mishap or malfunction is traceable to that aspect. Thus, instead of risk being shared, it is sheeted home to one or a few network members, with the likely consequence of fragmenting the collaboration.

A further potential service benefit from utilizing multiparty networks is the opportunity to learn, or to develop new ideas, about solutions or improvements to service problems. Again, this derives from the very factor that in other respects makes networks problematic: the differences among their participants. In this case, the different capabilities and knowledge bases of the parties can be brought together to generate new insights into how to deal with problems.

Huxham and Vangen (2005) point to another reason for entering into a network arrangement: that there is no other way to tackle a major societal or moral problem, such as poverty, crime, climate change drug abuse or indigenous disadvantage. These types of issues, which are receiving increasing attention under the rubric of 'wicked problems', are intractable ones that cannot be ignored but which are necessarily cross-organizational and cross-sectoral in their nature (Roberts 2000; APSC 2007; Head and Alford 2008).

To the extent that these kinds of networks actually implement solutions to such problems, then they warrant attention in our analysis. But often these kinds of multiparty arrangements are directed instead to deliberation or problem solving, that is, to deciding what to do about them. These deliberative processes are not unimportant, but as will be discussed below, they play an enabling rather than a central role for the service-delivery networks which are the focus here.

But service benefits and costs only tell part of the story. Another significant aspect of networks is their *relationship* costs – the costs of deciding what services are to be provided by whom and how, as well as those of ensuring that they are delivered. Networks typically are not subject to hierarchical command, nor do they tend to have recourse to 'high-powered' incentives (Frant 1996) such as monetary rewards tied to performance. Consequently, they tend to determine what to do, and to establish what constitutes good performance, through deliberative mechanisms such as steering committees or meetings. In general, the more complex the service, the more parties are involved and the more variegated their inter-relationships, then the more time-consuming are these deliberative processes.

At first sight, it might seem that the *Text4baby* initiative must have been prone to high relationship costs, given the large and diverse range of parties to the network. But three factors seem to have mitigated this problem. First, it had a powerful backer in the White House, which could exercise 'convening power' to get the project going. Second, there was widespread commitment to the idea. Bornstein (2011b) cites an on-line comment that 'Text4baby is an excellent entry point to forge new alliances because it's hard to find anybody who is anti-baby.' Third, the interdependence among the parties was relatively loose, in that each additional party's contribution was additive rather than jostling for a piece of an already crowded turf. For example, some states are advertising the programme through their Medicaid service or on birth certificates, while libraries, churches, health care providers and professional associations have all signed up to disseminate information about it.

But in other networks the relationship costs can be very high, because of the number and variety of parties involved, and must be weighed against the perceived service benefits. Among these relationship costs, all of them aggravated exponentially by the multiplicity of parties, are:

- the process of building trust among the providers;
- the effort of scheduling and arranging meetings, when it is difficult to find mutually convenient times;
- the time spent in meetings themselves;
- the length of negotiation about multiple factors;
- the time taken to bring new representatives of participating organizations 'up to speed';
- the task of communicating outside meetings, either verbally, electronically or in print.

These and other costs have been known to contribute to what Huxham and Vangen (2005: 69) refer to as 'partnership fatigue'. Their findings from a detailed field study of twelve collaborative networks make for sober reflection:

> The overwhelming conclusion from our research is that seeking collaborative advantage is a seriously resource-consuming activity so is only to be considered when the stakes are really worth pursuing. Our message to practitioners and policy makers alike is *don't do it unless you have to*.
>
> (2005: 13, emphasis in original)

On top of the service and relationship benefits and costs, there are also strategic implications to consider. On the benefit side, government may derive legitimacy from participation in a network, or perhaps more to the point, diminish its legitimacy by refusing to take part. Certainly its involvement in the *Text4baby* initiative did no political harm to the Obama administration (and did not require it to try to get some funds appropriated by Congress for the programme). On the cost side, a government organization may be concerned about a network taking over responsibility for a core competence, which is important for government to retain in the long run. This was not a problem in the *Text4baby* case, since it was a completely new concept over which no-one had previously had ownership. Like many networks, it involves an expansion rather than a handing over of an existing core competence.

Thus, the multiplicity of parties in networks constitutes a two-edged sword: it complicates the task of managing provision of services, but also offers opportunities for capitalizing on that complexity.

Managing in networks

Just as they do in one-to-one relationships, government organizations seek to get external providers in networks to act consistently with the purposes for which the government is part of the network, and because of their 'special position' (noted above), they tend to have more unique resources at their disposal. The challenge of eliciting contributions of time and effort from parties in a network is made more difficult by the multiplicity of providers. Offering extrinsic incentives may be effective with some parties, but they may be at odds with others, undermining their intrinsic, social or normative motivations. In this context, the best approach may not be to seek to reward providers for doing things they otherwise would not do, but rather to seek to affirm or engender goal-congruence – that is, to argue for and pursue a purpose to which the parties agree.

One version of this is to call for the establishment of a 'shared vision' or 'common purpose.' Sometimes this is code for 'everyone should agree with the purpose I propose', and is put forward in complete unawareness of the reality that the parties actually have quite divergent interests. But it is not always thus. One of the main factors driving the active participation of various providers in *Text4baby* was that in broad terms they endorsed it, as evidenced by the aforementioned comment that 'it's hard to find anybody who is anti-baby.' Thus, there is a role for network leaders in articulating a purpose that more or less genuinely brings together and represents the terms in which the various parties support the enterprise.

But while this affirms a general mission, it does not banish the differences they may have over issues such as resources, techniques and processes. Moreover, the multiplicity of parties increases the range of differing interests among them. However, this greater variation of interests offers an opportunity as well as a problem. The fact that interests are different does not necessarily mean they are in conflict; they could simply be different. This raises the possibility that the differences can be dovetailed, such that each party concedes something of lesser value for something of greater value in a negotiated arrangement, with the result that each gains more than it loses – commonly known as a win/win outcome. The interesting point about these arrangements is that the greater the number of differing interests there are on the table, the more variables there are in play, and hence the more ways of constructing win/win solutions. In multiparty networks, the presence of more parties increases the likelihood of differing interests being on the table, and hence the potential for dovetailing differences (Lax and Sebenius 1986; Brown 1991).

Both the framing of a shared purpose and the dovetailing of differences usually call for deliberative processes, of which the most common type will be some kind of joint forum or committee in which the relevant parties are represented. The joint forum itself does not do the work of implementation or service delivery; that is done by the network members. Its role is to reconcile and opti- mize the respective goals and interests of the parties. This raises another motivation which may also incline network members to contribute time and effort: a sense of ownership, grounded in a perception that the deliberative process is a fair one. We saw in Chapters 7 and 8 that procedural justice is an important motivator of co-production by clients or regulatees. As Tyler (1990) showed, people's willingness to obey the law is enhanced if they feel that it is procedurally fair, even if they are personally disadvantaged by its specific application to them. In the same way, it is reasonable to assume that people will accept the consensus of a group with which they have been deliberating, even if their own position has only been partially accepted, if they feel that they have received a fair hearing and that others' arguments have been well made. Thus an important motivator may stem from the very workings of the group itself.

However, as discussed above, ensuring that everyone feels they have received a fair hearing is likely to add to the relationship costs, since it usually entails more time spent in deliberative processes. But at least a partial solution to this problem lies in adopting a contin- gent approach to deliberation. Thomas (1995) offers a framework for thinking about public participation in public decisions which seeks to avoid staging a full-dress consultation process every time. He proposes a menu of participation options, including but not limited to autonomous management decision, public consultation, and public decision – not unlike Arnstein's 'ladder of citizen par- ticipation' (1969). Thomas' distinctive contribution is to propose that each of these is suitable in some circumstances but not in oth- ers. One advantage of this, relevant to the discussion here, is that in some circumstances less resource-intensive or time-consuming deliberative approaches may be suitable, thereby reducing relation- ship costs. However, the very nature of the network means that it is unlikely that its members will agree on a particular mech- anism, and no single party or bloc of parties will be able to dictate one.

All of these activities in managing in a network – framing purposes, finding win/win solutions, structuring and leading delib- erative processes – call for particular managerial capabilities on the part of those acting on behalf of network members. Rather than relying on managerial control based on hierarchical authority, they call for the exercise of indirect influence, such as persuasion, negotiation, or meaning making. These are the arts of leadership, broadly defined, rather than of management.

Chapter 10

A Contingency Framework for Decisions about Externalization

This book has considered a variety of types of external providers available to government organizations, both organizational – private companies, voluntary sector agencies, and other government organizations – and individual – volunteers, clients and regulatees. We have explored the various forms they take, the types of circumstances in which it is most appropriate to utilize them, and how their contributions can best be elicited. This chapter seeks to draw them together, by laying out a framework for making decisions among them. It argues that whether to utilize an external provider, and what type, is a contingent matter: it depends on the circumstances. This requires judgements about purposes, identification of who might be involved, and analysis of several types of benefits and costs.

Understanding purposes

The starting point for analysing whether and how to externalize any public sector activity has to be: what value are we seeking to produce? What benefits to the public do we expect to derive from the performance of this function? In other words, why are we doing this?

The implication here is that there is, or at least should be, some purpose for what is currently being done. The activity is not an end in itself, but rather a means to some end beyond that activity. Reasonable people would agree that a public sector function should never be performed merely for its own sake, but rather because it serves some purpose that is important to the citizenry. This much is obvious, even banal, but what makes it significant is *that there may be alternative means to the same end*. Indeed, the less proximate the end is to the existing means (that is, the more intermediate steps there are between cause and effect), the more likely it is that there will be alternative means to the same end. This does not mean that we should adopt an approach that amounts to 'whatever it takes'. As will be discussed below, there will usually be other values at stake, and these must constrain or qualify whatever means are deployed towards the end in question. Nevertheless, it is useful in the first instance to imagine as broad a range of means as possible.

Take the example of policing. One way of conceiving of the purpose of a police force is to patrol the streets and other public places, thereby providing a visible presence. This activity is not performed because officers enjoy parading around in uniforms. Nor is it solely a matter of the number of criminals that police on the beat apprehend directly, although that is not unimportant. It is also a matter of the deterrent effect of a visible police presence, thereby contributing to a reduction in crime. But even these benefits don't exhaust the potential value created by police patrols. To the extent that police on the beat are perceived to reduce crime, they also contribute to another important feature of value to the public: they reduce the *fear* of crime, thereby allowing citizens to lead more secure and presumably happier lives, all else being equal.

Notice that we have here three different ways of framing the purpose of a police force. The first – deploying a visible police presence on the streets – can be seen as an *output*. The second – reducing crime – can be seen in this context as an *intermediate outcome*, whereas the third – reducing fear of crime – can be seen as an *ultimate outcome*. Significantly, as we move along the chain of programme logic from outputs to ultimate outcomes, we also call forth a wider range of means to achieving the purpose.

If the purpose is to deploy more 'cops on the beat', then there are a few alternative means to do so. One might be to engage volunteers as uniformed community police officers, able to deal with minor problems and call in more fully fledged officers as required. In the same vein, the police could enter into partnerships with other government agencies, such as local councils, whose parking officers could be enlisted to carry out para-policing activities. Similarly, the police could extend something it already does, and outsource more policing functions, such as back office paperwork, to private contractors, freeing up uniformed staff. Even more radically, it might contract out front-line policing roles to private security firms. (Of course, these types of options start to raise very real concerns about the externalization of the coercive powers of the state, concerns which must at the very least subject these options to qualification – as will be discussed below.)

If, however, the purpose is to reduce crime, then other means *in addition* to increasing the number of police on the beat might be undertaken. The police themselves might be better trained to more effectively interdict criminals, meaning that increased crime-reduction is possible with the same number of police. Or the same result could be achieved by providing officers with better equipment that increases their effectiveness. More broadly, the police might enlist members of the community in addressing the social context that encourages crime. A minimal version of this might be to establish local 'Neighbourhood Watch' (or 'block-watching') groups that keep an eye on each other's properties and notify police of suspicious behaviour by strangers. A more full-blooded version might involve, for example, programmes to provide bored, alienated youth with activities that engage their interest and offer alternatives to gang membership or drug use.

But if the mission is to mitigate *fear* of crime, still broader means could be utilized, in addition to those mentioned above. Some of these could be aimed at making the surrounding urban environment feel safer. For instance, better street lighting or surveillance cameras could render dark or remote locations less daunting.

In fact, we know that in many police jurisdictions, a statistically demonstrable reduction in actual crime can be, somewhat perversely, accompanied by an increase in the public's fear of crime. The reason is that the mass media, often urged on by opposition politicians, tend to highlight more violent crimes, creating an impression of a crime wave. This suggests another way that police could reduce fear of crime: by undertaking extensive media publicity, driving home the message that crime is actually becoming less frequent and/or less serious.

All these options underscore the fact that the more the organization or programme focuses on ultimate ends rather than intermediate means, the more scope there is to imagine alternative ways of achieving the purpose.

Take another example: hospital heart surgery. Its purpose is clearly important: to avoid deaths, in this case of those at risk from heart impairment, such as congenital, ischemic or valvular heart disease. Heart or coronary surgery serves this purpose, often in emergency operations, by repairing or replacing heart parts that have malfunctioned. This is referred to as tertiary treatment.

However, the purpose of avoiding deaths from heart disease can also be achieved by secondary or primary care. In secondary treatment, heart disease may be alleviated by pharmaceuticals, which for instance moderate the heartbeat rate, prescribed by consultant physicians. The intention is to reduce or delay the likelihood that heart disease will result in a malfunction such as a heart attack. In primary care, the intention is to prevent heart disease from developing in the first place. The doctor, usually a general practitioner, emphasizes factors such as the patient's diet and exercise to decrease the incidence of obesity and its consequent stress on the heart. Notice again that each type of treatment relies not only on different types of medical personnel but also on differing levels of engagement of other professionals and of the patients themselves in contributing to the avoidance of heart-related deaths.

In summary, an understanding of the ultimate purpose of a given public sector activity opens up the possibility of identifying a broader range of means beyond that activity. It enables the unearthing of *prospective* external processes which might contribute to the achievement of the requisite outcomes.

But it should be emphasized that focusing on outcomes does not mean that we should do 'whatever it takes' to deliver them. Some ways of achieving purposes may be at odds with other important values, which must necessarily qualify the primary goal. For instance, the goal of reducing crime could conceivably be achieved effectively by granting police more powers to search premises and question subjects. But these powers may give licence to methods which are at odds with our conception of the rule of law, such as extorting confessions or planting evidence. In the inter-connected world of the public sector, it is usually likely that the pursuit of the ultimate purpose, framed in outcome terms, is constrained by, or subject to, the acknowledgement of other values, typically framed in process terms. This is taken up further in the discussion of strategic benefits and costs below.

If understanding ultimate purposes is useful, how then do we identify them? The answer is simple in form although potentially difficult in practice: to ask and keep asking 'What for?', up to the point where there seem to be no further usable answers. For example, in Australia, Britain, Canada and New Zealand, war veterans' administrations make payments for health and other services, as well as income benefits in some cases, to veterans. They also make payments to veterans' families, especially where the military personnel have been killed or injured. The proximate purpose is to provide adequate income or medical services for the veterans and their families. This is obviously a private benefit for the individual veterans, but it may also create value for the collective citizenry. To the question 'Why should more of our tax dollars go to veterans or their families?', the likely answer is that it concurs with our conception of fairness. In this perspective, the citizenry owes a debt to those who have served their country in war, being put in harm's way in order to defend against military threat. But if we then ask 'Why should veterans' benefits be fair?', we unearth another purpose beyond that. This is that we need to send a clear signal to those who might enlist in the future that they will be treated well once they return from war service, and their families will be looked after if they don't return, or are badly injured. In other words, people's propensity to enlist in the future will be affected by how they perceive previous ex-service personnel to have been treated in the past.

Posing these kinds of questions calls for imagination and judgement rather than science. It may be difficult to be sure if, in asking them, one has arrived at the ultimate outcome of a given activity. But even progressing in asking 'What for?' only a step or two beyond the proximate output is likely to enable the discovery of some additional possible means for achieving purposes that matter to the citizenry. The next section puts forward a methodology for identifying these alternative means.

Who should be involved?

Having identified the outcome(s) at stake, two related questions arise:

1 what specific activities do or could lead to the achievement of the outcome(s); and
2 who is or might be involved in those activities?

Answering these questions amounts to drawing a 'public value chain'. This notion is part of a constellation of ideas – such as the supply chain, the value chain, programme logic, backward mapping, and causal mapping – that can be used for understanding the causal links in the production of outcomes (see Elmore 1980;

Porter 1985; Handfield and Nicholls 1999; Fredendall and Hill 2001; Bryson *et al.* 2004).[1]

Tying together these ideas with the notion of externalization, the 'public value chain' encompasses a wider array of potential contributors to achieving public purposes than simply government organizations. It seeks to identify which external actors play a role in achieving the organization's purpose, and to delineate two kinds of interactions:

1 those between the government organization and external parties; and
2 those between or among the external parties.

Interactions of the first type can be identified from either of two perspectives. One is to start with the government organization, mapping its existing internal process for producing the output or outcome for which it is responsible, and then build in the links to other processes and actors in the external environment, such as contractors, partners, clients, volunteers or regulates. This is most useful when the output in question seems to be largely the responsibility of the government organization.

The other approach is to start by mapping the activities performed by a key external actor, such as a private firm or voluntary sector organization, then trace the points at which the government organization (or other actors) impinge on that process. This is most useful when the government's role is primarily to influence the external actor to act consistently with its purposes rather than to take over the external party's production role. Regulation is the most salient example of this.

Let us begin with the first of these (that is, starting with the government organization), using a simplified example of a government agency providing programmes for the unemployed. Its desired outcome is for as many unemployed people as possible to secure and retain viable, sustainable jobs. (For the purposes of this example, it is assumed that the assessment and payment of benefits to the unemployed are handled by a separate government agency, such as a social security department – although in some countries these functions are combined in the same agency, for reasons we will discuss later.) Figure 10.1a sets out the relevant activities. Let us say for illustrative purposes that those shaded in grey are the activities performed in whole, or part, by the government

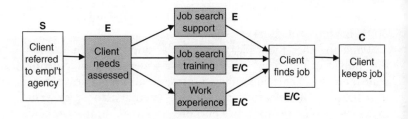

FIGURE 10.1a   *Initial public value chain for an employment agency*

employment agency, whereas the others are those performed by external parties such as contracted providers, clients or other public sector organizations.

Thus the process begins when the employment agency has a newly unemployed person referred to it from the social security agency, and conducts an assessment of the client's needs. From that it determines whether the client is what might be called 'job-ready', and can be left to search for work themselves with agency support in the form of access to media job ads and computer facilities, or even be provided with referrals to appropriate vacancies (that is, job matching) from the agency's database. If they are not assessed as 'job-ready', they may first need other support, such as job search training, skills training, or work experience. Upon successful completion of training or work experience, the client is again provided with job search support. If all goes well, the client then secures a job and beyond that manages to keep it for a sustained period of time.

Notice that the ultimate outcome – unemployed people getting sustainable jobs – depends on the productive contribution of at least one external party: the clients. As discussed in Chapter 8, programmes for the unemployed cannot realize their purposes unless their clients, engage with labour market programmes and actively search for work. Moreover, their willingness to engage in this effort is in some cases due to the activity of another party external to the employment agency: the social security agency. Under the 'mutual obligation' regimes of welfare-to-work programmes in most OECD countries, the continuing receipt of unemployment benefits is

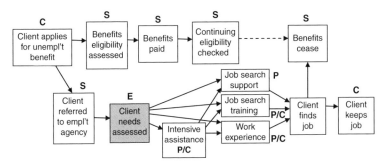

Key: E = activity performed by employment agency; S = by social security agency,
C = by client; P = by contracted provider.

FIGURE 10.1b   *Modified public value chain for an employment agency*

contingent on ongoing active search for work, or participation in programmes. This is why some countries have merged their employment and social security agencies.

Thus far, we have described an existing state of affairs in terms of the distribution of productive contributions between the government agency in question and external providers. But here we come to two essentially useful aspects of the public value chain. One is that it enables us to identify opportunities to redistribute responsibilities among the various producing parties. For instance it may be that the labour market programmes operated by the employment agency – job search support and training and work experience – could be performed by other parties, such as private sector personnel firms or non-profit community agencies, perhaps under contractual or collaborative arrangements, as shown in Figure 10.1b.

The second useful aspect is that the public value chain invites us to reconsider whether the current set of activities – regardless of who performs them – are the right ones for achieving the ultimate purpose. It could be that additional steps between the existing ones would make the whole process more effective. It could be that some activities are unnecessary. Or it could be that some activities could usefully be replaced by others. For example, the process could be elaborated to handle the particular circumstances of disadvantaged long-term jobless clients. For these people, not only their job-readiness but also their profound demotivation, and more generally

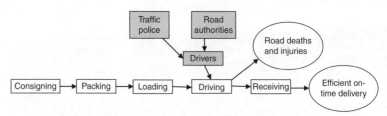

FIGURE 10.2a   *Core production process for road freight transport*

their incapacity to cope with social interactions, constitute powerful barriers to them getting work, because their experience over
lengthy periods has been deeply demoralizing with repeated rejection by prospective employers. In this situation, conventional job
training or job search support is unlikely to be effective. So in addition to conventional programmes, they are likely to need intensive
assistance which help them to take initial steps towards confidence
and social competence, such as opportunities to volunteer, peer support forums, or basic literacy classes. In turn, this modified set of
activities might dictate changes in the set of providers, as shown in
Figure 10.1b.

The alternative approach starts with the external party's activities. An example is the regulation of road freight transport, specifically to reduce the number of deaths and injuries due to accidents –
not only of freight drivers and workers, but also of other motorists.
It does not make economic sense for the regulators, in this case
the traffic police and the road authority to be in the business of
moving freight from one place to another. Rather the regulator's
concern is to mitigate the negative externalities of that primary
activity. It is useful, therefore, to map the processes in that primary activity in order to provide reference points for regulatory
intervention.

Figure 10.2a sets out the core production process in freight transport, from consigning goods at one end of the journey to receiving
them at the other.

Historically, in their efforts to reduce the road toll, authorities
have directed their attention primarily to the driving function. They
have sought to encourage or compel drivers not to speed, nor to
drive while intoxicated or drugged, and to keep their vehicles safe.
This has entailed both the mounting of media campaigns and the

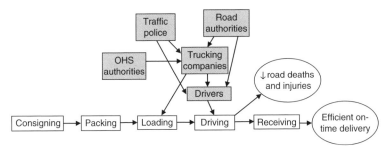

FIGURE 10.2b   *Elaborated production process for road freight transport*

application of penalties for infringements. Road authorities have also sought, within available resources, to make the roads themselves safer, for example by eliminating accident 'black spots' or installing crash barriers along road shoulders.

However, there are other possible factors contributing to the road toll besides the behaviour of truck drivers and the condition of the roads. For a start, drivers are not autonomous actors in performing their roles. They are subject to powerful pressure by their employers (or by freight forwarding companies in the case of owner-drivers), fuelled by highly competitive market demands, to meet tight deadlines, which induces them to drive at high speeds. They are also forced to drive for excessively long periods of time, which puts them at risk of falling asleep at the wheel, or induces them to take drugs to keep them awake. Drivers are also under pressure to overload their vehicles, which impairs braking performance and makes accidents more lethal when they do occur. This is an occupational safety issue as well as one of road safety. Thus the mapping of the core production process unearths at least two other external parties: trucking companies (employers or freight forwarders), and occupational health and safety (OHS) authorities, as shown in Figure 10.2b. Trucking companies in particular should be enlisted, or even conscripted, into the cause of promoting safe loading and driving practices in the expectations they impose on their drivers.

In fact, at least one regulator has explicitly applied this type of analysis. Australia's National Transport Commission, charged with introducing uniform national safety standards for all jurisdictions, in concert with the states, focused on what it called the 'chain of responsibility' in road transport, with legal and other types of interventions aimed at several points in the chain, similar to those in Figure 10.2b (Padula 2008).

These two examples show how the public value chain can help identify alternative contributors to the production process, beyond the currently understood set. In each case, the steps in the analysis are simple in form but require the exercise of judgement:

- First, identify the current core production process, either of the government organization internally or of the external party the government agency seeks to influence.
- Second, for each step in the production process, ask if there are any other as yet unsurfaced processes on which that step depends, either inside or outside the organization.
- Third (and this is likely to occur in tandem with the previous step), for each identified process, ask which actors affect whether and/or how it is performed. It can be helpful at this stage to refer to all of the different types of parties set out in the book (see Table 1.1 for a summary): other government agencies, private firms, voluntary agencies, volunteers, regulatees and clients.
- Fourth, having established a picture of the current state of play, discern whether any of the steps should be elaborated, eliminated, or amended.
- Fifth (again, probably in tandem with the fourth step), check for each step whether there any alternative parties which could conceivably perform that step.

Emerging from this analysis should be some potential candidates for external providers. But this does not mean these providers should necessarily be engaged by the organization. Whether to do so is a matter of careful analysis, comparing the benefits and costs of utilizing these potential providers to those of existing providers. These issues are taken up in the following sections.

Weighing up costs and benefits

As spelt out in Chapter 2, there are three types of costs and benefits to externalization. First, and most obviously, there are those relating to the service itself, encompassing on the one hand, benefits such as the effectiveness, efficiency or quality of the service compared to doing it in-house or via a different type of externalization, and on the other hand, the price charged by the external provider. Second, there are costs and benefits in managing the relationship with the external party. Third, there is the impact – positive or negative – of externalization on the strategic positioning, power or capabilities of the government organization itself. This third factor – strategic costs and benefits – can in a sense be considered as a prior issue to the other two categories of costs and benefits. To the extent that it seems likely to threaten the organization's core capabilities or power, then externalizing an activity should not proceed, and it becomes irrelevant whether the other types of costs are outweighed by the benefits.

The analysis employs a case example, about the contracting out of some child protection services to an ethnic community agency in Massachusetts (drawing on Varley 1994).

In 1989, the Massachusetts Department of Social Services (DSS) put a proposal to Latino community organization La Alianza Hispana (LAH): that LAH enter into a contract to provide child protection services to Latino children and families in Boston – a role hitherto performed mostly by DSS. The arrangement would fall under DSS's Partnership Agency Services (PAS) programme, a new scheme intended to enlist voluntary sector agencies while bringing order and consistency to the Department's dealings with them. For DSS, a key consideration was that it would enable the provision of more culturally sensitive services in ethnic communities – an especially important factor in child protection. The proposal was that LAH take on the case management of Latino clients, which involved: deciding what services (for example, counselling, parent training, many of them funded by DSS) a child and its family required, and arranging for their delivery; monitoring parents in addressing their problems such as drug abuse or family violence; guiding the case through the legal system; maintaining case records; and monitoring the child's well-being. Alongside these functions, LAH would perform the role of conducting an investigation of the family if a complaint was made about child neglect or abuse, and where necessary launch court action to take the child from its home and put it in foster or group care. In return, LAH would receive the same amount (that is, US$63,000) per standard caseload (15–20 cases per social worker) as DSS spent on its own workers' caseloads. Under the PAS programme, DSS would also provide training and information for caseworkers and computer facilities, compatible with those of the department, for record-keeping and tracking.

LAH had until then provided a range of different services in the Hispanic community, many of them government-funded, in areas such as education and health, but had no direct experience in child protection, although it had provided 'soft' services designed to prevent family breakdown – also funded by DSS. But LAH's board and management had misgivings about entering the field of child protection. Apart from concern about the funding level and the general complexity of the work – which even DSS found challenging – they were particularly concerned about the prospect of taking on a 'policing' role, intervening in Latino families through measures such as investigating complaints and where necessary recommending removal of at-risk children. This was likely to undermine LAH's considerable standing in Latino communities. On the other hand, they recognized that it would be valuable if the services were provided in a more culturally appropriate fashion than DSS social workers at times did.

After some negotiation, DSS and LAH came to an agreement. DSS had made concessions which persuaded the sceptical members of LAH's board. Most importantly, they had agreed that LAH would not have to investigate families or remove children from their homes; these tasks would be conducted by DSS. The Department also undertook to provide LAH with all the training and technical help it would need. LAH began working under the contract early in 1989. However the terms of the relationship changed in later years in ways that had significant implications for the benefits and costs to DSS.

At first sight, this seemed like a good arrangement for DSS, and hence for the citizenry it served. The Department was hoping to tap the reputation, networks and community knowledge of LAH to provide child protection services that were more culturally appropriate to Latino families. Thus, externalizing to a Hispanic agency offered the prospect of capitalizing on its specialized capacities, which derived from its structural position. In effect, LAH seemed able to perform this service better than DSS. Moreover, this would occur at no greater cost to DSS than if it did the work using its own staff. These elements comprised the *service* benefits and costs, and they added up to a valuable deal: DSS would get a better service for about the same price.

But these were not the only benefits and costs of externalizing child protection services. As Chapter 2 has made clear, there are also *strategic* benefits and costs to weigh up. In this case the main strategic benefit to DSS was the possibility that some of LAH's lustre in the eyes of the Latino community would rub off onto the Department in respect of other programmes. On the other side of the ledger there could have been a potential strategic cost in handing over child protection work in the Latino community (especially the 'policing' aspect) to LAH, thereby divesting DSS of what should be one of its core competences: the application of legal authority. But two factors obviated this risk: first, that DSS continued to do some of this work in-house, thereby keeping a knowledge base; and second, that the eventually negotiated agreement spared LAH the responsibility of performing the policing role. Thus, overall it seems that the strategic benefits of this externalization were net positives, albeit modest.

However, the third category of benefits and costs – those to do with the *relationship* itself – were on balance quite problematic for DSS, and as things turned out may well have constituted reasons not to go ahead with the contract. Most of the relationship costs – actual or potential – arose from the complex nature of the service itself.

First, there were challenges to do with the *choice of the provider*. DSS had simply recognized LAH as a key Latino social service organization and approached it to take on a new service. It did not really delve into whether LAH was capable of delivering this particular service. It was not enough for DSS to rely on what LAH said it was *willing* to do. It was also important to understand what it was *able* to do. LAH seemed to have had experience in providing services to families, but thus far, these had only been of a preventive kind. It hadn't delivered the more interventive types of services sought by DSS, even allowing that it didn't initially have to do the policing role. DSS should have looked more closely at the agency's past record and current capabilities. This would have required investing some effort into research, such as interviews with key stakeholders and analysis of documents, which in turn would have had a cost in time and money. However, this cost would not of itself have been large relative to the size of the contract – a couple of person-weeks at the most – and therefore would have been simply a factor to consider rather than a make-or-break issue. Of course, if such an investigation found that there were questions about LAH's ability to deliver the service, then this would most likely necessitate other costs that were more significant, especially those to do with monitoring the agency's performance.

Second, there were potential costs in *defining the service*. Surprisingly, given the nature of the service, these costs turned out to be relatively modest in what was actually implemented. The reason was that the arrangement was part of the PAS programme, which standardized case practice across the whole child protection system, so that in effect a set of service specifications was already in place. This raises the question as to whether a 'one size fits all' set of practices would adequately represent what is required from a specific service such as child protection for Latino families. However, it appears LAH was likely to be able to infuse its performance of these codified functions with its specialized and often tacit knowledge. DSS effectively was relying on LAH to bring its norms to the role.

But whether this led to good outcomes was affected by the third and most important relationship cost: *ascertaining whether the service had been provided*. There was considerable information-asymmetry, on a couple of levels, which aggravated the problem by increasing the distance between DSS and the affected families. One was between LAH and its clients. To the extent that it relied on the parents – often single mothers – to care properly for their children, its service outcomes were partly out of its control. It needed therefore to keep close tabs on what was happening in the families for which it was responsible, especially those showing signs of being at greater risk of child harm or abuse. With relatively limited resources, high caseloads and frequent staff turnover due to burnout, this was a challenge. The second level is between DSS and LAH. Again, with limited resources, it was difficult for the department to monitor the agency's child protection. One reason is the dispersed nature of the work. Visiting case families requires time, so that with up to 20 cases per social worker, checking on the actual work of more than a few requires resources. DSS would need to ascertain what proportion of cases should be audited to be a credible deterrent to lax performance by LAH. Even where a large proportion of cases can be checked, it can be hard to tell the difference between good and bad work. What does it mean, for example, if children give slightly hesitant positive replies when asked if they are being treated well? Or if they are getting poor grades in school? It can take time to delve into what is really going on in these families.

This information-asymmetry might not have been a problem if there had been sustainable trust between the two organizations. But as we shall see, the level of trust, which was only modest to begin with, steadily declined to almost zero as the relationship progressed. Instead, these circumstances called for a rigorous regime of monitoring of LAH by DSS.

To some degree, DSS at the outset relied on the trust it had in LAH's established reputation, and LAH seemed to reciprocate to a point. But as the partnership continued, serious problems arose in the relationship, partly stemming from the terms of the initial agreement, and partly from subsequent changes to DSS's policy and resources. For the first year or two of the PAS programme (1989–90), DSS kept in close contact with LAH and provided its staff with training, technical assistance and informal advice. But LAH (like other PAS agencies) had trouble meeting its contractual obligations. With its limited salary budget, its child protection staff were typically young and inexperienced, overwhelmed not only by higher than average caseloads but also by PAS's paperwork requirements. DSS started receiving a number of complaints about LAH from parents, courts and others.

At this stage, the prudent thing for DSS to do would be to improve its resourcing to enable lower caseloads and better social worker salaries. But budget cuts precluded this. Worse, the department was forced to cut its own staff and rationalize its regional offices. This meant that DSS was less able to help the PAS agencies. Then, in 1991, the state eliminated most of the PAS programme, leaving only those agencies serving minorities and a couple of other special categories. It also cut out the regional offices entirely, in the process eliminating all further PAS monitoring. For the next two years, agencies such as LAH floundered, so much so that in 1993 the regional offices were reinstated, along with additional resources to help restore some support for the agencies. But by then it was too late: LAH's child protection work was demoralized and chaotic. At the same time, DSS announced that LAH would henceforth be required to perform the policing role of removing children from their families as part of work, thereby breaching the key initial understanding on which the relationship was founded. All trust between the two organizations had evaporated.

This might not have been an insuperable obstacle – although it was hardly ideal – if instead DSS had been able systematically to monitor LAH's work. But as the preceding account indicates, it was unable to undertake any monitoring after the dismantling of the regional offices. The perhaps inevitable consequence came in February 1994, when police, responding to a tip-off, attended a house in Boston and found six young children of a 26-year old Latino drug-addict mother, living in appalling conditions – starving in a faeces-strewn room, one with untreated third-degree burns inflicted by his mother's boyfriend. The family had been one of LAH's cases, but the agency hadn't visited them for five months. In the ensuing public media frenzy, DSS had no choice but to cancel LAH's contract.

Given the high stakes involved, the high level of information-asymmetry demanded that DSS invest considerable resources in systematically monitoring its performance. Because it didn't, the contract failed, with tragic consequences. This case powerfully illustrates how in complex services, characterized by high levels of information-asymmetry, ascertaining whether the service has been provided can be costly.

It also throws light on the final category of relationship costs: *inducing good performance by the provider*. Not only did the budget cuts and departmental reorganizations reduce DSS capacity to monitor, but they also reduced its capacity to offer positive support to encourage good performance. On the one hand, it was less able to foster greater *willingness* by LAH to perform well through the nurturing of a better relationship. On the other hand, it was less able to enhance LAH's *ability* to provide a good service through training, information, advice and access to technical assistance. Doing these things would have cost money, which DSS, beset by budgetary stringency, did not have. Once again, this relationship management task had costs attached to it.

All of these categories of benefits and costs are summarized in Table 10.1. They show that while there were substantial service benefits, as well as a modest strategic advantage, in externalizing child protection services to Latino families, there were considerable relationship costs, on a scale that was not supportable by DSS's budget. For each identified benefit or cost, this summary table represents, first, an estimate of the gain or loss, and second, the likelihood that it will be incurred. It is compiled on the basis of judgement, not of inserting numbers into categories. But it can be assisted by recourse to quantitative data – for example, the purchase price, or the avoidable costs of choosing the provider

TABLE 10.1   *Benefits and costs of externalizing Latino child protection services to LAH*

Type	Benefits	Costs
Service	Improved effectiveness, equity and service quality arising from greater cultural sensitivity in child protection services (significant effect possible, actual realization unsure).	Purchase price no greater than the cost of in-house provision.
Strategic/ organiza-tional	Possible enhanced standing of DSS in Latino community (modest effect).	–
Relationship		Costs of choosing the provider (modest). Costs of defining the service (modest). Costs of ascertaining if service has been provided (significant). Costs of inducing good performance by the provider (significant).

(for example, person-weeks devoted to researching the provider, or more broadly to tender processes).

A contingency framework

We have now considered the various elements that go towards constructing a contingency framework. Its underlying premise is that there is no 'one right way' to deliver public services. Whether they are carried out in-house or by an external party, and by which

224

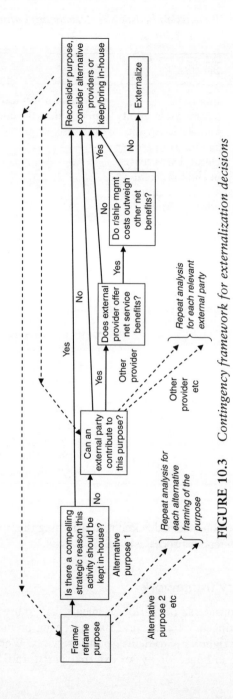

FIGURE 10.3 *Contingency framework for externalization decisions*

type of external party, depends on the circumstances. The framework is illustrated in Figure 10.3. It suggests a set of decision rules, and a logic of progression in applying those rules, in the form of a decision tree, bringing together the understanding of purposes, the public value chain, and the different types of benefits and costs, discussed in this chapter.

The reference point is clarity about the purpose, preferably framed in outcome terms. With that clear, the first question to ask concerns one of the types of benefits and costs, namely, strategic ones. Put in terms that call for a threshold decision, it asks: *is there a compelling strategic reason why this activity should be kept in-house?* In particular, would externalization result in a loss of core competences that would be very hard to retrieve once lost? Or would it lead to a decisive undermining of the government organization's reputation or authorization? These are issues that can be decisive reasons not to externalize even where doing so appears to be warranted in terms of other types of costs and benefits. At the very least, they might call for a reconsideration of the scope of the activity being considered for externalization.

From there, the analysis proceeds from the 'what' to the 'who', asking the question: *are there any external parties that might contribute to this purpose?* This is unearthed by the use of the public value chain, to identify any players who are somehow involved in the production of the outcome in question. If there are none, and it appears that mobilizing hitherto uninvolved parties would be prohibitively difficult, then the most sensible course of action is likely to be to retain the services in-house. If, on the other hand, there are some external parties that might play a role in producing the service, then they can be subject to assessment as to whether it would be worthwhile to engage these types of providers. This entails consideration of the other two types of benefits and costs.

Thus the next question is: *does the external provider offer (or seem likely to able to provide) net service benefits* – that is, will the service benefits exceed the purchase price? This is a matter not only of the relative value but also of the probability of it being delivered. Where an external provider-type is judged not to offer net service benefits, then consideration should be given to alternative external parties, and where there are none, to in-house production of the service. Where there is a likelihood of net service benefits, there is still another hurdle for the external provider to cross before a decision is made in favour of externalization: *do the relationship management costs outweigh other net benefits?* Again, where the relationship costs are considerable, then either alternative providers should be subject to a similar analysis, or the service should be delivered by in-house providers.

Only when it has successfully passed through four hurdles – strategic benefits and costs; availability of an external provider; net service benefits; and net relationship costs – should a service be externalized. At each hurdle, the decision is a matter of judgement rather than precise science, albeit judgement supported by analytical rigour where possible.

Instead of presuming on the basis of ideology, fashion, political convenience or transient budgetary circumstances that an activity should be externalized or alternatively conducted in-house, a contingency approach aims to choose the best option for the circumstances. Its touchstone is concern for what is likely to bring about the greatest value to the public.

Chapter 11

Organizational Capabilities for Managing External Provision

Although the focus of this book has been on work done by parties *external* to the government organization, it is obvious that this significantly changes the work done by public servants *within* that organization. In addition to, or sometimes even instead of, delivering services themselves, these public servants are also engaged in the work of getting external parties to deliver. Instead of having direct managerial control over the people and other resources needed to produce services, they have to exercise influence on the external providers indirectly. As a consequence, they have to engage in new tasks and develop new skills and knowledge. At the same time, if they are to be successful, the organization within which they work has to change its systems, structure and culture, to facilitate the new roles the staff adopt, and also has to relate to its environment in new ways. Moreover, these external relationships have to be managed in a context where the very structure and processes of government puts obstacles in their way.

This chapter considers these capabilities. It first identifies the *tasks* involved in externalization, as well as the governmental *barriers* to performing them. On that basis it analyses: the competencies needed by *individual* public sector staff dealing with external providers; how the government *organizations* in which they work need to equip themselves to take best advantage of externalization; and how the public *environment* needs to be encouraged to change to facilitate these new orientations.

The tasks in managing externalization

The tasks required for externalization are distilled from the discussion in the foregoing chapters, and can be grouped into two broad categories. One comprises those tasks involved in *moving to or from externalization*, which includes:

- Deciding whether and what to externalize (or internalize). This involves either actively identifying or passively receiving proposals for externalization, and more or less rigorously weighing up the benefits and costs of doing so. At a more strategic level, it might involve either rethinking or affirming the current portfolio of activities.
- Determining whom to engage (or disengage). At one level, this involves delineating the *type* of external provider to engage (for example, non-government organizations, clients or volunteers?). At another level, especially if the type of external provider is a private business or non-profit organization, it involves choosing, approaching or discovering a particular provider within that category.

The other category includes those tasks involved in *managing the ongoing relationship(s)* with the external provider(s). These are manifold and complex, but at a minimum they include:

- Defining expectations of what is to be delivered. This can range from laying down or negotiating a set of service-specifications, through discussing and agreeing a shared set of desired outcomes, to forging an understanding that each party will do the 'right thing' as unfolding circumstances require.
- Ascertaining/checking whether it has been delivered. This can range from tight monitoring of performance to informal agreement that each party will raise any issues they have from time to time.
- Motivating/enabling the external provider(s) to deliver as expected. This involves utilizing motivators and facilitators appropriate to the situation and the type of external provider.
- Maintaining channels of communication and mechanisms of influence to enable expectation-definition, ascertainment/checking and motivation/enablement to occur. This involves ensuring that there is some type of relationship through which the parties can reasonably hope to be able to communicate with each other.

The relative weight of these tasks varies according to a couple of factors. One is the stage of the relationship between the government organization and the external provider(s). (See also Ring and Van de Ven 1994; Bardach 1998: ch. 8; Spekman *et al.* 1998; Noble and Jones 2006.) And because this relationship will evolve over time, it calls for varying tasks and capabilities. One way to think about this is a 'life-cycle paradigm' which views the development of collaboration as a series of stages, typically: pre-conception, initiation, formalization, operation and termination.[1] In this schema, our first category of tasks (moving to and from externalization) are more relevant to the first one or two and the last of these stages, whereas managing the relationship is more relevant to the operation or delivery phase.

Another way the weight of the tasks varies is according to who performs them. There are a number of roles within the organization engaged in externalization. We might look, for instance, at how the responsibilities of public servants vary at different levels from chief executive officer down to line employee (Goldsmith and Eggers 2004: 159–71). Here we simply distinguish between two broad roles:

- Those whose primary responsibility is to manage the relationship with the external party on behalf of the government organization, in direct dealings with them. Terms abound to describe this role including relationship manager, boundary spanner, networker, broker, delegate, and more exotically 'collabronaut' and 'boundroid' (Williams 2002: 107). We will generally use the term *representative* for this role and this may relate to positions such as contract officers, partnership managers, volunteer coordinators, client service officers, and regulatory inspectors and information officers.
- The *senior management* of the government organization, including its chief executive and members of the top management team, to whom the representative ultimately reports.

Bear in mind that these are roles, not positions. In some situations, they may be combined in the same individual – for instance in a smaller organization. Or the representative role may be only a subsidiary aspect of the substantive jobs of other staff, such as policy analysts or programme managers. But it is worth drawing the distinction between these roles because the tasks associated with them tend to differ. In general, the tasks involved in moving to or from externalization are more likely to be the domain of senior management, whereas those involved in managing the ongoing relationship(s) with the external provider(s) are more the province of representative. To the extent that these roles are positionally separate – and they usually are, if not always – this has implications for the work of each. For senior management, there is a need to see that the relationship manager is acting in such a manner as to ensure that the relationship is delivering on the expectations inherent in the original decision to externalize. For the relationship manager, it means balancing the need, on the one hand, to build and maintain a good relationship with the external provider, and on the other, to retain the confidence and support of his/her home organization. However, as the following section explains, some inherent features of government mean that these requirements cannot always be easily reconciled. Our focus here will be mainly on the relationship manager, bringing in observations about senior management where they are important.

Governmental obstacles to managing externalization

Thus far in this book, we have canvassed the particular complexities of the external parties – companies, non-profit agencies, volunteers, regulatees and clients. But there also complexities associated with the government side of the relationships. Government organizations, by their very nature, have different goals to those of the other parties. Their basic purpose is to serve the public interest, whereas other entities have purposes reflecting their particular organizational or sectional interests. Sometimes these purposes will be congruent with each other, sometimes they will be in conflict with each other, and sometimes they will just be different. Even where they are congruent, there may be agreement about ends but disagreement about means. These divergences dictate a need for mechanisms of coordination, such as contracts, trust-based collaboration, mission alignment, sanctions or client convenience.

But public sector organizations are subject to a number of structural and operational imperatives inherent in the workings of government. These factors, which constitute the ways in which public sector management is inherently different from private sector management, have long been documented in a wide public policy and administration literature. (See, for example, Rainey *et al.*

1976; Allison 1980; Perry and Kraemer 1983; Perry and Rainey 1988; Moore 1995; Alford 2001.) Each of them poses challenges to the effective use of one or more of the coordination mechanisms examined in this book and as summarized in Table 11.2.

Accountability

A range of distinctive accountability mechanisms permeate governmental processes, including financial reporting obligations, public service employment protocols, freedom of information laws, expenditure delegations, and government purchasing rules and procedures (Rainey *et al.* 1976: 236; Day and Klein 1987: 6–9; Wilson 1989: 113–29; O'Faircheallaigh *et al.* 1999: ch. 13.) These mechanisms are, of course, the stuff of the 'red tape' which clogs bureaucratic arteries and fuels caricatures of the public service. Many of them have arisen, however, for reasons which made sense at the time they were established. Simply put, the authorizing environment grants both legal authority and financial resources to government organizations to pursue mandated public purposes (Moore 1995: 71), but in return, expects that those resources will be used in ways consistent with the terms on which they have been granted. Specifically, in the separation of powers, legislative bodies are concerned to ensure that executive government is accountable in its exercise of the law and spending of public money. The processes installed to hold public servants to account for them are revised from time to time, and when scandals or other accountability problems occur they become more onerous. Over time, they can ossify into rigid and elaborate systems, with accretions upon accretions of accountability obligations (Barzelay and Armajani 1990: 307–8).

The accountability factor is reinforced by the government-wide nature of input and process regimes. When the authorizing environment grants resources to the public sector, it tends to do so to government as a corporate entity, rather than to individual organizations within the sector. In particular, taxes are paid into what in some countries is called consolidated revenue, of which the Treasury or Budget Office is the custodian. These procedural obligations are experienced by individual departments as 'one-size-fits-all' government regulation, which takes insufficient account of the specific circumstances of the agency, but at the same time are unnecessary for achieving the spirit of the law (Bardach 1998: 122).

These mechanisms interact in problematic ways with the key modes of coordination. First, they can discourage good contracting practice. We know, for example, that instead of encouraging specification of outputs, as discussed in Chapter 4, government oversight bodies often over-emphasize process specifications in the rules they lay down for public agencies engaging in procurement of services, depriving providers of flexibility to seek better ways of achieving results (Behn 1999).

Second, they can undermine trust in collaborative partnerships, by constraining the scope for public servants representing government organizations to adjust when unexpected circumstances arise. It may make good sense, in terms of the public value created by the partnership, for the public servant to allow some leeway to a non-government organization that is having trouble achieving an agreed performance requirement or deadline. But the bureaucrat's hands may be bound by the requirements of financial management processes or purchasing rules. On the other hand, the public servant may decide to look the other way over minor breaches of accountability protocols, reasoning that this facilitates more valuable outcomes for the public. But in a democracy with a vigilant political opposition and a probing media, a small transgression can become a partnership-threatening scandal.

To the extent that accountability mechanisms prescribe tight monitoring procedures which are characteristic of classical contracting, they can actually diminish trust. Rigid monitoring of a non-government partner conveys a message of mistrust, prompting cautious disclosure in reply, with the potential for an ongoing low-trust spiral. A similar argument can be made about volunteers.

Third, rigid accountabilities can limit the scope for responsive regulation, which, as Chapter 7 shows, is the most effective approach for inducing positive compliance by regulatees. If their ability to exercise discretion is curtailed, regulators find it difficult to apply the appropriate mix of persuasion and punishment. At the same time, accountability is especially important for regulators, since they are authorized to exercise public power.

In a similar vein, strict accountabilities may circumscribe the opportunities for eliciting client co-production, which typically calls for responsiveness on the part of the public agency. The standardization, implicit in accountability rules, militates against personalization of service offerings and can produce less than optimal services and outcomes.

Intra-governmental complexity

Intra-governmental complexity is an issue that strikes both within government organizations and between them. It arises because there are many inter-connections between government activities, in inputs, processes and/or outcomes. These inter-connections are more common to public than private organizations, for two reasons. One is that government 'produces' public value, which comprises things such as, the provision of social order and of the conditions for the operation of the market, remedies to various forms of market failure such as public goods and externalities, and the promotion of distributional or procedural equity (Moore 1995: 10; Bozeman 2002). By their very nature, these values are more likely to entail inter-linkages among programmes involved in delivering them, for example, because they address overlapping needs or client groups.

The other reason for inter-connections is that democratic governments are inevitably responsible for a wide variety of differing purposes, some of which conflict with or diverge from each other. These arise from, among other things: the influencing efforts of competing interests; mismatches between government-wide and organization-specific purposes; commons problems; divergences between procedural and distributional equity, and among different types of each; conflicting interests between current and future generations; and contradictions between short- and long-term goals. The job of government is to coordinate, balance or otherwise mediate among these contending purposes.

Both these factors generate overlapping or cross-cutting structural and operational arrangements, either between or within government organizations. These arrangements affect contracting by complicating the monitoring of outsourced services. They do this by increasing the extent to which external factors impinge on providers' ability to perform, thereby making it difficult to attribute success or blame when monitoring performance. Similarly, they complicate partnerships from time to time by subjecting them to demands at odds with their original purposes.

Cross-cutting structural arrangements also pose challenges for partnerships, as well as for dealings with regulatees and clients, by complicating the messages coming from one side or the other. For instance, a government social welfare department, structured in a matrix of programmes and regions, might enter into a partnership with a voluntary agency for the delivery of an ensemble of services for a client group with complex needs, such as mildly intellectually disabled people who are homeless and have drug abuse problems. In its relationship with the department, the non-profit may find that there are differing policy emphases between, say, the intellectual disability and drug treatment programme divisions, both represented in the departmental team with which it deals in a particular regional office. In these circumstances, the agency will be unsure as to which particular message from the department it should attach credence to, and therefore how much it can trust what the department as a whole is saying. Similarly, a company dealing with different branches of a regulatory authority might at best be confused and at worst take the opportunity to exploit the situation if the branches conveyed inconsistent expectations. Lastly, clients' capacity to engage in co-production with an agency may be diluted if they find they have to deal with different organizational 'gateways' for different services.

Turbulence

Simply put, the turbulence factor is that policies, strategies and resource commitments typically change frequently in government organizations, for reasons inherent in governmental processes. The environment in which public organizations and their managers operate is a political one, unlike the market environment that private sector executives populate (Rainey *et al.* 1976: 236–7; Allison 1980: 294–6). The most obvious example of turbulence is that, in a democratic society, governments are replaced periodically at elections, and with them the policy priorities, funding parameters and even public administration structures and processes are also subject to change (Allison 1980: 287–8). More generally, however, governmental priorities shift in response to the currents and eddies of democratic politics between elections; new problems arise, interest groups wax and wane in power, and the public mood changes. As the former British Prime Minister Harold Wilson once said, a week is a long time in politics.

This environmental turbulence adds to the difficulty of contractual specification by increasing the level of uncertainty, which as discussed in Chapter 4 makes it harder to know in advance what services will usefully be required at given points during the life of the contract. At the same time, it must be acknowledged that contractors focusing on specific services can be more agile in response to change than an organization responsible for a wide array of complex services.

Perhaps more tellingly, turbulence can constrain and even damage the development of trust, not only with partners but also with regulatees. The democratic electoral cycle formally limits the time horizon for which undertakings can be made to non-government partners, thereby constraining the degree to which 'gifts' signal a commitment. At the same time, shifts in governmental priorities can force public servants to renege on commitments, and be perceived by the partner as breaching trust. For instance, a new minister may change the objectives of the organization or programme to ones at odds with those for which the partnership is working, and which may have been developed through lengthy dialogue between the partners. The government may cut funding below the level originally earmarked for the programme. The department head may initiate a reorganization which removes from the government partner body a function significant to the partnership. Or a central agency such as Treasury may mandate new reporting processes which override flexible arrangements the partners had developed in establishing the relationship, and which may require a major resource investment or reallocation for providers to comply.

If such breaches are small or infrequent, or they occur against a backdrop of well-embedded trust, they can be handled by the mutual adjustments which trust facilitates. Moreover, the public servants representing the organization may be able to disclaim responsibility and express regret for a decision taken at a higher level. But if the breach is particularly serious, or occurs repeatedly, then the partner loses faith not so much in the good intentions of individual public servants as in their ability to uphold their side of the relationship, and may initiate retaliatory action against the government organization such as working to the letter of the contract.

Another corrosive effect of turbulence on partnerships is the frequent organizational restructuring to which it typically gives rise, as governments respond to shifting community priorities, operational pressures, or political whim. External partners often find that the entity with which they thought they had a partnership has changed its name or shape. Most significantly, the public servants with whom they deal are frequently moved around from job to job. The result is that they rarely get to deal with an individual government representative long enough to build up the personal ties that are critical to the building of trust.

Cultural differences

A fourth factor is that there may be mismatches between the organizational cultures of the respective partners. This is important in situations requiring the active cooperation of people in the partnering organizations. There is a substantial literature demonstrating that it is very difficult to get an organization to pursue particular purposes, or activities directed toward them, if the beliefs and values of its staff are at odds with those purposes. Conceivably (but perhaps not desirably), it may be possible to apply such measures as performance management, incentive pay, organizational restructuring or even fear of dismissal as means to induce performance consistent with the purposes of a partnership, but if the organizational culture is inconsistent, none of these devices is likely to bring about more than external or perhaps grudging compliance. At a subterranean level, culture can act as a 'drag' on the more formal and explicit aspects of organizational functioning (Schein 2004).

This problem is likely to be heightened if the partnership is between a government organization and a non-government one, for two reasons, both specific to the public sector (Sinclair 1991). The first is that the public sector employs a lot of professional specialists, whose training and work socialization orients them strongly to professional values and beliefs which may be divergent with those relevant to a partnering situation (Ferlie and Geraghty 2005). Government necessarily makes use of professional staff because many of its functions are ones which require specific expertise but which private sector firms usually do not seek to provide, because they are public goods or there is some other market failure precluding or limiting private provision. Examples are meteorologists, ambulance paramedics, wildlife and habitat conservation scientists, rail safety engineers, lawyers in regulatory agencies, public hospital medical staff, social workers, military officers, or public defenders. All of these and many others have strong cultural norms and beliefs – for instance, the Hippocratic oath for doctors, due process for lawyers, duty of care for social workers – that come from their training and socialization. These values and beliefs can be challenged by policies or practices sought of them as part of a partnership. This can be true not only of cross-sectoral partnerships, but also of partnerships within the public sector – for instance one between police and social workers dealing with truancy. It is also very relevant for organizations calling on volunteers, who can be the target of resistance and negativity from employed staff of those organizations. Consider the case of the Brotherhood of St Laurence in Australia, a major faith-based provider of social services on behalf of the government. They argued that major value clashes were developing in the employment services model because policy changes, which required them to 'breach' clients for non-compliance knowing they would have their welfare payments suspended, conflicted with their beliefs (Brotherhood of St Laurence 2005).

The second reason is that, as mentioned in Chapter 2, whether they are professional specialists or not, government staff tend to be bearers of a 'public service ethic' (Dingwall and Strangleman 2005), which may diverge from the values and beliefs of staff working for private firms or non-profit/voluntary agencies. This 'public service orientation' (Clarke and Stewart 1986) entails a commitment to public purposes and to values such as probity and fairness, for which public servants may be willing to 'go the extra mile', as well as an understanding of proper behaviour in functions such as, public expenditure, recruitment and selection, and procurement. It has been shown that public sector employees attach greater importance to the normative purposes of their organization of public service as a whole than do their private sector counterparts (see Perry and Wise 1990; Perry 1996; Crewson 1997; Houston 2000; Parker and Bradley 2000; Rainey 2003.) This orientation may (or may not) be experienced by non-government partners as red tape or obstruction, but it is nevertheless grounded in basic cultural norms which are difficult to dismiss.

The representative's dilemma

All of these issues pose challenges for the representative in most of the types of relationship – with firms, non-profits, other government organizations, volunteers, regulatees, and clients – we have considered. Accountability, complexity, turbulence, and cultural difference all constitute ways in which the public sector pulls the front-line delegate away from a productive relationship with the external provider.

A capabilities framework for managing externalization

The tasks outlined above, and the governmental obstacles to performing them, delineate the parameters of the job for public servants managing externalization. They must make good judgements about external parties – about when and how to get them to deliver services – but they must also understand and manage the complexities of their own public sector side of the relationship. In effect, they must optimize within constraints.

This challenge calls for capabilities at three levels.[2] The first concerns the competencies of the individual public servant – primarily those of the relationship manager, but also to some extent those of senior managers when making decisions about particular instances of externalization. The second concerns the capabilities of the organization – how its senior managers arrange structures and processes to facilitate the tasks of relationship managers and to mitigate organizational obstacles to their work. The third relates to the wider environment within which these individuals and organizations operate – how government-wide structures and processes might be configured to enable the other two levels to better handle externalization. Figure 11.1 illustrates these levels. They are explored in the remainder of this chapter.

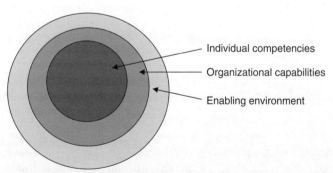

FIGURE 11.1   *A capabilities framework for managing external relations*

Source: Adapted from OECD (2011: 34).

Individual competencies

There has been a lot of attention to the skills and knowledge required of those people referred to as 'boundary spanners'. The various typologies display substantial consensus about necessary competencies, with differences only at the margins (see also Aldrich and Herker 1977; Tushman and Scanlan 1981; Sullivan and Skelcher 2002; Ramarajan *et al.* 2011). Here we adopt but reframe these competencies to align with the tasks involved in externalization discussed above (namely, moving to/from externalization and managing the relationship), as set out in Table 11.1.

These existing schema constitute useful starting points for identifying the relevant competencies, but they are limited in that their

TABLE 11.1 *Competencies for externalization identified in the literature*

Competencies for moving to/from externalization	*Competencies for managing the relationship*
Agranoff 2004	
• Orchestrating the agenda	• Balancing accountabilities
• Creativity	• Creativity
• Recognizing expertise	• Sharing administrative burden
	• Patience and interpersonal skills
	• Sensitivity to roles and responsibilities
	• Incentivize collaboration
Goldsmith and Eggers 2004	
• Big picture thinking	• Big-picture thinking
• Negotiation	• Negotiation
• Risk analysis	• Mediation
• Ability to tackle unconventional problems	• Ability to tackle unconventional problems
• Strategic thinking	• Strategic thinking
	• Interpersonal communications
	• Team building

TABLE 11.1   *(Continued)*

Competencies for moving to/from externalization	Competencies for managing the relationship
Bingham *et al.* 2008 • Network design • Designing evaluatory frameworks	• Structuring governance for the collaborative group • Negotiating ethically • Facilitating meetings • Managing conflict • Engaging the public
Williams 2010 • Brokering • Entrepreneurial • Innovative and creative • Tolerates risk	• Networking • Managing accountabilities • Appreciates different modes of governance • Political skills and diplomacy • Inter-personal relationships • Communication, listening and empathizing • Building trust • Tolerance of diversity and culture

focus is mostly on collaborative partnerships. The list needs modification to take account of contracting and of relationships with volunteers, regulatees and clients, for which the major tasks remain the same but some of the competencies vary. Table 11.2 sets them out, and they are discussed further below.

As Table 11.2 indicates, many of the competencies are similar across types of externalization. One group of them relates to moving to or from externalization, and includes competencies necessary for deciding *whether* to externalize (big-picture and systems thinking and creativity) and *to whom* to externalize (judging people).

In exercising these competencies we can see that talented representatives are lateral thinkers who are creative problem solvers; they can also weigh up whether a particular person or category of persons will be good providers.

The other group relates to the management of the relationship. This involves on the one hand *understanding* of the parties' needs, motivations and power-resources, or what have been referred to as 'interpreter' competencies: interpersonal skills, listening skills, building trust, and tolerance of difference (Williams 2010: 11). Effective representatives are exceptional communicators who can 'talk the talk' and learn the languages of different organizations; they are able to read the external environment and switch roles accordingly. On the other hand, managing the relationship effectively involves *influencing* parties, through motivating people, diplomacy, negotiation and communication skills – what have been referred to as 'reticulist' skills (Williams 2010: 11). Thus representatives need to be skilled negotiators who can manage and resolve conflict; who can exercise influence without formal power; who can understand relationships and can manage these effectively through the development of shared goals, trust and empathy; who have the savvy to navigate environments with dispersed power configurations; and who can work across cultures – a demanding list indeed.

These types of relationship-management skills and knowledge loom large in the literature on outsourcing and partnering, as well as in our commonsense understanding. But focusing on them overlooks another important competency for managing the relationship: the same type of big-picture thinking and creativity necessary for moving to or from externalization. These competencies are important because *they enable relationship managers to better address the inherently governmental obstacles to externalization.* Confronted with contending imperatives – for instance, between a provider's need for some leeway and a governmental requirement for accountability – a relationship manager who can see the bigger picture and think laterally is more likely to find ways to reconcile them, or to trade them off in a wider package of measures. An interesting example is the Solution Brokers operating in the Indigenous Affairs area in Australia. These are individuals who are empowered to broker deals between communities, government organizations, private and non-profit organizations (Blackman *et al.* 2010). This

TABLE 11.2 Competencies for different types of externalization

Tasks	Types of externalization				
	Contracting to other organizations (private, non-profit, other government)	Collaboration with other organizations (private, non-profit, other government)	Calling on volunteers	Enlisting regulatees as contributors	Clients as co-producers
Moving to/from externalization	Big picture/systems thinking Creativity Judging people	Big picture/systems thinking Creativity Judging people	Big picture/systems thinking Creativity Judging people	Big picture/systems thinking Creativity Judging people Segmentation	Big picture/systems thinking Creativity Understanding client needs Segmentation

Managing the relationship	Output-clarity	Outcomes orientation	Outcomes orientation	Understanding regulatory outcomes	Client focus
	Negotiation skills	Negotiation skills	Negotiation skills	Negotiation skills	Communication skills
	Communication skills	Communication skills	Communication skills	Communication skills	Building trust
	Ability to structure incentives	Building trust	Building trust	Building trust	Tolerance of diversity
	Understanding of accountabilities	Tolerance of diversity	Tolerance of diversity	Tolerance of diversity	Systems thinking
	Creativity	Ability to motivate	Ability to motivate	Ability to motivate	
	Systems thinking	Understanding of accountabilities		Understanding of accountabilities	
	Ability to monitor performance	Creativity			
		Big-picture thinking			
		Diplomacy			

kind of ability to cope with governmental obstacles depends importantly on being able to read their environment:

> A key area of expertise and knowledge lies in an understanding of the context in which they operate – the roles, responsibilities, cultures, operating systems, accountabilities and motivations of individuals and agencies working in a particular inter-organizational domain. This is a picture of complexity and interdependence and the value of boundary spanners is their ability to appreciate and analyse the connections, links and interrelationships in this system.
>
> (Williams 2005; cited in Williams 2010: 22)

Another competency, relevant to the barrier of cultural difference, is a tolerance of diversity – which at its most developed is a capacity to put oneself in others' shoes.

In addition to these generic competencies for managing externalization, there are also some more specific, albeit analogous competencies for certain types of external provision. One of them is the use of clients as co-producers. When deciding whom to involve, there is a need not so much for judgements of specific providers' motives and capacities as of the needs of groups of people, that is, clients. This carries over into a need for client focus in managing the relationships with them. Client focus in turn calls for the ability to segment client groups, so that rather than a 'one size fits all' mantra, specific offerings can be made to each group, thereby increasing the likelihood of a positive response in co-production terms. The ability to segment is also important in appealing to regulatees as contributors, since they differ in their 'compliance postures'. A key competency for contracting – an ability to structure incentives – is slightly different from but analogous to one for collaboration: an ability to motivate. The difference lies in the fact that collaboration calls for non-material motivators in addition to material incentives. Both, however, require an ability to understand what motivates providers, as we considered at length in Chapter 3.

Organizational capabilities

If representatives are to deploy their competencies in managing externalization effectively, the organizations for which they work will likely need to change. Their senior managers need to pay attention to the organization's routines, structures and processes (Teece *et al.* 1997; Eisenhardt and Martin 2000). These capabilities both encourage the development of individual competencies and harness them in pursuit of organizational goals. We focus on four key areas that are crucial for effective externalization: human resource management; organizational structures; culture; and portfolio management.

Human resource management

If representatives are important to the effective management of external relationships, so too is their selection, job design, training, career paths and appraisal. These functions are the domain of human resource management. Yet often organizations do not give them due weight in the way they manage their own representatives. Typically, representatives are appointed because they have content knowledge of the service covered by the relationship, or even because they used to be involved in running that service. This content knowledge is necessary, but not sufficient: it does not include the competencies in relationship management we have discussed.

Instead, the organization needs to adopt a more strategic approach to managing people, so that they have the right staff for the new requirements and to ensure they are motivated to perform these roles effectively. Various aspects of this have been stressed by many government organizations and international agencies over the past several years, but progress appears to be slow against a range of these recommendations (England and Herrera 2005; United Nations 2005). First, government organizations need to undertake workforce planning in the light of the new orientation: assessing the skills and attributes required to pursue the organization's strategies, modelling the current workforce, forecasting potential supply (both internal and external) and setting out strategies to either recruit or invest in learning and development to address this. The importance of such capabilities has enjoyed considerable attention for some time (see Cotten 2007).

Related to this is ensuring that individuals have the set of skills and attributes that enable boundary spanning activity to be undertaken effectively – in other words, recruiting and selecting, investing in training and development, and ensuring that the mix of rewards and opportunities provided through strategic job design works to attract and retain those who hold such valuable skills (Tushman and Scanlan 1981).

Performance management systems are critical here in tying many of these factors together. Designed well, they should make it clear to individuals how their work ties to the broader organizational goals and activities, they should set out clear expectations of behaviour and then bestow rewards for achieving these. For example, if the boundary spanning activity required for effective management of external relations is highly valued by organizations then it will be central to the appraisal of an individual's performance, and representatives will be rewarded accordingly.

In the end, this is a story of alignment – ensuring that the right people are in the right jobs, at the right time to deliver on the organization's goals – and of the fostering of HRM capabilities that can *enable* the development of boundary spanning competencies. Despite the focus on these ideas for many years, however, there is a widespread belief that governments have either failed to invest in the development of these types of skills and competencies to recalibrate organizational systems, incentives, rewards and cultures to facilitate their use. (See, for example, Pollitt (2003) on joined-up government and also Parston and Timmins (1998).)

Structures

Formal structures are an important part of organizing for externalization, because they set out the rules and procedures that govern behaviour, identify roles, and map the relationships between different parts of the organization (Ogawa and Bossert 1995: 227). Structures are therefore critical to boundary spanning activity, collaboration and partnering, and cross-boundary working within government.[3] These formal structures interact with cultures and impact on behaviour and relationships, therefore playing an important role in the management of externalization. This makes the process of organizational design critical because they can enable or block the effective management of externalization, with mismatches between structures and the relationship leading to poor outcomes. Failing to reconfigure structures will also undermine attempts at developing individual competencies:

> It seems there is only limited benefit to be derived from changing an individual if institutions remain unchanged. The leadership crisis at the end of the century did not produce significant structural change. It requires a larger effort than most individuals can produce to turn round an institution.
>
> (Hewison 2006: 16)

The importance of structural change was recognized in a major Australian report on tackling wicked problems, which noted that 'existing public sector institutions and structures were, by and large, not designed with a primary goal of supporting collaborative inter-organisational work' (Australian Public Service Commission 2007: 17). And a British report on cross-boundary working noted that 'simply removing barriers to cross-cutting working is not enough; more needs to be done if cross-cutting policy initiatives are to hold their own against purely departmental objectives' (Cabinet Office 2000: 5). Despite such calls to action, traditional notions of accountability still tend to drive public sector structures, with functional structures – anathema to more collaborative or holistic approaches – continuing to dominate (Perri 6 1997).

The emerging focus on externalization has given rise to three types of structural changes, partly overlapping and partly divergent, and each with its own set of problems:

- *Alignment of internal organizational structures with external parties.* For example, when the United States Internal Revenue Service decided in the mid-1990s to reorient itself from a 'one size fits all' enforcement approach to one of helping taxpayers meet their obligations, it reorganized its structure from a function-based one (for example, finance, administration, compliance, and so on) to one based on different groups of taxpayers, such as, individuals, small business, large business (Alford 2009: 140). By contrast, a key problem in the management of the three contracted providers in the metropolitan public transport network by the Transport Department in Victoria, Australia was the mismatch between the department's structure and the operators. Each of the providers had to deal with four different functional branches to get their business done (Watts 2004).
- *Outcome- or problem-oriented networks.* These structures group together heterogeneous parts of a department or even of a public sector on the basis of a particular problem, usually a large one, or a desired higher-order outcome. For example, in the late 2000s, the Dutch tackled the problems of social integration arising from immigration by establishing a Programme Ministry for Housing, Communities and Integration, with a small staff and the task of coordinating and influencing other relevant government agencies (Rijksoverheid 2007). The Scottish government organized its public service into six directorates, responsible for

the five strategic objectives of the government as a whole and linked together in a National Performance Framework.[4]

- *Matrix-like structures*. These arrangements try to overcome the difficulties that arise from the two types of structural change outlined above. Client-focused and outcome-focused imperatives cut across each other and across functional structures, and these tensions usually manifest as competition over resources. One way this has been dealt with in the past is by establishing a matrix structure. However, this is no silver bullet; it is generally troubled by having to cope with contending reporting requirements. A more modest version is what we might call a 'shifting projects' model, wherein staff are pulled together from time to time to work on a project, then regrouped differently when the project finishes and another begins. This is the arrangement consulting firms utilize, and it is close to what organization theorist Henry Mintzberg has called 'adhocracy'; typically however such approaches require a large support staff and infrastructure.[5]

The structural approach we are suggesting is different to the hyperactive restructuring that characterized some public sector systems during the 1990s and 2000s, and is more focused on adaptation and agility as a means of responding to turbulence.[6] In the UK there have been fairly innovative structural reconfigurations in the National Health Service, with some purchasing agencies moving away from functional structures toward more networked, matrix approaches (Ferlie and Pettigrew 1996). This has involved the use of multi-disciplinary teams, staff taking on more mixed portfolios of tasks, and the emergence of 'matrix hopping' activity as employees engaged in more boundary spanning behaviour (Ferlie and Pettigrew 1996: s88). There are a wide variety of network configurations that can be used to deal with the increasingly complex web of relationships: government can act as the central integrator in a hub-and-spokes model; a prime contractor model can be used; or another party can be employed to act as the network integrator (see Goldsmith and Eggers 2004). All, of course, have benefits and costs, and government needs to be willing to experiment to find a good fit.

Culture mapping and matching

A third organizational challenge is the different cultures of government organizations and external providers. Some degree of 'fit' with the culture(s) of other organizations in the partnership can be fostered through two devices. One is to engage in 'cultural mapping' of each organization, to better understand the core values and beliefs animating each culture (Sinclair 1991: 327; Schein 2004: ch. 11). From that it should be possible to identify the values and beliefs which are: (1) shared by members of the partner organizations; (2) conflicting between them; and (3) different but not in conflict. Obviously the presence of shared values and beliefs is conducive to fostering mutual trust but, more typically, cultures are divergent in some way. Here it can be particularly useful to identify dovetailing values and beliefs. By celebrating and acknowledging the differences, the respective parties receive 'gifts' of mutual recognition without generating divergence between them. The other device for bringing about 'fit', employed most usefully alongside cultural mapping, is to foster frequent and extensive mutual exposure between the members of the participating entities. Mechanisms such as cross-organizational secondments and internships or joint meetings in which each party explains what it does and how it works can enable each to gain a better picture of what makes the others tick, and hopefully less attribution of adverse motives to the other.

Portfolio management

One means of attempting to address the twin challenges of accountability and intra-governmental complexity is through an approach known as portfolio management (Goldsmith and Eggers 2004: 21). The increasing complexity that comes with multi-party relationships and the associated demand for government organization to simultaneously manage an increasing number of relationships requires a new approach. Even if there has been much written on *specific types* of relationships, there has been remarkably little on how to go about doing this across a complex constellation of relationships – for instance, how to analyse the interaction effects of different modes of operating, how to clarify purposes, how to monitor across the portfolio, and how to weigh up the various costs and benefits for different relationships. This is, in our view, one of the fundamental challenges for public sector leaders in the twenty-first century.

The focus of the portfolio approach is on optimizing networks, by coordinating multiple partners, managing the tension that emerges between competition and collaboration, and analysing and rationalizing the portfolio of relationships, to cut costs and minimize dependency. The end aim is to enable the organization to ensure that the bundle of relationships in which they are involved are not in conflict, or redundant and that they 'square with the strategic framework that drives the agency's activities' (Goldsmith and Eggers 2004: 151). More specific benefits sought include: the harmonization of contractual provisions; economies of scale and related cost reduction; an evidence base for future negotiations; more judicious contracting and relationship management, with government better able to negotiate across the portfolio of providers and increased flexibility.

The case of the U.S. Department of Education's Office of Federal Student Aid (OFSA) illustrates this approach (Goldsmith and Eggers 2004: 151). OFSA spent more than US$450 million per annum on technology contracts – some 82 per cent of their budget – but had little coordination across them. A new Chief Executive arrived to find:

> We had a vendor here, a vendor there, a vendor here, all on different contract timelines, all on different contract terms, all with different technology platforms, all with different businesses.
>
> (Goldsmith and Eggers 2004: 151)

She undertook an exercise where she layered all the contracts on top of each other and assessed whether they were aligned with the strategic goals of the organization. Finally, she found that OFSA had no real idea of how these contracts related to each other, there were no common purposes, and no method of coordinating between them to deliver the value that the organization wanted. Armed with this information she was able to move vendors to a more integrated approach, inviting them to merge multiple contracts together. The result was that OFSA moved from having five separate IT systems to a single one, and costs were reduced by some US$100 million per year.

Organizational capabilities build on individual competencies to enable strategies to combat the main governmental obstacles we have identified. Where these HRM, structural, cultural and portfolio management capabilities combine effectively, organizations should be better able to address turbulence, as they will have enhanced agility and adaptability. More flexible accountability approaches – such as portfolio management – suggest ways to attenuate the worst aspects of traditional accountability. Intra-governmental complexity can be tackled through re-engineering and combining rewards, structures and cultures to encourage cross-boundary relationships in pursuit of value.

Enabling environment

The enabling environment refers to the government-wide structures, processes, norms, rules, regulations and policy frameworks that set the parameters for organizational action. They include systems governing procurement, budgeting, sector-wide personnel frameworks, and probity, and their custodians are central agencies such as the Prime Minister or Premier (or the President), the Treasury or the Public Service Commission. Whatever their label, these central agencies act toward the rest of their public sectors, in effect, as regulators. When they adopt a traditional stance toward their regulatory role, they create severe constraints for line departments. In particular, their rules and regulations take the form of 'one size fits all' prescriptions. Worse, they are designed to avert 'worst case' scenarios, rather than enable effective day-to-day operations. The net result is an intra-public sector version of what was described in Chapter 7 as 'regulatory unreasonableness' (Bardach and Kagan 1982). Consequently they are the wellsprings of many of the previously explored governmental obstacles to externalization, and can be at odds with the granting of autonomy to agencies and programme leaders to adopt contingent approaches. For example, countries that have adopted across-the-board output budgeting, which include most of the Anglo-American democracies, limit the capacity of agencies to harness multiple functions toward over-arching *outcomes*.

But although they are inherent to the operation of the public sector, they are not entirely impervious to amelioration. Just as the field of regulation more generally has developed ways to facilitate the achievement of regulatory outcomes while minimizing unnecessarily adverse impacts on regulatees, so too are intra-public sector regulators developing more optimal approaches. Here we consider two of them.

The first is flexibility, in budgeting and rule-application. In budgeting, a number of countries are introducing greater flexibility. There has for some time been flexibility across time-periods, enabling agencies to combine the allocations for say, three years, and spend it flexibly within that period. There has also been flexibility across agencies, wherein funds from several departments are pooled and applied to a particular project or programme, as occurred with the previously mentioned Dutch programme ministries' focus on social integration.

An as yet untried, but not to be dismissed, variant is flexibility across budget categories (for example, inputs, outputs and outcomes). There is no logical reason, for instance, why budget regulations could not be framed so that a particular allocation could be for an outcome, an output, or even an input – all within the same budget. Against this, it may be argued that it would be hard to compare 'apples and oranges', but doing that is exactly what elected politicians have to do now, and have always done, not only with budgets but in setting policy priorities. There would still be a need to account for how the money was spent, to ensure it accorded with the stated intent of the legislature, but that need not interfere with the essence of a more contingent approach.

In rule-application, for instance in areas such as procurement practice, personnel management systems and ensuring probity, there is room for concern that flexibility might leave the door open for inefficiency or corruption. But as foreshadowed, the regulatory field has developed an approach that has proven to be effective at reducing the regulatory burden while heightening the regulatory impact: responsive regulation, as discussed in Chapter 7. There is no reason why line agencies could not be held to account, utilizing the same mix of help, persuasion and sanctions as, for instance, private companies, through a suitably tailored version of the regulatory pyramid (Ayres and Braithwaite 1992).

The other approach – easily combinable with responsive regulation – is risk management. Instead of promulgating rules to deal with many eventualities, no matter how unlikely they are occur, this entails framing regulations and penalties to anticipate only those eventualities of high likelihood and high potential harm – that is, according to their risk. For the heads of central agencies it means constructing accountability regimes across the sector, which enable sufficient flexibility for agencies and programmes to deploy the most suitable managerial devices for their purposes, while ensuring that fundamental probity and other obligations are adhered to.

Conclusion

Our focus through the bulk of this book has been on working with external providers to deliver public services. Externalization involves two key tasks – *moving to or from externalization* and *managing the ongoing relationships* this involves. The obstacles to doing this, from the public organization side of these relationships, have been canvassed here: accountability, intra-governmental complexity; turbulence; and cultural differences. Individually and together, these challenges present tensions and dilemmas for those that have to manage these relationships.

However, we argue that, in the end, public sector organizations *must* develop the capability to manage these complex portfolios and networks of external providers. And not simply as discrete providers engaged in a narrow part of the service delivery story, but as interconnecting webs of providers focused on the production of public value. To guide organizations in doing this, we develop a capabilities framework that brings together individual, organizational, and environmental factors. This is no simple task, we admit; however the failure to do so takes us back to the various costs and benefits we set out in Chapter 2 of this book. Without a focus on developing these capabilities the costs of externalization are likely to overshadow any expected or desired benefits.

Conclusion: The New World of Public Service Delivery

For at least fifty years, 'one best way' has been the answer to government's problems. In the post-war era, when services were delivered by the government's own employees, the quest was to make them work more efficiently, so managerialist reforms – for example, focusing on results, programme budgets, devolution and performance measurement – were the keys to better government. In the 1980s, the answer changed. Better and cheaper government would come from handing public services over to private enterprise, in a new era of contractualism – separating purchasers from providers, and subjecting providers to classical contracting and competitive tendering. By the turn of the twenty-first century, the answer changed again. More integrated and responsive public services would come from greater collaboration – between government agencies, private firms and non-profits – and network governance was the one best way.

In fact, none of these waves of reform eliminated what had come before. Rather, each phase overlaid its predecessor, so that today, public managers deal with a whole variety of external providers, through an array of relationships. This book embraces the different kinds of externalization, which have become common place for public servants. But it begs the question: what's next?

It may be that there is a new public sector reform panacea waiting in the wings. But in this book we offer a different answer: *there is no 'one best way'*. Instead, the new world of public service delivery is one where there are different ways for different circumstances. Finding these new paths calls for a broader perspective, going beyond solutions such as contracts, collaboration or co-production on their own. This book puts forward such a perspective, in several respects.

First, it is about questioning the way we think of *purposes*. One of the characteristics of traditional public administration, even if it was more true of the stereotype than the reality, was that ends tended to be defined, if they were thought of at all, as whatever the

254

organization was already doing. Thus the current functions were by definition the purposes of the enterprise – that is, means and ends amounted to the same thing. Not surprisingly, this usually meant that alternatives to the (then) current in-house production arrangements were not considered.

The New Public Management from the 1980s onwards, in its various forms, shifted the emphasis to results, at least in its rhetoric. But its focus tended to be on a narrow definition of results, namely *outputs*, that is, the 'products' emerging from the in-house production process or from contractors to whom closely specified services were outsourced. As we have seen, this approach had shortcomings that became more salient as governments increasingly contracted out more complex tasks, took on complex, multi-faceted problems, engaged more and different parties to share in tackling them, and engaged with citizens in deliberation about them. In particular, it limited the scope for imagining alternative ways of achieving *outcomes*. Now there is an emerging trend in public sector management to think expansively about ultimate purposes, and concomitantly about means of realizing them. The key concern in this emerging trend is to optimize what is of value to the public.

Second, the book is about broadening the *range of actors* who might contribute to the achievement of desired public purposes, from government organizations and their contracted providers to a range of others. Here we have specifically considered various types of organizations as partners, as well as volunteers, regulatees and clients. But we have also suggested that the web of potential participants is wider still, and could include acquaintances, neighbours, relatives and others who have some connection to any of the above. We have put forward a diagnostic device – the public value chain – as a method for unearthing potential contributors.

Third, the book offers a more complex and, we hope, nuanced set of factors to consider in *deciding whether to externalize* to any of the parties identified through the analysis of the public value chain. This involves taking account not only of the service benefits and costs, but also those of managing the relationship and those affecting the strategic situation of the government organization and the values it provides. Rather than re-igniting the sterile debate about whether services should be delivered by the private or the public sector, we argue that it all depends on the context and the nature of the service. In some cases, the circumstances will be such that the adoption of externalization is not just a nice idea, but in fact is inevitable, because of inter-dependencies between the governmental and non-governmental actors. The question in that situation is not whether to externalize but how best to do so. To help identify those situations, we have put forward the notion of a 'public value chain'

Fourth, it entertains a wider array of *factors inducing external parties to contribute* to public service delivery. On the one hand, it extends the range of motivators beyond those appealing to economic self-interest (such as material rewards or sanctions) to embrace non-material motivators such as intrinsic rewards, social solidarity and normative appeals. On the other, it also recognizes the importance of making it easier for external parties to contribute, either by making their expected tasks simpler or by enhancing their capacity to do them.

Finally, it makes it clear that these new ways of delivering services also call for a *broader conception of the work of public servants*. Not only do they deliver services themselves, but they also engage in activities designed to induce others to contribute to their delivery, such as applying sanctions or incentives, re-engineering service-delivery tasks to make them more interesting or convenient to external parties, mobilizing peer groups, or representing purposes that attract support. This is usually more challenging work, but has the potential to be more absorbing and rewarding.

As we move further into the twenty-first century, the challenges confronting societies will force governments to consider new means of organizing and of engaging with other parties; to rethink public service delivery. This is redrawing the traditional boundaries of public sector organizations, and reshaping their work. They will face new challenges, which we have identified and sought to address in this book. But as the book also illuminates, there will be new possibilities for doing things of value for the public.

This 'new world of public service delivery' is not some overarching vision for the future, but rather the everyday challenge for public managers in many parts of the world. They no longer have the luxury of managing in simple service delivery models, but must contend with and weave together multiple providers, with various motivations, using the full range of mechanisms to manage them – and do these things simultaneously. This will be a risky enterprise, but also potentially a very rewarding one.

Notes and References

1 Mapping the Changing Landscape of Public Service Delivery

1. The UK government, among others, has tried to convert clients into roles more like those of private sector paying customers, under its personalization agenda, casting them as budget holders who can exercise choices in markets (see Clarke *et al.* 2007: 41–2). However, to the extent that this money is bestowed by government, this merely makes them beneficiaries one stage removed.
2. Or what Schaeffer and Loveridge (2002) call 'leader–follower relationships'.

2 Benefits and Costs

1. An important explanation of how specialization generates value is the concept of the experience curve, 'whereby costs fall with cumulative production' (Abell and Hammond 1979: 106). It has been found to be measurable and predictable for a range of products and services. Organizations that have been producing something for longer have had more opportunity to increase labour efficiency, improve work methods, develop new production processes, change the resource mix or standardize the product (Abell and Hammond 1979: 112–13).
2. For instance, the US Department of Housing and Urban Development in Kansas City engaged a tenant association to work with a private company on aspects of the redevelopment of a housing project, ensuring local concerns were taken into account.
3. Primary care (or primary health) partnerships often perform this role, calling on a variety of health care providers on an 'as needs' basis. By contrast, if the agency makes its own investment in an integrated set of processes, it finds it harder to adjust these to changing conditions.
4. In Australia's Landcare and Environment Action Program in the 1990s, the employment service provided a wage subsidy to young jobless people, while government conservation agencies provided them with training as they worked on local land conservation projects, with the result that both employment and conservation objectives were achieved (LEAP 1993).
5. For an example, see the Saline Wetlands Conservation Partnership in Nebraska's Lincoln Park (Malmstrom, 2009).

3 Motivations and Mechanisms

1. In the UK, for example, the New Labour reforms were inspired by the notion that 'actors are rational, self-interested and likely to respond in a predictable way to incentives and constraints' (Stoker and Moseley 2010: 10).
2. For a fascinating look at life on the production line, see Hamper (1991).

3. Interestingly, intrinsic motivation has attracted attention not only from psychologists but also some economists, including Bruno Frey and colleagues who have undertaken extensive research on the interplay between motivation and motivators. See for example, Frey and Meier (2002).

4. On intrinsic motivation see Deci (1975); Lepper and Greene (1978); and Deci *et al.* (1999). On growth and development, classic studies include: Maslow (1954); Alderfer (1969); and Hackman and Lawler (1971).

5. See for example, Kreps (1997); Besley and Ghatak (2003) for such a tendency.

6. On psychology, see Satow (1975); Piliavin and Charg (1990); Piliavin (2001); Batson and Powell (2003); and Safrilsyah *et al.* (2009). On sociology, see Healy (1994); Fehr and Gintis (2007). On anthropology, see Henrich (2006). On political science, see Ostrom and Walker (2003); Fowler and Kam (2007). On behavioural economics, see Frey (1992); Gintis *et al.* (2005); Fehr and Fishbacher (2005); Sigmund (2007). On biology, see Kiers *et al.* (2003); Wenseleers and Ratnieks (2006). And on neurology, see de Quervain *et al.* (2004).

7. Ayres and Braithwaite (1992: 27–8) use the example of a nursing home, which provides the minimum standard of care for clients in a nursing home and then once this is fulfilled pursues profit maximization.

8. An interesting example was developed in the Shire of Meekatharra in the state of Western Australia, where local police and local government, working together, devised a scheme to reward the good behaviour of young people with free passes to the local swimming pool (ABC News 2007).

9. See Weiner and Mander (1978); Deci and Ryan (1985); Kohn (1993); Elliot *et al.* (2000); see also Reeson and Tisdell (2008) on the first point.

10. In serious cases, even public shaming may be utilized, for example where those who have committed crimes are made to 'face' their victims and their community through restorative justice processes which aim to make the perpetrator understand the effect of their behaviours. On restorative justice see the extensive work of John Braithwaite. For a substantial catalogue of examples see http://www.restorativejustice.org/.

11. On the rewards side, merit pay for teachers has been correlated with higher test scores (Dee and Keys 2004), and schemes in Brazil, the UK and the USA have shown that when rewards are given to students or parents, school attendance rates improve (Gauri 2001; UNDP 2006; and see Trouton *et al.* 2005 for a summary). In the United Kingdom, the 100 per cent Attendance Club offers a range of rewards from football tickets, to tickets to Disney on Ice for school pupils in Newcastle where they have perfect school attendance. And in the United States, the Star Project encourages students to get and maintain excellent grades through monetary incentives which can be used to fund educational expenses (Trouton *et al.* 2005).

When drug users have been offered financial rewards there is a higher rate of sobriety. The Contingency Management for Adolescent Drug User scheme administered by the University of Vermont in the USA (Trouton *et al.* 2005), uses a range of vouchers to encourage pro-social behaviours amongst young people, and clinic workers award them when participants return drug-free urine tests. Rewards increased in value the longer participants remained drug-free, and the programme linked with parents to ensure ongoing participation and even provided rewards for parents where they actively engaged in reinforcing aspects of the scheme. Financial incentives can also be used to drive up enhance quality levels in health services (Conrad and Perry 2009), improve immunization rates in developing countries (Fairbrother *et al.* 2001, cited in Conrad and Perry 2009), encourage patients to comply with medical advice and take prescribed medications (Giuffrida and Torgenson 1997, cited in Gauri 2001) and increase appointment attendance rates for patients with depression (Post *et al.* 2006, cited in Jochelson 2007).

On the other side of the coin, sanctions have also worked through the use of deposit bonds. In these schemes participants pay a monetary bond which they forfeit if they breach their agreement. Innovative examples include a smoking cessation scheme where the group was penalized where individuals smoked; and a programme where bonds were returned when individuals completed a full course of treatment for tuberculosis (Jochelson 2007).

12. The 'classic' on this topic is Kerr (1975).
13. There is growing empirical evidence that test scores do in fact miss the mark in this fashion; cf. Holmstrom and Milgrom (1991), Harvey-Beavis (2003). A recent scandal in Atlanta in the United States illustrated the dangers of fixing high-powered incentives on test scores (including individual rewards and workplace perks) and included allegations that teachers provided students with the correct answers, and that some held weekend pizza parties so they could 'fix' student tests to ensure that their school performance expectations set by the superintendent (see Severson 2011a, 2011b). Many of the teachers and principals confessed to 'cheating' and investigators argued that the superintendent and her administration had over-emphasized test results and under-emphasized integrity and ethics. In the midst of the scandal a parent (and former teacher) noted, 'It becomes a question of what it means to be educated ... Does it mean the highest test score? I would argue it does not. This is part and parcel of a general dysfunction that isn't particular to Atlanta public schools'. Worse still was the prospect that because many students had their scores inflated they were denied access to the remedial education they actually needed.
14. See Lave and Frank (1990) for a discussion of payment system effects on healthcare, including psychiatric care, and the length of stay of patients.
15. The classic study is Hackman and Lawler (1971) and several studies have confirmed and elaborated this in the time since. See for example, Weiner and Mander (1978); Oldham and Cummings (1996); Latham and Pinder (2005).
16. See Satow (1975) on the link between social approval and helping behaviours and Izuma *et al.* (2010: 629) on the neuroscience example.
17. Volunteers help out with ancillary work in hospitals in many countries, freeing professional medical and administrative staff to perform their core tasks (Handy and Srinivasan, 2004), 'Friends of the National Park' support national parks in countries ranging from Canada, the United States and Britain to Australia and Indonesia, not only with monetary donations but also with work on such things as clearing trails or repairing huts. For example see www.fnpf.org/ www.friendsofthesmokies.org/aboutus; www.pc.gc.ca/pn-np/ab/banff/edu; www.friendsofflindersranges.org.au.
18. In the Allied nations, the fight against fascism in the Second World War was widely supported, whereas the war in Vietnam in the 1970s was controversial to the public of those countries, and this was reflected in the lack of enthusiasm to enlist by comparison with the Second World War (Segal *et al.* 1999). More recently, army recruiters find that the difficulty of attracting volunteers to the

military increases with the growing unpopularity of the Iraq war (Krepenevich 2005; Korb and Duggan 2007).

19. Similar campaigns have been waged in many countries in the cause of reducing water consumption and wastage, limiting greenhouse gas emissions, getting people to quit smoking, encouraging recycling or persuading property owners to render their homes more fire-proof (for an excellent discussion see Dolan *et al.* 2010; and for a discussion of the social marketing context see Brennan and Binney 2010). In most cases, this has entailed attempting to communicate how the individual's own interest will be better served by the requisite behaviour.

20. In Ireland the volume of plastic bags used by shoppers had concerned policy makers and the general public for many years (Collins *et al.* 2003). It was estimated that 1.28 billion bags (325 bags per person) were consumed each year, costing retailers $50 million; just 0.5 per cent were ever recycled. Previous attempts to encourage recycling of bags had not had any significant effects, largely because consumers were apathetic. In 2001 the government introduced a levy of € 0.15 per plastic bag widely known as the 'PlasTax', and combined this with a major public education campaign. The campaign explained why the levy was being introduced and how consumers could adopt new behaviours to avoid the cost. The combination of education and financial incentives produced major changes in consumer behaviours and also generated support for the adoption of the levy itself. That the funds collected were earmarked for an environmental fund helped link the levy to broader environmental goals. Combining material and non-material motivators can, in such cases, produce positive outcomes.

21. There is also a related phenomenon known as the 'spillover effect', which adds to the problem. Thus, not only will our school-age child demand to be paid every time he is asked to do the particular task of homework, but he will also seek it when asked to do other tasks, such as mowing the lawn.

22. See also Reeson and Tisdell (2008). Similar arguments have been made by Makris (2009) who argued that intrinsic motivation reduces the power of material incentives.

23. See Frey and Jegen (2001: 594) and the arguments put forward by Reeson and Tisdell (2008) and Makris (2009).

24. A survey of 18 laboratory studies in economics found strong experimental support for the thesis (Frey and Jegen 2001), as did a meta-analysis of 128 studies by psychologists (Deci *et al.* 1999). Empirical studies in the fields of labour supply and work motivation, services, siting problems, common pool resources, constitutional design and tax evasion also lend it strong weight (Frey and Jegen 2001).

25. This has been the finding of research in the field of corporate regulation (Grabosky and Braithwaite 1986; Garoupa 2000; Engelen 2003; Gunningham *et al.* 2003).

26. See Vandenbergh (2003) for a discussion on norms and environmental compliance. See also Paternoster and Simpson (1996) on shaming.

27. However, a 1973 study found strong empirical support for it, in particular that the rate of donation was higher among those not offered any payment (Upton 1973).

28. The Mindspace report (Dolan *et al.* 2010) by the Institute for Government in the United Kingdom and the report by the Centre for Strategic Analysis (Oullier

and Sauneron 2010) on improving public health in France being two excellent examples.

29. The favourite example from Richard Thaler, one of the economists who published the book *Nudge*, is the case of how a simple act of etching pictures of flies in the urinals at Amsterdam airport encouraged men to aim at a target when urinating, thereby reducing spillage by 80 per cent . This, he has argued, shows that small acts can change behaviours, often without requiring any additional effort from individuals (see Sommer 2009). For extensive examples see www. nudges.org the blog developed by Thaler and Sunstein.

30. See Patrick Wintour (2010) on the British 'nudge unit' and Sommer (2009) on Sunstein as the 'nudger in chief' in the United States.

31. See Phillips and Rowley (2011) on the limitations of nudge strategies and the need to make major changes. For some general criticisms of the approach see Stoker and Moseley (2010). Popular media critiques have also appeared in the UK, for example, Rowson (2011).

32. See French and Raven (1959) for the various bases of power for social influence.

4   Outsourcing and Contracting to Other Organizations

1. See Office of the Inspector of Custodial Services (2004); Department of Justice (2005) where the year following the breakout is referred to as a time of 'reflection, recovery and renewal for the Court Security and Custodial Services ... contract' (p. 3).

2. For a full discussion on the range of contractual forms see Macneil (1978); Williamson (1979); and Williamson (1985).

3. See Hodge and Greve (2008) on this point. They set out five families of arrangements: institutional cooperation for joint production and risk-sharing, long-term infrastructure contracts, public policy networks, civil society and community developments, urban renewal and development projects (p.94).

4. Broad and fairly all-encompassing definitions are provided by Domberger and Fernandez (1999); and also Skelcher (2005).

5. For example, in the UK it is common to distinguish between infrastructure PPPs (physical capital infrastructure) and personal service PPPs which we would consider to be a form of outsourcing, even where this is a longer-term arrangement. Domberger and Fernandez (1999) consider both large-scale infrastructure projects and on-going service delivery contracts as forms of PPPs. Here we simply consider PPPs and outsourcing as the dominant forms of *contracting*. This aligns with the work of Teisman and Klijn (2002) who specifically noted that the PFI scheme in the UK was a form of contracting rather than partnering. In part this tends to reflect how PPPs have been treated in practice in many settings that is, as 'a business relationship, underpinned by a long-term contract' (Hodge and Greve 2008: 95).

6. European Commission (2004). The case of the Dublin Region Waste Water Scheme in the Republic of Ireland, opened in 2003, is a good example of a DBO (design, build, operate) PPP. The government launched a large-scale Water Services Investment Programme in 2000 which was heavily reliant on PPPs, and the Dublin Region treatment plant was part of this scheme. After

an international bidding process a contract was awarded to an international consortium to design and build the facility and then operate it for 20 years. Interestingly, in this case, the finance for the project, some € 265 million, was a combination of funds from the European Union, national and local government, rather than the private consortium. The contractor is paid to operate the plant by the municipal government who collects fees from non-domestic consumers with fees reflecting, in part, the amount of untreated discharges made by these users, and allocations from the National Government. The contractors are required to maintain the plant and cover the operational costs, whilst the assets remain publicly owned. The incentives are such that the operators *should* focus on increasing efficiency so that operating and maintenance costs are minimized, and therefore profit is maximized. The detailed case is set out on pp. 36–8.

7. Across the world a veritable 'shopping list' of projects can be seen: from Portugal's National Road Programme, the high speed rail link for Thalys trains in the Netherlands, reconstruction and maintenance of roads in Argentina, construction of police stations, prisons and courts in France, the building of shipping terminals and industrial parks in the Philippines, the Athens airport in Greece, through to the upgrading of water facilities in Romania and ports and education facilities in the Republic of Korea. See Blöndal (2005); and Webb and Pulle (2002), for an extensive range of examples. Detailed cases are presented in European Commission (2004); and Kim *et al.* (2011).

8. On the case of the Mildura hospital see Blöndal (2005); on the cleanliness of PFI hospitals see Jameson (2010); and on the Indian expressway see City of London (2008).

9. For discussions on this point see Webb and Pulle (2002); Williams (2003); Bevir (2009).

10. A range of points on this topic are set out in Webb and Pulle (2002); Williams (2003); Blöndal (2005). For an excellent analysis of costs of PFI initiatives in Scotland see Hellowell and Pollock (2007).

11. On the evidence question, see Pollock *et al.* (2007), who examine the UK Treasury evidence, or lack thereof, for claims about the success of PFIs in terms of costs and time over-runs. On the risk issue see Edwards and Shaoul (2002); and also Pollock *et al.* (2011).

12. On the cost issue, it is said that the payments made to investors in the Edinburgh Royal Infirmary PFI in Scotland will, over the life of the arrangements, be more than twice the original capital cost of the hospital. A range of PPP scandals have fuelled the debate about their effectiveness. In Hungary, the M1 highway project, heralded as 'the finance project of the year' in 1995, soon collapsed under low patronage and threat from the automobile club to sue over high prices, resulting in its nationalization in 1999; shareholders lost € 60 million and the government incurred huge costs. In Mexico, a major toll-road operator collapsed in 1997 with the government stepping in and picking up a $US7.7 billion debt. See Pollock *et al.* (2011), for a full discussion on these cases.

13. See Smith (2007), for an excellent discussion on the diversity of non-profits and also their focus on complex social services.

14. See Van Slyke (2002) and Smith (2007) for a comprehensive discussion of these points.

15. On local government see O'Flynn and Alford (2008); and on Next Steps agencies in the UK see Talbot (2004).

16. Various forms of asset specificity are possible. Williamson (1991) refers to six: site specificity, physical asset specificity, human asset specificity, brand name capital, dedicated assets, and temporal specificity.

17. AIMS received an A$100,000 penalty (or rather reduction in its potential performance-linked bonus) when the death of the man, Charley Raymond Gamble, was ruled a death in custody by the Coroner. The performance measure in the contract has a zero deaths in custody standard (Department of Justice 2005). In this way it could be argued they were held to account *contractually* because they did not meet performance standards, however the broader strategic costs were borne by government.

18. The same company was found to be legally neglectful and to have abused the use of solitary confinement in its management of detention centres for asylum seekers and/or illegal immigrants in Australia; and came under criminal investigation in Britain when a man died from asphyxiation after guards held him down on an airplane. A previous detention centre provider (GEO Group) lost its contract with the Australian government in 2003 when an inquiry found that children in detention had been subjected to cruel treatment (Bernstein 2011). The use of private contractors, mainly large multinationals, in the management of detention centres in Australia has been extensive, but also highly controversial. Bernstein (2011) provides a good summary of the issues.

19. On The Centrelink case from Australia see Halligan (2007); and on the Next Steps agencies in the United Kingdom see Jenkins *et al.* (1988).

20. All information on the provision of lunches for Turkish civil servants is drawn from OECD (1997).

21. Where court security is defined as the 'provision of orderlies in lower courts, gallery guards in superior courts and perimeter security to the external premises and internal public areas of a court' and court custody is the 'deployment of dock guards in both higher and lower courts and the management of court custody centres attached to courts' (Department of Justice 2005: 10).

22. Interestingly the cooks and other staff were redeployed in the Ministry which meant that the *overall* labour cost savings to the Ministry were less clear; however there were significant reductions in the number of employees used in the specific catering service (OECD 1997).

23. G4S was recently awarded a A$70million, five-year contract for prisoner transport in the Australian state of Victoria – there were no other bidders. It also manages a prison, prisoner hospitals, and court buildings in Australia.

24. Department of Justice (2003). There were 19 performance indicators and they had an associated payment linked to achievement of the target relative to the risk, impact on services, and reputation effects associated with failure to perform. Performance standards related to things such as deaths in custody (0); self-harm (0); assaults on a member of the public (2); breaches of legislation (4); and incident of 'loss of control' (1) per annum.

25. For more on the dynamics of contracting see Hefetz and Warner (2004); and see UNISON (2011), for a discussion on the trend toward insourcing under fiscal constraints.

5 Partnering and Collaboration with Other Organizations

1. An Australian version is at www.neighbourhoodwatch.com.au.
2. See for example, UK; http://www.ourwatch.org.uk, USA; http://www.usaonwatch.org, New Zealand; http://www.ns.org.nz, Canada; http://www.blockwatch.com).
3. These issues are an important part of the literature on boundary spanning. See for example, Centre for Management and Policy Studies (2001), cited in Pollitt (2003: 39); and Star and Griesemer (1989).

6 Calling on Volunteers

1. Other areas of government utilizing volunteers include agricultural extension, national park support, environmental protection, land conservation, tax counselling for the elderly, rape prevention, small business counselling and training, and forests (Morley 1989; Brudney 1990; Osborne and Gaebler 1992; Brudney and Meijs 2009).
2. Perhaps a more controversial example is the use of volunteer police in the USA. In Fresno, California volunteer police now carry out many investigative tasks such as evidence collection, interviewing witnesses, and searching for missing persons; and in Mesa, Arizona volunteers have been training to swab for DNA, and dust for fingerprints (McKinley 2011).
3. For example, older volunteers at a school in Morecambe, England started to withdraw their participation after rigorous induction processes were adopted because, they argued, it would make them feel more like teachers than parents or grandparents helping out (Zimmeck 2001).
4. In Australia, a national survey by Volunteering Australia, a sector peak body, found that 'knowing that my contribution would make a difference' and 'personal belief for a cause' were much more significant reasons than 'what I would get out of the role' (Volunteering Australia 2009).
5. One example was the growing tension between paid staff and volunteers at a Country Fire Authority (CFA) station in Eltham, a suburb in Victoria, Australia which ended up in the press. The station employed 16 paid staff and had 50 volunteers, and was in an area especially prone to bushfires. A memo sent to all staff and volunteers set out new rules for the use of the mess hall, making it out of bounds to volunteers when the duty officer wanted to use it, and issued instructions that they should knock if they wanted to enter. Indeed, when paid staff were not on site, the mess hall would be locked. A volunteer fireman said, 'It is just a subtle thing but indicative of a larger-scale problem. I don't think volunteers are treated well and I'm getting tired of it.' Tensions were also emerging over who got access to new equipment (mostly paid staff) and training (all paid staff, some volunteers) (Dover 2010).

7 Regulatees as Contributors to Social Outcomes

1. In a sample of 36 Dutch Food Authority inspectors surveyed by Mascini and van Wijk, 17 believed there are more bad companies than good companies, 8

believed there are as many good as bad ones, and 11 believed there are more good companies than bad ones (2009: 33).

2. Sometimes this can seem almost comical: in Georgia, USA, funeral directors are fined for not having the correct number of caskets on display (eight) (Sheinin 2009), and in the European Union, Category I cucumbers must meet regulations in terms of length, curvature (no more than 10mm arc per 10cm of length), and colour (Geiger 2007). But in other cases, these actions (or lack thereof) have more profound consequences, as in situations where immigration staff can deport or detain asylum seekers on-the-spot without recourse to the regular 'justice system' (Weber 2003), or where regulators fail to comprehend and respond to menacing patterns in financial markets which result in a global financial meltdown (Avgouleas 2009; Crotty 2009; Goodman 2010).

3. The Tenant Service Authority (TSA) provides the 'backbone' of regulation, while boards and councillors who govern the actual delivery of housing self-regulate, and tenants are involved in both governance and delivery. For more information see: http://www.tenantservicesauthority.org/.

4. But it is not only in policing that voluntary compliance is cheaper. Substantial research shows that in areas as diverse as taxation and environmental protection, it is less costly for a regulatory agency if it can induce those whom it regulates to comply voluntarily (Scholz 1984; Parker 2000). For a counter case see Bratspies' (2003) analysis of voluntary compliance (or the failure of) in relation to the StarLink corn fiasco in the United States, the case of a genetically modified corn approved only for animal feed making its way into food products, which resulted in a widespread recall of popular food products. Fuhr and Bizer (2007) argue that administrative costs for government organizations can increase substantially alongside more voluntary regimes, especially in complex areas such as regulation of chemicals.

5. These points take us back to broader issues of citizen–state relations and demonstrate that coercion is not the only way that compliance can be encouraged.

6. This model echoes that put forward in the early research on criminal deterrence, which placed material self-interest at the centre of human motivation. As originally articulated by the economist Gary Becker (1967), it was argued that people rationally weigh the likely gains from a committing a crime against the certainty of being caught and the severity of the expected penalty. The higher the likelihood and harshness of the punishment, the less inclined was the criminal to break the law.

7. This reflects our analysis in Chapter 3, but also broader views and critiques of the concept of utility (see Etzioni 1988; 2008). For example, it tells us nothing of where preferences originate from. Etzioni's position is that they have their basis in pleasure and morality.

8. Fisse and Braithwaite (1983) studied the impact of adverse publicity on corporate offenders, and found that business executives attached considerable importance to a good reputation – not only because of its financial impact, but also for its own sake. In other words, they valued sociality as well as material self-interest (see also Hawkins 1984; Kagan and Scholz 1984; Gunningham 1991).

9. See McKie (1974) Kagan and Scholz (1984). Braithwaite's study of coal-mine safety enforcement (1985), for instance, found a number of cases where mining

companies, and more particularly mine managers, were committed to meeting their obligations about safety, even though it might cost money.

10. Mascini and Van Wijk (2009) provide an excellent example of this when they discuss the differences between established restaurants and street fairs where food preparation is done largely by volunteers on a one-off basis. Inspectors at some parts of the fair were fining vendors for not following procedures expected in established restaurants, whilst others did not think these regulations were appropriate for one-off events.

11. See Bratspies (2003) on the StarLink corn case in the United States where the company at the centre of the case, Aventis, was required to put tags on the StarLink seed sacks stating that the product was to only be used for animal feed, non-food purposes, and not for human food. This was intended to ensure that growers did not contaminate the food chain with corn grown from the product under an agreement with the regulatory agency. Many of the tags, however, were ambiguous. That is, they may have complied with the 'letter of the law' but the meaning was open to interpretation by growers. For example, one batch included a tag that stated 'under this purchase agreement, customer or any user may: use this hybrid corn seed or any non-hybrid corn seeds found herein, for the purpose of producing grain for feeding or processing' (p.621). There were no other statements on the seed sacks which explicitly indicated restrictions in the use of the seed.

12. Indeed for some it can be lucrative because voluntary adoption of regulations and standards can make them more attractive on the stock market (PricewaterhouseCoopers 2006).

13. In the state of New South Wales, in Australia, restaurants and cafes that breach food safety laws are listed on the Food Authority website for 12 months. Many governments in the United States and Europe have adopted this approach as a way of encouraging compliance.

14. For instance, firms with exceptional performance in the United States Occupational Health and Safety Administration's (OSHA) Voluntary Protection Program get high priority for assistance, low priority for enforcement inspections, and penalty reductions of up to 100 per cent. For more on trust in regulatory relationships see Six (2011).

15. In another case, an inspector explained, in great detail, problems with the storage of perishable goods to the operator of a Turkish supermarket. Afterwards, the inspector discovered that the man had simply nodded his head throughout the encounter because he did not speak a word of Dutch, the upshot being that none of the food storage practices actually changed.

16. Further, regulators, and officials at the 'business end' of regulation are likely to have predispositions about regulatees. In the Dutch food inspection case, for example, it was found that one team of inspectors were more likely to see business owners as amoral calculators, whilst the other team had a more nuanced view of those they regulated (Mascini and Van Wijk 2009). These differences create complex regulatory relationships at the coalface.

17. There have been critiques of the responsive regulation approach with claims that the discretion given to public servants or those given the power to 'respond', especially in sensitive areas of government policy is problematic. An example which highlights this is provided in Weber (2003) with an analysis

of discretion to detain asylum seekers on arrival in the United Kingdom. Here officers can exercise considerable discretion over the detention, or otherwise, of people at the border without evidence or justification, which would be required in other justice-like situations. Such cases have been heavily criticized by organizations such as Amnesty International who have called for more formal rules-based approaches to limit discretion. The Netherlands food inspection case makes the same point: officers inspecting the same case with the same facts responded in significantly different ways – from the application of a 2000 euro fine to a warning. Mascini and Van Wijk (2009) also report on a range of studies that raise concerns about the application of responsive regulation at the coalface.

18. For some caveats about responsive regulation, see Weber (2003); Mascini and Van Wijk (2009); Freiberg (2010).

19. Drawing on Braithwaite's work, Adams and Chandler (2004) explain this in terms of moving through the layers of restorative justice, deterrence and then incapacitation each of which relies of specific assumptions about those involved, that is, a restorative justice approach assumes a virtuous actor, deterrence a rational actor, and incapacitation an incompetent or irrational actor.

20. One example of the success of voluntary compliance is in the experience of the Occupational Health and Safety Administration (OSHA) in the USA (Parker 2000). Under the Voluntary Protection Program (VPP) the OSHA recognizes and rewards those who voluntarily incorporate comprehensive safety and health programmes into their management systems. Figures showed that of the 178 companies in the programme in 1991, nine sites had no injuries at all, with an overall injury rate 55 per cent below the expected average for similar industries. Workdays lost to injury were 51 per cent below similar industries, helping the OSHA to reach its broader policy outcomes.

21. Bratspies (2003) provides a detailed discussion of regulatory failure in the StarLink case in the United States which delves into such issues in detail and explores the broad ranging implications which included: costs of hundreds of millions of dollars for companies that had unwittingly included the corn in their products (for example, in taco shells), loss of sales to retailers, and more broadly a loss of public trust in the regulatory regime.

8 Clients as Co-producers

1. Sure Start was based on a similar programme in the US called Head Start.

2. In extreme cases substitution occurs because the government organization fails to perform a task adequately (if at all), an issue especially pertinent in developing or 'challenging' country settings. In Karachi, Pakistan, a failure of the police and the army to counter widespread criminal activity, civil disorder and political violence during the 1980s was the bedrock for an innovative co-production model (Joshi and Moore 2004). This differs substantially from Community Policing or Neighbourhood Watch approaches that have emerged in richer countries. Local business people, often the subject of kidnapping and one group that paid a high price for political disorder, along with the Governor, developed a model which involved the creation of the Citizens–Police Liaison

Committees (CPLC) – a group of prominent and highly esteemed business people (actual and potential 'clients' of the police service). The CPLC set up several projects including the establishment and maintenance of intelligence databases which the Karachi police access on a daily basis to help them solve crimes and enhance their performance. Further, they have conducted crime analysis, helped in kidnapping incidents, and provided police-related services to individuals. For example the CPLC worked with the Army Intelligence Team in nearly 800 kidnapping cases in the period 1990–2010, rounding up some 100 kidnapping groups and 350 criminals. This co-productive effort makes the police more effective and produces benefits for those 'would be clients' of the police, and the community more broadly.

3. A similar scheme, although looking at the physical conditions of neighbourhoods more broadly rather than just parks, has been introduced in Worcester in the United States (OECD 2011). Here again, mobile technology is used by residents from some of the most economically and socially challenged areas in Worcester who have been trained to monitor neighbourhood conditions on a regular basis – sidewalks, refuse, abandoned vehicles, buildings, and so on – and this is recorded and compiled for the municipal departments responsible for addressing these problems.

4. For more information on the Expert Patient programme see: http://www.expertpatients.co.uk/.

5. The accepted norm is that those who are able-bodied and unencumbered should not receive welfare payments, whereas the elderly, the disabled and sole parents of young children are 'deserving'. More recently, however, even the claims of the latter two are being challenged, especially in the US, but also in Australia.

6. In the UK in the late 2000s, the Coalition government in 2010 replaced a range of labour market programmes, including Labour's Flexible New Deal, with a single Work Programme, to be delivered by public, private and non-profit providers under contractual arrangements (DWP 2010). Meanwhile in the US, the decentralized nature of welfare-to-work arrangements means that many different types of programmes operate across the states and counties in the late 2000s.

7. In the case of the long-term unemployed, research has shown that sanctions tend to produce intermediate effects on the motivations of the unemployed rather than produce actual labour market outcomes (Riccio *et al.* 1994; Handler and Hasenfeld 1997; Finn *et al.* 1998; Millar 2000). On the latter, even the most positive verdict on sanctions, from the US Manpower Demonstration Research Corporation (MDRC) (2002), is somewhat qualified, arguing that programmes using reduced welfare payments as a sanction produced higher programme participation rates than those without these types of sanctions. However, beyond some threshold, sanctioning did not produce higher participation in employment. A synthesis by the RAND Corporation found that hardly any of the studies lending weight to this type of finding distinguished the impact of sanctions from that of other features of the programmes studied (Grogger *et al.* 2002: xxi). In particular, programmes emphasizing sanctions also tend to stress a 'work first' approach, which other research shows to be a little more effective than 'education first' (see below). Studies in the UK and Australia show a similarly unclear relationship between sanctioning and successful job placement (Considine 2001; Handler 2004).

8. Several studies have shown that sanctioning usually provokes non-compliant behaviour (see Hasenfeld and Weaver 1996; Weaver and Hasenfeld 1997). However, other studies find that sanctions prompt more active job search, or at least exit from welfare (Dolton and O'Neill 1996; O'Neill and Hill 2001; Saunders *et al.* 2001). What may help make sense of these contending findings is a more finely grained approach, which acknowledges some segmentation in responses by the unemployed, based on differing attitudes. This is offered by several studies that show varying responses to sanctioning among the unemployed, in which some are prompted to search energetically for a job, whereas others become resentful or demoralized, and avoid or give up seeking work (Vincent 2008).

9. TANF was set up under the Personal Responsibility and Work Opportunity Reconciliation Act 1996, and embodied President Clinton's promise to 'end welfare as we know it' (Handler 2004).

10. See, as one of many examples, the Friends of the Great Smoky Mountains National Park, at www.nps.gov/grsm/supportyourpark/ joinourfriends.htm.

11. The research on this issue shows that where clients feel that the process of negotiating the terms of the arrangement between them and the agency is fair, they are more likely to have a positive view of the specific obligations within it (REARK Research 1992; DEET 1995; Weaver and Hasenfeld 1997; Hasluck 2000; Pavetti *et al.* 2005).

12. A large study of programme implementation across 59 programme offices covering 70,000 clients in the US found that 'personalized client attention' was one of the most significant factors having large positive effects on employment outcomes (Bloom *et al.* 2001: 40). In the UK New Deal, one-to-one sessions between Employment Service advisers and clients during the initial Gateway phase were seen by clients as one of the best elements of the New Deal. They were seen to have helped in improving the frequency and quality of job search activity, and in increasing their confidence and motivation (Winterbotham *et al.* 2001). Relatedly, clients tend to be better motivated where they have the opportunity to build up a good relationship with the front-line worker, who thereby is better able to understand and act on the particular client's needs (Hasluck 2000: 47; see also White *et al.* 2008a and 2008b).

11 Organizational Capabilities for Managing External Provision

1. Sullivan and Skelcher (2002: 119). We could also delineate pre-partnership collaboration, partnership creation and consolidation, programme delivery and termination and succession as stages.

2. Complementary schemas are discussed in Goldsmith and Eggers (2004); OECD (2010).

3. See Ramarajan *et al.* (2011) on boundary spanning activity; Huxham and Vangen (2000) on collaboration and partnering and O'Flynn *et al.* (2011) on cross-boundary working within government.

4. As at September 2011, the directorates were Learning and Justice; Finance; Enterprise and Environment; Health and Social Care; Governance and

Communities; and Services and Groups. For more information see: http://www. scotland.gov.uk/About/Directorates.

5. See Whitely (2006) on consulting firms and Mintzberg (1979: 432) on adhocracy.

6. See Pollitt (2007) on hyperactive reform; Roberts (2000) on adaptive con- figurations; and see Jupp and Younger (2004) and AGRAGA (2010) on agility.

Bibliography

ABC News (2007) 'Meekatharra to Reward Good Youth Behaviour', *ABC News*, 7 December, accessed on 19 June 2010 at http://www.abc.net.au/news/stories/2007/12/07/2112272.htm

Abell, D. and Hammond, J. (1979) *Strategic Marketing Planning: Problems and Analytical Approaches*, Englewood Cliffs, NJ: Prentice-Hall.

ABS (Australian Bureau of Statistics) (2006) *Voluntary Work, Australia, 2006*, Canberra: ABS, accessed on 10 January 2011 at http://www.abs.gov.au/ausstats/abs@.nsf/mf/4441.0.

ACOSS (Australian Council of Social Services) (2001) *Breaching the Social Safety Net: The Harsh Impact of Social Security Penalties*, Strawberry Hills, NSW: ACOSS.

Adams, P. and Chandler, S. (2004) 'Responsive Regulation in Child Welfare: Systemic Challenges to Mainstreaming the Family Group Conference', *Journal of Sociology and Social Welfare*, 31(1): 93–116.

Advisory Group on Reform of Australian Government Administration (AGRAGA) (2010) *Ahead of the Game: Blueprint for the Reform of Australian Government Administration*, Canberra: Commonwealth of Australia.

Agranoff, R. (2003) *Leveraging Networks: A Guide for Public Managements Working Across Organizations, New Ways to Manage Series*, Arlington: IBM Endowment for The Business of Government.

Agranoff, R. (2007) *Managing Within Networks: Adding Value to Public Organizations*, Washington, DC: Georgetown University Press.

Airely, D., Bracha, A. and Meier, S. (2009) 'Doing Good or Doing Well? Image Motivation and Monetary Incentives in Behaving Prosocially', *American Economic Review*, 99(1): 544–55.

Alderfer, C. (1969) 'An Empirical Test of a New Theory of Human Needs', *Organizational Behavior and Human Performance*, vol. 4: 142–75.

Aldrich, H. and Herker, D. (1977) 'Boundary Spanning Roles and Organizational Structure', *The Academy of Management Review*, 2(2): 217–30.

Alexander, N. (2008) 'Public-Private Partnerships for Water Services in Africa, G-24', Policy Brief No. 32, Washington: Intergovernmental Group of Twenty Four.

Alford, J. (2001) 'The Implications of "Publicness" for Strategic Management Theory', in G. Johnson and K. Scholes (eds), *Exploring Public Sector Strategy*, London: Prentice-Hall.

Alford, J. (2002) 'Defining the Client in the Public Sector: A Social Exchange Perspective', *Public Administration Review*, 62(3): 337–46.

Alford, J. (2009) *Engaging Public Sector Clients: From Service Delivery to Co-Production*, Basingstoke: Palgrave Macmillan.

Alford, J. (2011) 'Public Value from Co-production by Clients', in J. Benington and M. Moore (eds), *Public Value: Theory and Practice*, Basingstoke: Palgrave Macmillan.

271

Alford, J. and Hughes, O. (2007) 'Public Value Pragmatism as the Next Phase of Public Management', *American Review of Public Administration*, 38(2): 130–48.

Alford, J. and Speed, R. (2006) 'Client Focus in Regulatory Agencies: Oxymoron or Opportunity?', *Public Management Review*, 8(2): 313–31.

Allison, G. (1980) 'Public and Private Management: Are They Fundamentally Alike in All Unimportant Respects?', in R. Stillman (ed.), *Public Administration: Concepts and Cases*, 4th edn, Boston: Houghton Mifflin.

Alm, J., Jackson, B. and McKee, M. (1992a) 'Deterrence and Beyond: Toward a Kinder, Gentler IRS', in J. Slemrod (ed.), *Why People Pay Taxes: Tax Compliance and Enforcement*, Ann Arbor: University of Michigan Press.

Alm, J., McClelland, G. and Schulze, W. (1992b) 'Why Do People Pay Taxes?' *Journal of Public Economics*, 48: 21–38.

Almqvist, R. and Hogberg, O. (2006) 'Public-Private Partnerships in Social Services: The Example of the City of Stockholm', in G. Hodge and C. Greve (eds), (2005) *The Challenge of Public-Private Partnerships: Learning from International Experience*, Cheltenham: Edward Elgar.

Alter, C. and Hage J. (1993) *Organizations Working Together*, Newbury Park, CA: Sage Publications.

Anderson, S. (2001) 'Welfare Recipient Views about Caseworker Performance: Lessons for Developing TANF Case Management Practices', *Families in Society*, 82(2): 165–74.

Anheier, H. and Salamon, L. (2000) 'Nonprofit Institutions and the Household Sector', in United Nations Statistics Division (ed.), *Household Accounting: Experience in Concepts and Compilation*, Series F, No. 75 (Vol. 1), New York: United Nations.

Ansoff, I. (1968) *Corporate Strategy*, New York: Penguin.

Applebome, P. (2010) 'A Jolt of Energy for a Much Trod-Upon Trail', *The New York Times*, 30 May.

APSC (Australian Public Service Commission) (2005) *State of the Service Report 2004*, Canberra: Australian Government Publishing Service.

APSC (Australian Public Service Commission) (2007) *Tackling Wicked Problems: A Public Policy Perspective*, Canberra: Australian Government Publishing Service.

Arnstein, S. (1969) 'A Ladder of Citizen Participation', *Journal of the American Planning Association*, 35(4): 216–24.

Aulich, C. and O'Flynn, J. (2007) 'John Howard: The Great Privatiser?' *Australian Journal of Political Science*, 42(2): 365–81.

Avant, D.D. (2007) 'Contracting for Services in U.S. Military Operations' PS, *Political Science & Politics*, 40(3), Research Library: 457.

Avgouleas, E. (2009) 'The Global Financial Crisis, Behavioural Finance and Financial Regulation: In Search of a New Orthodoxy', *Journal of Corporate Law Studies*, 9(1): 23–59.

Axelrod, R. (1984) *The Evolution of Cooperation*, New York: Basic Books.

Ayling, J., Grabosky, P.N. and Shearing, C. (2006) 'Harnessing Resources for Networked Policing', in J. Fleming and J. Wood (eds), *Fighting Crime Together: The Challenges of Policing and Security Networks*, Sydney: University of New South Wales Press: 60–86.

Ayres, I. and Braithwaite, J. (1992) *Responsive Regulation: Transcending the Deregulation Debate*, Oxford: Oxford University Press.

Baier, A. (1986) 'Trust and Antitrust', *Ethics*, 96(2): 231–60.

Bajari, P. and Tadelis, S. (2001) 'Incentives versus Transaction Costs: A Theory of Procurement Contracts', *The RAND Journal of Economics*, 32(3): 387–407.

Baldwin, R. and Black, J. (2008) 'Really Responsive Regulation', *Modern Law Review*, 71: 59–94.

Baldwin, R. and Cave, M. (1999) *Understanding Regulation: Theory, Strategy and Practice*, Oxford: Oxford University Press.

Bandura, A. (1986) *Social Foundations of Thought and Action: A Social Cognitive Theory*, Englewood Cliffs, NJ: Prentice-Hall.

Bardach, E. (1998) *Getting Agencies to Work Together: The Theory and Practice of Managerial Craftsmanship*, Washington, DC: Brookings Institution Press.

Bardach, E. (2000) *A Practical Guide to Policy Analysis: The Eightfold Path to More Effective Problem Solving*, New York: Chatham House Publishers.

Bardach, E. and Kagan, R.A. (1982) *Going by the Book: The Problem of Regulatory Unreasonableness*, Philadelphia: Temple University Press.

Barzelay, M. and Armajani, B. (1990) 'Managing State Government Operations: Changing Visions of Staff Agencies', *Journal of Policy Analysis and Management*, 9(3): 307–38.

Batson, C.D. (1991) *The Altruism Question: Toward A Social-Psychological Answer*, New Jersey: Lawrence Erlbaum Associates.

Batson, C.D. and Powell, A.D (2003) 'Altruism and Prosocial Behavior', in *Handbook of Psychology*, T. Millon and M. Lerner (eds), Hoboken, NJ: John Wiley & Sons.

Baum, J. and Oliver, C. (1992) 'Institutional Embeddedness and the Dynamics of Organizational Populations', *American Sociological Review*, 57: 540–59.

Becker, G.S. (1967) *Human Capital and the Personal Distribution of Income: An Analitical Approach*, Ann Arbor: University of Michigan.

Behn, R.D. (1999) 'Do Goals Help Create Innovative Organizations?' in H. Frederickson and J. Johnston (eds), *Public Management Reform and Innovation: Research, Theory, and Application*, Tuscaloosa, AL: University of Alabama Press.

Behn, R. and Kant, P. (1999) 'Strategies for Avoiding the Pitfalls of Performance Contracting', *Public Productivity and Management Review*, 22(4): 470–89.

Beinecke, R. and DeFilippi, R. (1999) 'The Value of the Relationship Model of Contracting in Social Services Reprocurements and Transitions', *Public Productivity and Management Review*, 22(4): 490–501.

Bénabou, R. and Tirole, J. (2003) 'Intrinsic and Extrinsic Motivation', *Review of Economic Studies*, 70(3): 489–520.

Bénabou, R. and Tirole, J. (2006) 'Incentives and Prosocial Behavior', *American Economic Review*, 96(5): 1652–78.

Bernstein, N. (2011) 'Companies Use Immigration Crackdown to Turn a Profit', *The New York Times*, 28 September 2011, accessed on 10 October 2011 at http://www.nytimes.com/2011/09/29/world/asia/getting-tough-on-immigrants-to-turn-a-profit.html.

Besley, T. and Ghatak, M. (2003) 'Incentives, Choice, and Accountability in the Provision of Public Services', *Oxford Review of Economic Policy*, 19(2): 235–49.

Betsill, M. M. and Bulkeley, H. (2004) 'Transnational Networks and Global Environmental Governance: The Cities for Climate Protection Program', *International Studies Quarterly*, 48(2): 471–93.

Bevir, M. (2009) *Key Concepts in Governance*, London: Sage.

Bingham, L.B., Nabatchi, T. and O'Leary, R. (2005) 'The New Governance: Practices and Processes for Stakeholder and Citizen Participation in the Work of Government', *Public Administration Review*, 65(5): 547–58.

Bingham, L.B., Sandfort, J. and O'Leary, R. (2008) 'Learning to Do and Doing to Learn: Teaching Managers to Collaborate in Networks', in L.B. Bingham and R. O'Leary (eds), *Big Ideas in Collaborative Public Management*, London: Sharp.

Blackman, D., Buick, F., Halligan, J., O'Flynn, J. and Marsh, I. (2010) *Australian Experiments with Whole of Government: Constraints and Paradoxes in Practice*, paper presented at International Research Society for Public Management conference, Berne, Switzerland, 7–10 April.

Blau, M. (1964) *Exchange and Power in Social Life*, New York: Wiley.

Blois, K. (1999) 'Trust in Business to Business Relationships: An Evaluation of its Status', *Journal of Management Studies*, 36(2): 197–215.

Blöndal, J. (2005) 'Market-type Mechanisms and the Provision of Public Services' *OECD Journal on Budgeting*, 5(1): 79–106.

Bloom, D. (1997) *After AFDC: Welfare-to-Work Choices and Challenges for States*, New York: Manpower Demonstration Research Corporation.

Bloom, H., Hill, C. and Riccio, J. (2001) *Modeling the Performance of Welfare-to-Work Programs: The Effects of Program Management and Services, Economic Environment, and Client Characteristics*, New York: Manpower Demonstration Research Corporation.

Bloom, D. and Michalopoulos, C. (2001) *How Welfare and Work Policies Affect Employment and Income: A Synthesis of Research*, New York: Manpower Demonstration Research Corporation.

Bornstein, D. (2011a) 'Mothers-to-Be Are Getting the Message', NYTimes.com, 7 February 2011, accessed on 8 February 2011 at http://opinionator.blogs.nytimes.com/2011/02/07/pregnant-mothers-are-getting-the-message.

Bornstein, D. (2011b) 'Making the Text-to-Mom Connection', NYTimes.com, 2 February, accessed on 8 February 2011 at http:// opinionator.blogs.nytimes.com/2011/02/11/making-the-text-to-mom-connection.

Boseley, S. (2008) 'Overweight People could be offered Cash to Lose Pounds', *Guardian*, 24 January 2008 accessed on 9 July 2010 at http://www.guardian.co.uk/society/2008/jan/24/health.publicservices.

Boston, J. (1994) 'Purchasing Policy Advice: The Limits to Contracting Out, *Governance*, 7(1): 1–30.

Bovaird, T. (2004) 'Public-Private Partnerships: From Contested Concepts to Prevalent Practice', *International Review of Administrative Sciences*, 70(2): 199–215.

Bovaird, T. (2007) 'Beyond Engagement and Participation: User and Community Co-production of Public Services', *Public Administration Review*, 67: 846–60.

Bower, J. (1970) *Managing the Resource Allocation Process: A Study of Corporate Planning and Investment*, Boston, MA: Harvard Business School.

Boyle, D., Clark, S. and Burns, S. (2006) *Hidden Work: Co-production by People Outside Paid Work*, York: Joseph Rowntree Foundation.

Boyle, D. and Harris, M. (2009) 'The Challenge of Co-production. How Equal Partnerships between Professionals and the Public are Crucial to Improving Public Services', paper produced for NESTA, London, UK.

Boyne, G. (1998) 'Bureaucratic Theory Meets Reality: Public Choice and Service Contracting in U.S. Local Government', *Public Administration Review*, 58(6): 474–84.

Bozeman, B. (2002) 'Public-Value Failure: When Efficient Markets May Not Do', *Public Administration Review*, 62(2): 145–61.

Braithwaite, J. (1985) *To Punish or Persuade: Enforcement of Coal Mine Safety*, Albany: State University of New York Press.

Braithwaite, V. (1995) 'Games of Engagement: Postures within the Regulatory Community', *Law and Policy*, 17(3): 225–55.

Braithwaite, V. (2003) 'A New Approach to Tax Compliance', in V. Braithwaite (ed.), *Taxing Democracy: Understanding Tax Avoidance and Evasion*, Aldershot: Ashgate Publishing.

Braithwaite, V., Braithwaite, J., Gibson, D. and Makkai, T. (1994) 'Regulatory Styles, Motivational Postures and Nursing Home Compliance', *Law and Policy*, 16: 363–94.

Bratspies, R. (2003) 'Myths of Voluntary Compliance: Lessons from the StarLink Corn Fiasco', *William & Mary Environmental Law and Policy Review*, 23(3): 593–649.

Brennan, L. and Binney, W. (2010) 'Fear, Guilt and Shame Appeals in Social Marketing', *Journal of Business Research*, 63(2): 140–6.

Breyer, S.G. (1993) *Breaking the Vicious Circle: Toward Effective Risk Regulation*, Cambridge, MA: Harvard University Press.

Bridgman, P. and Davis, G. (2004) *The Australian Policy Handbook*, Sydney: Allen & Unwin.

Brotherhood of St Laurence (2005) 'Job Network Proposal = conflict of interest', media release, 6 May, Melbourne, Australia, available at http://www.bsl.org.au/mediareleases.aspx?id=252.

Brown, E. (1999) 'The Scope of Volunteer Activity and Public Service', article prepared for the Amateurs in Public Service conference held at Duke University, 12 November.

Brown, K., Waterhouse, J. and Flynn, C. (2003) 'Change Management Practices: Is a Hybrid Model a Better Alternative for Public Sector Agencies?', *International Journal of Public Sector Management*, 16(3): 230–41.

Brown, L.D. (1991) 'Bridging Organizations and Sustainable Development', *Human Relations*, 44(8): 807–31.

Brown, T. and Potoski, M. (2003) 'Managing Contract Performance: A Transaction Costs Approach', *Journal of Policy Analysis and Management*, 22(2): 275–97.

Brown, T. and Potoski, M. (2004) 'Managing the Public Service Market', *Public Administration Review*, 64(6): 656–68.

Brown, T.L., Potoski, M. and Van Slyke, D.M. (2006) 'Managing Public Service Contracts: Aligning Values, Institutions and Markets', *Public Administration Review*, 66(3): 323–31.

Brudney, J. (1990a) *Fostering Volunteer Programs in the Public Sector: Planning, Initiating, and Managing Voluntary Activities*, San Francisco: Jossey-Bass.

Brudney, J. (1990b) 'The Availability of Volunteers: Implications for Local Governments', *Administration and Society*, 21(4): 413–24.

Brudney, J.L. (1999) The Perils of Practice: Reaching the Summit, *Nonprofit Management and Leadership* 9(4): 385–98.

Brudney, J. (2000) *Advancing Public Management: New Developments in Theory, Methods and Practice*, Washington, DC: Georgetown University Press.

Brudney, J. and England, R. (1983) 'Toward a Definition of the Co-production Concept', *Public Administration Review*, 43(1): 59–65.

Brudney, J., Fernandez, S., Ryu, J. and Wright, D. (2005) 'Exploring and Explaining Contracting Out: Patterns Among the American States', *Journal of Public Administration Research and Theory*, 15(3): 393–419.

Brudney, J. and Gazley, B. (2003) 'Federal Volunteerism Policy and the States: An Analysis of Citizen Corps', in Keon S. Chi (ed.), *The Book of the States*, Lexington, KY: The Council of State Governments.

Brudney, J. and Meijs, L.C. (2009) 'It Ain't Natural. Toward a New (Natural) Resource Conceptualization for Volunteer Management', *Non Profit and Voluntary Sector Quarterly*, 38(4): 564–81.

Bryson, J., Ackermann, F., Eden, C. and Finn, C. (2004) *Visible Thinking: Unlocking Causal Mapping for Practical Business Results*, Chichester: Wiley.

Busch, T. and Gustafsson, O. (2002) 'Slack in the Public Sector', *Public Management Review*, 4(2): 167–86.

Butler, J. (1991) 'Toward Understanding and Measuring Conditions of Trust: Evolution of a Conditions of Trust Inventory', *Journal of Management*, 17(3): 643–63.

Cabinet Office (2000) *Wiring it Up: Whitehall's Management of Cross-Cutting Policies and Services*, A Performance and Innovation Unit Report, London: The Stationery Office.

Cabinet Office (2008) *Modernising Commissioning, Increasing the Role of Charities, Social Enterprises, Mutuals and Cooperatives in Public Service Delivery*, London: The Stationery Office.

Carter, P. (2004) 'How to Discipline Private Contractors, *Slate*, 4 May 2004, accessed on 22 August 2010 at http://www.slate.com/id/2099954.

Chatterjee, P. (2004) *Iraq, Inc: A Profitable Occupation*, New York: Seven Stories Press.

Child, J. and Faulkner, D. (1998) *Strategies of Co-operation: Managing Alliances, Networks and Joint Ventures*, Oxford: Oxford University Press.

Choi, Y.C. (1999) 'The Politics of Transaction Costs', *Public Money & Management*, October–December: 51–6.

Cialdini, R.B. (1989) 'Indirect Tactics of Image Management: Beyond Basking', in R.A. Giacolone and P. Rosenfeld (eds), *Impression Management in the Organization*, Hillsdale, NJ: Erlbaum, pp. 45–56.

City of London (2008) 'Developing India's Infrastructure through Public Private Partnerships: A Resource Guide', prepared by Research Republic for the City of London, England.

Clark, P. and Wilson, J. (1961) 'Incentive Systems: A Theory of Organizations', *Administrative Science Quarterly*, 6: 129–66.

Clark, S., Burt, M., Schulte, M. and Maguire, K. (1996) *Coordinated Community Responses to Domestic Violence in Six Communities: Beyond the Justice System*,

Washington, DC: Urban Institute, accessed on 22 August 2010 at http://www. urban.org/url.cfm?ID=406727.

Clarke, J., Newman, J., Smith, N., Vidler, E. and Westmarland, L. (2007) *Creating Citizen-Consumers. Changing Publics and Changing Public Services*, London: Sage.

Clarke, M. and Stewart, J. (1986) 'Local Government and the Public Service Orientation', *Local Government Studies*, 12(3): 1–8.

Clary, E., Snyder, M. and Ridge, R. (1992) 'Volunteers' Motivations: A Functional Strategy for the Recruitment, Placement, and Retention of Volunteers, *Nonprofit Management & Leadership*, 2: 333–50.

Clary, E.G., Snyder, M., Ridge, R.D., Copeland, J., Stukas, A.A., Haugen, J., *et al.* (1998) 'Understanding and Assessing the Motivations of Volunteers: A Functional Approach, *Journal of Personality and Social Psychology*, 74(6): 1516–30.

Clary, E., Snyder, M. and Stukas, A. (1996) 'Volunteers' Motivations: Findings from a National Survey', *Nonprofit and Voluntary Sector Quarterly*, 25: 485–505.

Coase, R. (1937) 'The Nature of the Firm', *Economica*, 4: 386–405.

Coase, R. (1960) 'The Problem of Social Cost', *Journal of Law and Economics*, 3(1): 1–44 .

Cohen, S. and Eimicke, W. (2008) *The Responsible Contract Manager: Protecting the Public Interest in an Outsourced World*, Washington, DC: Georgetown University Press.

Coleman, J. (1990) *Foundations of Social Theory*, Cambridge, MA: Belknap Press.

Collins, J., Thomas, G., Willis, R. and Wilsdon, J. (2003) 'Carrots, Sticks and Sermons: Influencing Public Behaviour for Environmental Goals', a Demos/Green Alliance report produced for Department for Environment, Food and Rural Affairs, London: DEMOS.

Commission on Wartime Contracting in Iraq and Afghanistan (2009a) 'At What Cost? Contingency Contracting in Iraq and Afghanistan', Interim Report to Congress, June, Washington, United States of America.

Commission on Wartime Contracting in Iraq and Afghanistan (2009b) 'Lowest-Priced Security Not Good Enough for War-Aone Embassies', Special Report on Embassy Security Contracts, 1 October, Washington, United States of America.

Commission on Wartime Contracting in Iraq and Afghanistan (2011) 'At What Risk? Correcting Over-Reliance on Contractors in Contingency Operation', Second Interim Report to Congress, February, Washington, United States of America.

Confederation of British Industry (2007) *Going Global: The World of Public Private Partnerships*, London: Confederation of British Industry.

Conrad, D. and Perry, L. (2009) 'Quality-Based Financial Incentives in Health Care: Can We Improve Quality by Paying For It?' *Annual Review of Public Health*, 30: 357–71.

Considine, M. (2001) *Enterprising States: The Public Management of Welfare to Work,* Cambridge: Cambridge University Press.

Corbett, T. (1996) 'Understanding Wisconsin Works (W-2)', *Focus*, 18(1): 53–4.

Corcoran, J. and McLean, F. (1998) 'The Selection of Management Consultants: How Are Governments Dealing with this Difficult Decision? An Exploratory Study', *International Journal of Public Sector Management*, 11(1): 37–54.

Cotten, A. (2007) *Seven Steps of Effective Workforce Planning*, Washington: IBM Center for the Business of Government.

Crewson, P. (1997) 'Public Service Motivation: Building Empirical Evidence of Incidence and Effect', *Journal of Public Administration Research and Theory*, 7: 499–518.

Crosby, B. and Bryson, J. (2005) *Leadership for the Common Good: Tackling Public Problems in a Shared-Power World*, San Francisco: John Wiley.

Crosby, B., Bryson, J. and Stone, M. (2010) 'Leading Across Frontiers: How Visionary Leaders Integrate People, Processes, Structures and Resources', in S. Osborne (ed.), *The New Public Governance: Emerging Perspectives on the Theory and Practice of Public Governance*, London: Routledge.

Crotty, J. (2009) 'Structural Causes of the Global Financial Crisis: A Critical Assessment of the "New Financial Architecture"', *Cambridge Journal of Economics*, 33(4): 563–80.

Cubbin, J., Domberger, S. and Meadowcroft, S. (1987) 'Competitive Tendering and Efficiency: The Case of Hospital Cleaning', *Fiscal Studies*, 8(3): 49–58.

Dasgupta, P. (1988) 'Trust as a Commodity', in D. Gambetta (ed.), *Trust: Making and Breaking Co-operative Relations*, Oxford: Basil Blackwell.

Day, P. and Klein, R. (1987) *Accountabilities: Five Public Services*, London: Tavistock Publications.

de Quervain, M.R., Fischbacher, U., Treyer, V., Schelthammer, M., Schnyder, U., Buck, A. and Fehr, E. (2004) 'The Neural Basis of Altruistic Punishment', *Science*, 305: 1254–8.

Deci, E. (1975) *Intrinsic Motivation*, New York: Plenum Press.

Deci, E., Koestner, R. and Ryan, R. (1999) 'A Meta-analytic Review of Experiments Examining the Effects of Extrinsic Rewards on Intrinsic Motivation.' *Psychological Bulletin*, 125: 627–68.

Deci, E. and Ryan, R. (1985) *Intrinsic Motivation and Self Determination in Human Behavior*, New York: Plenum Press.

Dee, T., and Keys, B. (2004) 'Does Merit Pay Reward Good Teachers? Evidence from a Randomized Experiment', *Journal of Policy Analysis and Management*, 23(3): 471–88.

Deery, S., Plowman, D. and Walsh, J. (1997) *Industrial Relations: A Contemporary Analysis*, Sydney: McGraw-Hill.

DEET (1995) *Longitudinal Cohort Study of Jobseekers 18+ Years Old*, Canberra, ACT: Department of Employment, Education and Training.

deHoog, R (1990) 'Competition, Negotiation or Co-operation: Three Models for Service Contracting', *Administration and Society*, 22(3): 317–40.

Deming, W.E. (1982) *Quality, Productivity and Competitive Position*, Cambridge, MA: MIT Press.

Department of Corrective Services (2010) *Contract for the Provision of Court Security and Custodial Services*, Annual Report 2009/10, Government of Western Australia, Perth, Australia.

Department of Justice (2003) *Contract for the Provision of Court Security and Custodial Services*, Annual Report, Government of Western Australia, Perth, Australia.

Department of Justice (2005) *Contract for the Provision of Court Security and Custodial Services*, Annual Report, Government of Western Australia, Perth, Australia.

DfE (Department for Education) (2010) *The Impact of Sure Start Local Programmes on Five Year Olds and their Families*, University of London.

Dilulio, Jr, J.T. (2003) 'Response: Government by Proxy: A Faithful Overview', *Harvard Law Review*, 116(5): 1271–84.

Dingwall, R. and Strangleman, T. (2005) 'Organizational Cultures in the Public Services', in E. Ferlie, L. Lynn and C. Pollitt (eds), *The Oxford Handbook of Public Management*, Oxford: Oxford University Press.

Diver, C.S. (1980) 'A Theory of Regulatory Enforcement', *Public Policy*, 28: 257–301.

Dobes, L. (2006) *Managing Consultants: A Practical Guide for Busy Public Sector Managers*, Canberra: ANU E-Press.

Dolan, P., Hallsworth, M., Halpern, D., King, D. and Vlaev, I. (2010) *Mindspace: Influencing Behaviour Through Public Policy*, London: Institute for Government.

Dolton, P. and O'Neill, D. (1996) 'Unemployment Duration and the Restart Effect: Some Experimental Evidence', *The Economic Journal*, 106: 387–400.

Domberger, S. (1989) 'The Impact of Competition on Pricing and Quality of Legal Services', *International Review of Law and Economics*, 9(1): 41–56.

Domberger, S. (1993) 'Privatisation: What Does the British Experience Reveal?' *Economic Papers*, 12(2): 58–68.

Domberger, S. (1994) 'Public Sector Contracting: Does It Work?', *Australian Economic Review*, 27(3): 91–6.

Domberger, S. (1998) *The Contracting Organization: A Strategic Guide to Outsourcing*, Oxford: Oxford University Press.

Domberger, S. and Fernandez, P. (1999) 'Public-Private Partnerships for Service Delivery', *Business Strategy Review*, 10(4): 29–39.

Domberger, S. and Rimmer, S. (1994) 'Competitive Tendering and Contracting in the Public Sector', *International Journal of the Economics of Business*, 1: 439–53.

Donahue, J. (1989) *The Privatization Decision: Public Ends, Private Means*, New York: Basic Books.

Donahue, J. and Zeckhauser, R. (2011) *Collaborative Governance: Private Roles for Public Goals in Turbulent Times*, Princeton: Princeton University Press.

Donaldson, L. (1990) 'The Ethereal Hand: Organizational Economics and Management Theory', *Academy of Management Review*, 15(3): 369–81.

Dover, G. (2010) 'Public Sector Volunteering: Committed Staff, Multiple Logics, and Contradictory Strategies', *Review of Public Personnel Administration*, 30(2): 235–56.

Downs, A. (1957) *An Economic Theory of Democracy*, New York: Harper & Row.

DWP (Department of Work and Pensions) (2010) *The Work Programme Prospectus – November 2010*, London: DWP.

Eberts, R., Hollenbeck, K. and Stone, J. (2000) 'Teacher Performance Incentives and Student Outcomes', paper presented at the National Academy of Sciences Conference, 17–18 December, Irvine, California.

Edelenbos, J. and Klijn, E.H. (2007) 'Trust in Complex Decision-Making Networks: A Theoretical and Empirical Exploration', *Administration and Society*, 39(1): 25–50.

Edwards, P. and Shaoul, J. (2002) Partnerships: For Better, for Worse? *Accounting, Auditing and Accountability Journal*, 16(3): 397–421.

Ehrlich, I. (1973) 'Participation in Illegitimate Activities: A Theoretical and Empirical Investigation', *Journal of Political Economy*, 81(3): 521–65.

Ehrlich, I. and Posner, R. (1974) 'An Economic Analysis of Legal Rule-Making', *Journal of Legal Studies*, 3: 257–86.

Eisenhardt, K. and Martin, J. (2000) 'Dynamic Capabilities: What Are They?' *The Strategic Management Journal*, 21(10–11): 1105–21.

Ekeh, P. (1974) *Social Exchange Theory: The Two Traditions*, Cambridge, MA: Harvard University Press.

Elliot, A., Faler, J., McGregor, H., Campbell, W., Sedikides, C. and Harackiewicz, J. (2000) 'Competence Valuation as a Strategic Intrinsic Motivation Process', *Personality and Social Psychology Bulletin*, 26(7): 780–94.

Ellis, S. (1996) *The Volunteer Recruitment (and Membership Development) Book*, Philadelphia: Energize, Inc.

Elmore, R. (1980) 'Backward Mapping: Implementation Research and Policy Decisions', *Political Science Quarterly*, 94: 601–16.

Engelen, P. (2003) 'Can Reputational Damage Restrict Illegal Insider Trading?' *European Journal of Crime, Criminal Law and Criminal Justice*, 11(3): 253–63.

England, S. and Herrera, R. (2005) 'Conserving Government's Most Valuable Resource', *Outlook No. 2*, Accenture.

English, L. (2005) 'Using Public-Private Partnering to Deliver Social Infrastructure: The Australian Experience', in G. Hodge, and C. Greve (eds), *The Challenge of Public-Private Partnerships: Learning from International Experience*, Cheltenham: Edward Elgar.

Entwistle, T., Martin, S. and Enticott, G. (2005) 'The Politics of Performance Improvement', *Local Government Studies*, 31(5): 541–54.

Etzioni, A. (1988) *The Moral Dimension – Towards a New Economics*, New York: Free Press.

Etzioni, A. (2008) 'The Moral Dimension Revisited' in A. Etzioni, *Twenty Years of The Moral Dimension: Toward a New Economics* (Discussion Forum), *Socio-Economic Review*, 6(1): 135–73.

European Commission (2004) *Resource Book on PPP Case Studies, Directorate-General Regional Policy*, Brussels, Belgium: EC.

European Commission (2004) *Green Paper on Public-Private Partnerships and Community Law on Public Contracts and Concessions*, Brussels: European Commission.

Exworthy, M., Powell, M. and Mohan, J. (1999) 'The NHS: Quasi-market, Quasi-hierarchy and Quasi-network?' *Public Money & Management*, 19(4): 15–22.

Fahey, C., Walker, J. and Sleigh, A. (2002) 'Training can be a Recruitment and Retention Tool for Emergency Service Volunteers', *Australian Journal of Emergency Management*, 17(3): 3–7.

Fairbrother, P., Paddon, M. and Teicher, J. (2002) *Privatisation, Globalisation & Labour: Studies from Australia*, Sydney: The Federation Press.

Fehr, E. and Falk, A. (2002) 'Psychological Foundations of Incentives', *European Economic Review*, 46(4–5): 687–724.

Fehr, E. and Fishbacher, U. (2005) 'Human Altruism – Proximate Patterns and Evolutionary Origins', *Anal Kritik*, 27: 6–47.

Fehr, E. and Gintis, H. (2007) 'Human Motivation and Social Cooperation: Experimental and Analytical Foundations', *Annual Review of Sociology*, 33: 43–64.

Feigenbaum, H., Henig, J. and Hamnett, C. (1998) *Shrinking the State: The Political Underpinnings of Privatization*, Cambridge: Cambridge University Press.

Ferlie, E. and Geraghty, K. (2005) 'Professionals in Public Service Organizations: Implications for Public Sector "Reforming"', in E. Ferlie, L. Lynn and C. Pollitt (eds), *The Oxford Handbook of Public Management*, Oxford: Oxford University Press.

Ferlie, E. and Pettigrew, A. (1996) 'Managing Through Networks: Some Issues and Implications for the NHS', *British Journal of Management*, 7 (special issue): S81–S99

Ferris, J. (1984) 'Coprovision: Citizen Time and Money Donations in Public Service Provision', *Public Administration Review*, 44(4): 324–33.

Ferris, J. (1986) 'The Decision to Contract Out: An Empirical Analysis', *Urban Affairs Quarterly*, 22(2): 289–311.

Finn, D. (2002) 'Joining up Welfare and Work: The Role of "Private Public Partnerships" in British and Australian Welfare Reform', paper presented at the International Conference on 'Knowledge, Networks and Joined-Up Government', Melbourne.

Finn, D., Blackmore, M. and Nimmo, M. (1998) *Welfare-to-Work and the Long Term Unemployed: 'They're Very Cynical'.* London: Unemployment Unit and Youthaid.

Finn, P. (2005) 'Forecasters Feeling Some Official Heat', *Washington Post*, 1 March.

Fisher, J.C. and Cole, K.M. (1993) *Leadership and Management of Volunteer Programs: A Guide for Volunteer Administrators*, San Francisco: Jossey-Bass.

Fisse, B. and Braithwaite, J. (1983) *The Impact of Publicity on Corporate Offenders*, Albany: State University of New York.

Flynn, N. (2007) *Public Sector Management*, 5th edn, London: Sage.

Flynn, R., Williams, G. and Pickard, S. (1996) *Markets and Networks: Contracting in Community Health Services*, Buckingham: Open University Press.

Fowler, J. and Kam, C. (2007) 'Beyond the Self: Social Identity, Altruism and Political Participation', *Journal of Politics*, 69(3): 813–27.

Fox, A. (1974) *Beyond Contract: Work, Power and Trust Relations*, London: Faber.

Frant, H. (1996) 'High Powered and Low Powered Incentives in the Public Sector', *Journal of Public Administration Research and Theory*, 6(3): 365–81.

Frederickson, H. and Smith, K. (2003) *The Public Administration Theory Primer*, Boulder, CO: Westview Press.

Freiberg, A. (2010) *The Tools of Regulation*, Leichhardt, Australia: The Federation Press.

Fredendall, L. and Hill, E. (2001) *Basics of Supply Chain Management*, London: St Lucie Press.

French, J. and Raven, B. (1959) 'The Bases of Social Power', in D. Cartwright (ed.) *Studies in Social Power*, Ann Arbor, MI: Institute for Social Research.

Frey, B. (1992) 'Tertium Datur: Pricing, Regulating and Intrinsic Motivation', *Kyklos*, 45(2): 161–84.

Frey, B. (1997a) *Not Just for the Money: An Economic Theory of Personal Motivation*, Cheltenham: Edward Elgar.

Frey, B. (1997b) 'A Constitution for Knaves Crowds Out Civic Virtues', *The Economic Journal*, 107(July): 1043–53.

Frey, B. and Jegen, R. (2001) 'Motivation Crowding Theory', *Journal of Economic Surveys*, 15(5): 589–611.

Frey, B.S. and Meier, S. (2002) 'Pro-Social Behavior, Reciprocity or Both?' Working Paper Series (107), Institute for Empirical Economic Research, University of Zurich, accessed on 21 February 2011 at http://ideas.repec.org/p/zur/iewwpx/107.html.

Fuhr, M. and Bizer, K. (2007) 'REACh as a paradigm shift in Chemical Policy – Responsive Regulation and Behavioural Models', Journal of Cleaner Production, 15: 327–34.

Garoupa, N. (2000) 'Corporate Criminal Law and Organizational Incentives: A Managerial Perspective', Managerial and Decision Economics, 21(6): 243–52.

Garvey, J. (2010) 'Rewards for Recycling may Encourage People to Create Waste', Guardian, 8 June 2010, accessed on 18 September 2010 at http://www.guardian.co.uk/environment/cif-green/2010/jun/08/rewards-for-recycling-create-waste.

Gaskin, K. (2003) A Choice Blend: What Volunteers Want from Organisation and Management, London: Institute for Volunteering Research.

Gaster, L. and Squires, A. (2003) Providing Quality in the Public Sector: A Practical Approach to Improving Public Services, Maidenhead: Open University Press.

Gaston, K. and Alexander, J. (2001) 'Effective Organisation and Management of Public Sector Volunteer Workers: Police Special Constables', International Journal of Public Sector Management, 14(1): 59–74.

Gauri, V. (2001) Are Incentives Enough? Payment Mechanisms for Health Care Providers in Developing Countries, Washington: World Bank.

Gazley, B. and Brudney, J. (2005) 'Volunteer Involvement in Local Government after September 11: The Continuing Question of Capacity', Public Administration Review, 65(2): 131–42.

Geiger, S. (2007) 'The Strange Curvature of the Cucumber', The German Times, January, accessed on 16 October 2010 at http://www.german-times.com/index.php?option=com_content&task=view&id=94&Itemid=34.

Gerrard, M. (2001) 'Public-Private Partnerships', Finance & Development, 38(3), International Monetary Fund, accessed on 19 October 2010 at http://www.imf.org/external/pubs/ft/fandd/2001/09/index.htm.

GHK (2010) 'Study on Volunteering in the European Union' (National Report for the Netherlands), accessed on 2 February 2011 at http://ec.europa.eu/citizenship/eyv2011/doc/National%20report%20NL.pdf.

Gibbs, J.P. (1968) 'Crime, Punishment, and Deterrence', Social Science Quarterly, 49: 157–62.

Gintis, H., Bowles, S., Boyd, R. and Fehr, E. (2005) Moral Sentiments and Material Interests: the Foundations of Cooperation in Economic Life, Cambridge, MA: MIT Press.

Glanz, J. and Lehren, A. (2010) 'Use of Contractors Added to War's Chaos in Iraq', The New York Times, 23 October.

Glass, J. and Hastings, J. (1992) 'Stress and Burnout: Concerns for the Hospice Volunteer', Educational Gerontology, 18(7): 717–31.

Goldsmith, S. and Eggers, W. (2004) Governing by Network: The New Shape of the Public Sector, Washington, DC: Brookings Institution Press.

Goodman, P. (2010) 'Rule No. 1: Make Money by Avoiding Rules', The New York Times, 21 May.

Gore, A. (1993) From Red Tape to Results: Creating a Government that Works Better and Costs Less, New York: Times Books.

Gottschalk, P. (2005) 'Can Work Alter Welfare Recipients' Beliefs?' *Journal of Policy Analysis and Management*, 24(3): 485–98.

Gough, I. (1979) *The Political Economy of the Welfare State*, London: Macmillan.

Gouldner, A. (1960) 'The Norm of Reciprocity; A Preliminary Statement', *American Sociological Review*, 25: 161–78.

Grabosky, P. (1995a) 'Using Non-Governmental Resources to Foster Regulatory Compliance', *Governance*, 8(4): 527–50.

Grabosky, P. (1995b) 'Counterproductive Regulation', *International Journal of the Sociology of Law*, 23: 347–69.

Grabosky, P. and Braithwaite, J. (1986) *Of Manners Gentle: Enforcement Strategies of Australian Business Regulatory Agencies*, Melbourne: Oxford University Press.

Grant, A. (2007) 'Relational Job Design and the Motivation to Make a Prosocial Difference', *Academy of Management Review*, 32(2): 393–417.

Grant, A. (2008) 'Does Intrinsic Motivation Fuel the Prosocial Fire? Motivational Synergy in Predicting Persistence, Performance, and Productivity', *Journal of Applied Psychology*, 93(1): 48–58.

Grasmick, H. and Green, D. (1980) 'Legal Punishment, Social Disapproval and Internalization as Inhibitors of Illegal Behavior', *Journal of Criminal Law and Criminology*, 71: 325–35.

Gray, B. (1996) 'Cross-Sectoral Partners: Collaborative Alliances among Business, Government and Communities', in C. Huxham (ed.), *Creating Collaborative Advantage*, London: Sage.

Gray, W. and Scholz, J. (1991) 'Analyzing the Equity and Efficiency of OSHA Enforcement', *Law and Policy*, 13: 185–214.

Greve, C. (2008) *Contracting for Public Services*, London: Routledge.

Grogger, J., Karoly, L. and Klerman, J. (2002) *Consequences of Welfare Reform: A Research Synthesis*, Working Paper DRU-2676-DHHS, Santa Monica, CA: RAND Corporation.

Grönroos, C. (1990) *Service Management and Marketing: Managing the Moments of Truth in Service Competition*, Lexington, MA: Lexington Books.

Gunningham, N. (1991) 'Private Ordering: Self-Regulation and Futures Markets: A Comparative Study of Informal Social Control', *Law & Policy*, 13: 297–326.

Gunningham, N. and Grabosky, P. (1998) *Smart Regulation: Designing Environmental Policy*, Oxford: Oxford University Press.

Gunningham, N., Kagan, R. and Thornton, D. (2003) *Shades of Green: Business, Regulation and Environment*, Berkley, CA: Stanford University Press.

Hackman, J. and Lawler, E. (1971) 'Employee Reaction to Job Characteristics', *Journal of Applied Psychology*, 55: 259–86.

Halachmi, A. and van der Krogt, T. (2005) 'The Role of the Manager in Employee Motivation', *Handbook of Human Resources Management in Government*, San Francisco: Jossey-Bass.

Hall, R., Clark, J., Giordano, P., Johnson, P. and van Roekel, M. (1977) 'Patterns of Interorganizational Relationships', *Administrative Science Quarterly*, 22(3): 457–74.

Hallam, R. (1995) *First Fruits of Reform: Minister's Review of Local Government in 1995*, Melbourne: Victorian Ministry of Local Government.

Halligan, J. (2007) 'Reform Design and Performance in Australia and New Zealand', in T. Christensen and P. Laegreid (eds), *Transcending New Public Management*, Aldershot: Ashgate.

Hamper, B. (1991) *Rivethead: Tales from the Assembly Line*, New York: Warner Books.

Handler, J. (2004) *Social Citizenship and Workforce in the United States and Western Europe: The Paradox of Inclusion*, New York: Cambridge University Press.

Handler, J. and Hasenfeld, Y. (1997) *We the Poor People: Work, Poverty, and Welfare*, New Haven, CN: Yale University Press.

Handfield, R. and Nichols, E. (1999) *Introduction to Supply Chain Management*, Upper Saddle River, NJ: Prentice Hall.

Handy, F. and Srinivasan, N. (2004) 'Valuing Volunteers: An Economic Evaluation of the Net benefits of Hospital Volunteers', *Nonprofit and Voluntary Sector Quarterly*, 33(1): 28–54.

Hardin, R. (1993) 'The Street-Level Epistemology of Trust', *Politics and Society*, 21(4): 505–9.

Hardy, B., Turrell, A. and Wistow, G. (1992) *Innovations in Community Care Management*, Aldershot: Avebury.

Hardy, C., Phillips, N. and Lawrence, T. (2003) 'Resources, Knowledge and Influence: The Organizational Effects of Interorganizational Collaboration', *Journal of Management Studies*, 40(2): 321–47.

Harvey-Beavis, O. (2003) 'Performance-Based Rewards for Teachers: A Literature Review', 3rd Workshop of Participating Countries on OECD's Activity, Attracting, Developing and Retaining Effective Teachers 4–5 June, Athens, Greece.

Hasenfeld, Y. and Weaver, D. (1996) 'Enforcement, Compliance, and Disputes in Welfare-to-Work Programs', *Social Service Review*, 70: 235–56.

Hasluck, C. (2000) *The New Deal for the Long-Term Unemployed: A Summary of Progress*, London: Working Age Research and Analysis Publications, Employment Service.

Hawkins, K. (1984) *Environment and Enforcement: Regulation and the Social Definition of Pollution*. Oxford: Clarendon Press.

Head, B. and Alford, J. (2008) 'Wicked Problems: The Implications for Public Management', Panel on Public Management in Practice, IRSPM, 12th Annual Conference, 26–28 March, Brisbane.

Healy, K. (1994) 'Altruism as an Organizational Problem: The Case of Organ Procurement', *American Sociological Review*, 69(3): 387–404.

Hefetz, A. and Warner, M. (2004) 'Privatization and its Reverse: Explaining the Dynamics of the Government Contracting Process', *Journal of Public Administration Theory and Practice*, 14(2): 171–90.

Hellowell, M. and Pollock, A. (2007) 'New Development: The PFI: Scotland's Plan for Expansion and its Implications', *Public Money & Management*, 27(5): 351–4.

Hendry, J. (2002) 'The Principal's Other Problems: Honest Incompetence and the Specification of Objectives', *Academy of Management Review*, 27(1): 98–113.

Henrich, J. (2006) 'Costly Punishment across Human Societies', *Science*, 312: 176–77.

Herzberg, F. (1959) *The Motivation to Work*, New York: John Wiley & Sons.

Herzberg, F., Mausner, B. and Bloch Snyderman, B. (1993) *The Motivation to Work*, New Brunswick, NJ: Transaction Publishers.

Hewison, R. (2006) *Not a Sideshow: Leadership and Cultural Values*, London: DEMOS.

Himmelmann, A. (1996) 'On the Theory and Practice of Transformational Collaboration: From Social Service to Social Justice', in C. Huxham (ed.), *Creating Collaborative Advantage*, London: Sage.

Hodge, G. (1996) *Contracting out Government Services: A Review of International Evidence*, Melbourne: Graduate School of Government, Monash University.

Hodge, G. (2000) *Privatization: An International Review of Performance*, Boulder, CO: Westview Press.

Hodge, G. (2005) 'Public-Private Partnerships: The Australasian Experience', in G. Hodge and C. Greve (eds), *The Challenge of Public-Private Partnerships: Learning from International Experience*, Cheltenham: Edward Elgar.

Hodge, G. and Greve, C. (eds) (2005) *The Challenge of Public-Private Partnerships: Learning from International Experience*, Cheltenham: Edward Elgar.

Hodge, G. and Greve, C. (2008) 'The PPP Phenomenon: Performance and Governance Insights', in J. O'Flynn and J. Wanna (eds), *Collaborative Governance: A New Era of Public Policy in Australia?* Canberra: ANU E Press.

Hodgkinson, V.A. and Weitzman, M.S. (1988) *Giving and Volunteering in the United States*, Washington, DC: Independent Sector.

Hodgkinson, V., Weitzman, M., Abrahams, J., Crutchfield, E. and Stevenson, D. (1996) *Nonprofit Almanac: Dimensions of the Independent Sector*, San Francisco: Jossey-Bass.

Hoggett, P., Mayo, M. and Miller, C. (2006) 'Private Passion, the Public Good and Public Service Reform', *Social Policy & Administration*, 40(7): 758–73.

Holmstrom, B. and Milgrom, P. (1991) 'Multitask Principal-Agent Analyses: Incentive Contracts, Asset Ownership, and Job Design', *Journal of Law, Economics, & Organization*, 7: 24–52.

Horne, M. and Shirley, T. (2009) *Co-production in Public Services: A New Partnership with Citizens*, London: Cabinet Office.

Hood, C. (1986) *Administrative Analysis: An Introduction to Rules, Enforcement, and Organizations*, Brighton: Wheatsheaf.

Hood, C. (2005) 'The Idea of Joined-Up Government: A Historical Perspective', in V. Bogdanor (ed.), *Joined-Up Government*, Oxford: Oxford University Press.

Hosmer, L. (1995) 'Trust: The Connecting Link between Organizational Theory and Philosophical Ethics', *Academy of Management Review*, 20(2): 379–403.

Houston, D. (2000) 'Public-Service Motivation; A Multivariate Test', *Journal of Public Administration Research and Theory*, 10: 713–27.

Hudson, B. (2004) 'Trust: Towards Conceptual Clarification', *Australian Journal of Political Science*, 39(1): 75–87.

Hughes, O. (2003) *Public Management and Administration; An Introduction*, 3rd edn, Basingstoke: Palgrave Macmillan.

Husock, H. and Scott, E. (1999) *Centrelink: A Service Delivery Agency in Australia*, KSG Case Study 1524.0, Cambridge, MA: Kennedy School of Government.

Hustinx, L. (2010) 'I Quit, Therefore I Am? Volunteer Turnover and the Politics of Self-Actualization', *Nonprofit and Voluntary Sector Quarterly*, 39(2): 236–55.

Hutter, B. (1997) *Compliance: Regulation and Environment*, Oxford: Oxford University Press.

Huxham, C. (ed.) (1996) *Creating Collaborative Advantage*, London: Sage.

Huxham, C. and Vangen, S. (2000) 'Leadership in the Shaping and Implementation of Collaboration Agendas', *Academy of Management Journal*, 43(6): 1159–75.

Huxham, C. and Vangen, S. (2004) 'Doing Things Collaboratively: Realizing the Advantage or Succumbing to Inertia?' *Organizational Dynamics*, 33(2): 190–201.

Huxham, C. and Vangen, S. (2005) *Managing to Collaborate: The Theory and Practice of Collaborative Advantage*, London: Routledge.

IAP2 (International Association for Public Participation) (2007) *IAP2 Spectrum of Public Participation*, accessed on 20 October 2010 at http://www.iap2.org/associations/4748/files/IAP2%20Spectrum_vertical.pdf.

Indigenous Studies Program (2005) Mulan 'Economic Strength and Healthy Kids', *Shared Responsibility Agreement, Agreements, Treaties and Negotiated Settlements Project*, University of Melbourne, Australia, accessed on 2 November 2010 at http://www.atns.net.au/agreement_print.asp?EntityID=3012.

Insinga, R. and Werle, M. (2000) 'Linking Outsourcing to Business Strategy', *Academy of Management Executive*, 14(4): 58–70.

Izuma, K., Saito, D. and Sadato, N. (2010) 'Processing of the Incentive for Social Approval in the Ventral Striatum during Charitable Donation', *Journal of Cognitive Neuroscience*, 22(4): 621–31.

Jackson, A. (2009) 'Mess Hall Limits Leave Bad Taste for CFA Volunteers', *The Age*, 18 November.

Jahiel, A. (1998) 'The Organization of Environmental Protection in China', *The China Quarterly*, 156: 757–87.

Jameson, A. (2010) 'PFI-Funded Hospitals Outshine Peers in Study of Cleanliness', *The Times*, 17 May.

Jamison, I. (2003) 'Turnover and Retention among Volunteers in Human Service Agencies', *Review of Public Personnel Administration*, 23(2): 114–32.

Janoski, T., Musick, M. and Wilson, J. (1998) 'Being Volunteered? The Impact of Social Participation and Pro-Social Attitudes on Volunteering', *Sociological Forum*, 13 (3): 495–519.

Janssen, M. and Mendyss-Kamphorst, E. (2004) 'The Price of a Price: On the Crowding Out and In of Social Norms', *Journal of Economics, Behavior and Organization*, 55(3): 377–95.

Jenkins, K., Caines, K. and Jackson, A. (1988) *Improving Management in Government: The Next Steps*, Efficiency Unit Report to the Prime Minister, London: HMSO.

Jensen, M. and Meckling, W. (1976) 'Theory of the Firm: Managerial Behaviour, Agency Costs and Ownership Structure', *Journal of Financial Economics*, 3: 305–60.

Jochelson, K. (2007) *Paying the Patient: Improving Health Using Financial Incentives*, London: King's Fund.

Johnson (1775) in Agassi, J. (1974) 'The Last Refuge of the Scoundrel', *Philosophia*, 4(2–3): 315–17.

Jolley, G. (2008) 'Contracting Regimes and Third-Party Governance: A Theoretical Construct for Exploring the Importance of Public Service Motivation of Private Sector Contractors', *International Public Management Review*, 9(2): 1–54.

Joshi, A. and Moore, M. (2004) 'Institutionalised Co-production: Unorthodox Public Service Delivery in Challenging Environments', *Journal of Development Studies*, 40(4): 31–49.

Jupp, V. and Younger, M. (2004) 'A Value Model for the Public Sector', *Accenture Outlook*, 1.

Kagan, R. (1984) 'On Regulatory Inspectorates and Police', in K. Hawkins and J. Thomas (eds), *Enforcing Regulation*, Boston, MA: Kluwer-Nijhoff Publishing.

Kagan, R. and Scholz, J. (1984) 'The "Criminology of the Corporation" and Regulatory Enforcement Strategies', in K. Hawkins and J. Thomas (eds), *Enforcing Regulation*, Boston, MA: Kluwer-Nijhoff Publishing.

Kahneman, D. and Tversky, A. (1979) 'Prospect Theory: An Analysis of Decisions under Risk', *Econometrica*, 47: 313–27.

Kavanagh, I. and Parker, D. (1999) 'Managing the Contract: A Transaction Cost Analysis of Externalisation', *Local Government Studies*, 26(4): 1–22.

Kelman, H. (1981) 'Reflections on the History and Status of Peace Research', *Conflict Management and Peace Science*, 5(2): 95–110.

Kennedy, D. and Sparrow, M. (1991) *On the Kindness of Strangers: The Origins and Early Days of FINCEN*, KSG Case C-16-91-1000.0, Cambridge, MA: Harvard University Press.

Kerr, S. (1975) 'On the Folly of Rewarding A, While Hoping for B', *Academy of Management Journal*, 18(4): 769–83.

Kettl, D. (1993) *Sharing Power: Public Governance and Private Markets*, Washington, DC: The Brookings Institution.

Kettl, D. (2010) 'Governance, Contract Management and Public Management', in *The New Public Governance*, Oxon: Routledge, pp. 239–54.

Kiers, E. Rousseau, R., West, S., Denison, R. (2003) 'Host Sanctions and the Legume-Rhizobium Mutualism', *Nature*, 425: 78–81.

Kim, J., Kim, J. and Choi, S. (2011) *Public-Private Partnership Infrastructure Projects: Case Studies from the Republic of Korea, Volume 2: Cases of Build-Transfer-Operate Projects for Ports and Build-Transfer-Lease Projects for Education Facilities*, Manila, Philippines: Asian Development Bank.

Kinsey, K. (1992) 'Deterrence and Alienation Effects of IRS Enforcement: An Analysis of Survey Data' in J. Slemrod (ed.), *Why People Pay Taxes*, Ann Arbor, MI: University of Michigan Press.

Kirkpatrick, I. (1999) 'The Worst of Both Worlds?: Public Services without Markets or Bureaucracy', *Public Money & Management*, October–December: 7–14.

Klepper, S. and Nagin, D. (1989) 'Tax Compliance and Perceptions of the Risks of Detection and Criminal Prosecution', *Law & Society Review*, 23: 209–40.

Klerman, J., Zellman, G., Chun, T., Humphrey, N., Reardon, E., Farley, D., Ebener, P. and Steinberg, P. (2000) *Welfare Reform in California: State and County Implementation of CalWORKs in the Second Year*, Los Angeles: RAND Corporation.

Klijn, E. and Koppenjan, J. (2000) 'Public Management and Policy Networks: Foundations of a Network Approach to Governance', *Public Management Review*, 2(2): 135–58.

Klijn, E., Koppenjan, J. and Termeer, K. (1995) 'Managing Networks in the Public Sector: A Theoretical Study of Management Strategies in Policy Networks', *Public Administration*, 73(3): 437–54.

Klijn, E.H. and Teisman, G. (2000) 'Governing-Public-Private Partnerships: Analysing and Managing the Process and Institutional Characteristics of Public-Private Partnerships', in S. Osborne (ed.), *Public-Private Partnerships: Theory and Practice in International Perspective*, London: Routledge.

Kohn, A. (1993) 'Why Incentive Plans Cannot Work', *Harvard Business Review*, September–October: 54–63.

Korb, L. and Duggan, S. (2007) 'An All-Volunteer Army? Recruitment and its Problems,' *PS: Political Science and Politics*, 40(July): 467–71.

Korczynski, M. (2000) 'The Political Economy of Trust', *Journal of Management Studies*, 37(1): 1–21.

Korpi, W. (1974) 'Conflict and the Balance of Power', *Acta Sociologica*, 17: 99–114.

Krepenevich, A. (2005) 'How to Win in Iraq', *Foreign Affairs*, September/October: 87–104.

Kreps, D. (1997) 'Intrinsic Motivation and Extrinsic Incentives', *The American Economic Review*, 87(2): 359–64.

Kristensen, O. (1987) 'Privatization', in J. Kooiman and K. Eliassen (eds), *Managing Public Organizations: Lessons from Contemporary European Experience*, London: Sage.

Lambright, K., Mischen, P. and Laramee, C. (2010) 'Building Trust in Public and Nonprofit Networks: Personal, Dyadic and Third-Party Influences', *American Review of Public Administration*, 40(1): 64–82.

Lane, J. (2000) *New Public Management*, London: Routledge.

Latham, G. and Pinder, C. (2005) 'Work Motivation Theory and Research at the Dawn of the Twenty-First Century', *Annual Review of Psychology*, 56: 485–516.

Lave, J. and Frank, R. (1990) 'Effect of the Structure of Hospital Payments on Hospital Costs', *Journal of Health Politics, Policy and Law*, 20(2): 327–47.

Lax, D. and Sebenius, J. (1986) *The Manager as Negotiator: Bargaining for Co-operation and Competitive Gain*, New York: Free Press.

Le Grand, J. (2003) *Motivation, Agency, and Public Policy: Of Knights & Knaves, Pawns & Queens*, Oxford: Oxford University Press.

Leadership Centre (nd) *Living Leadership*, London: Leadership Centre, accessed on 18 February 2011 at http://www.localleadership.gov.uk/current/publications/.

Leadership Development Commission (2004) *An Emerging Strategy for Leadership Development in Local Government*, London: LDC.

LEAP (1993) *National Curriculum Project for Landcare and Environment Action Program*, Frankston: ACTRAC.

Lee, E. (2010) *The New Public Management Reform of Social Service Nonprofit Organizations in Hong Kong: Nonprofit Regime Change and the Changing Politics of Welfare*, paper presented to the 14th Annual Conference of the International Research Society for Public Management, 7–9 April, Berne, Switzerland.

Leisink, P. and Steijn, B. (2008) 'Recruitment, Attraction, and Selection', in J. Perry and A. Hondeghem (eds), *Motivation in Public Management: The Call of Public Service*, Oxford: Oxford University Press, pp. 118–35.

Leone, R. (1986) *Who Profits: Winners, Losers, and Government Regulation*, New York: Basic Books.

Lepper, M. and Greene, D. (1978) *The Hidden Costs of Reward*, Hillsdale, NJ: Erlbaum.

Levi, M. (1988) *Of Rule and Revenue*, Berkeley: University of California Press.

Levine, C. (1984) 'Citizenship and Service Delivery: The Promise of Co-production', *Public Administration Review*, 44(2): 178–87.

Levitt, S. and List, J. (2008) 'Homo Economicus Evolves', *Science*, 319(5865): 909–10.

Levitt, S. and List, J. (2009) 'Field Experiments in Economics: the Past, the Present, and the Future', *European Economic Review*, 53: 1–18.

Lewicki, R. and Bunker, B. (1995) 'Developing and Maintaining Trust in Work Relationships', in R. Kramer and T. Tyler (eds), *Trust in Organizations: Frontiers of Theory and Research*, Thousand Oaks, CA: Sage Publications.

Lewis, R. and Booms, B. (1983) 'The Marketing Aspects of Service Quality', in L. Berry, G. Shostack and G. Upah (eds), *Emerging Perspectives on Services Marketing*, Chicago: American Marketing Association.

Linder, S. (1999) 'Coming to Terms with the Public-Private Partnership: A Grammar of Multiple Meanings', *American Behavioural Scientist*, 43(1): 35–51.

Lindert, P. (2004) *Growing Public: Social Spending and Economic Growth Since the Eighteenth Century, Vol. 1: The Story*, Cambridge: Cambridge University Press.

Lindhorst, T. and Mancoske, R. (1993) 'Structuring Volunteer Supports in a Buddy Program for People with AIDS', *Journal of Sociology and Social Welfare*, 20.1: 175–88.

Ling, T. (2002) 'Delivering Joined-Up Government in the UK: Dimensions, Issues and Problems', *Public Administration*, 80(4): 615–42.

Lodge, M., Wegrich, K. and McElroy, G. (2010) 'Dodgy Kebabs Everywhere? Variety of Worldviews and Regulatory Change', *Public Administration*, 88(1): 247–66.

Long, S. and Swingen, J. (1991) 'Taxpayer Compliance: Setting New Agendas for Research', *Law and Society Review*, 25(3): 637–83.

Lorange, P., Roos, J. and Bronn, P. (1992) 'Building Successful Strategic Alliances', *Long Range Planning*, 25(6): 10–17.

Lowndes, V. and Skelcher, C. (1998) 'The Dynamics of Multi-Organisational Partnerships: An Analysis of Changing Modes of Governance', *Public Administration*, 76(2): 313–34.

Luhmann, N. (1979) *Trust and Power*, Chichester: Wiley.

Lundvall, B. (1993) 'Explaining Interfirm Co-operation and Innovation: Limits of the Transaction-Cost Approach', in G. Grabher (ed.), *The Embedded Firm: On the Socioeconomics of Industrial Networks*, London: Routledge.

Lyons, B. and Mehta, J. (1997) 'Private Sector Business Contracts: The Text Between the Lines', in S. Deakin and J. Michie (eds), *Contracts, Co-operation and Competition: Studies in Economics, Management and Law*, Oxford: Oxford University Press.

Macneil, I. (1978) 'Contracts: Adjustment of Long-Term Economic Relations Under Classical, Neoclassical, and Relational Contract Law', *Northwestern University Law Review*, 72(6): 854–905.

Madrick, J. (2009) *The Case for Big Government*, Princeton University Press: Princeton.

Makkai, T. and Braithwaite, J. (1994) 'The Dialectics of Corporate Deterrence', *Journal of Research in Crime and Delinquency*, 31: 347–73.

Makris, I. (2009) 'A Systematic Inventory of Motives for Becoming an Orchestra Conductor: A Preliminary Study', *Psychology of Music*, 37(4): 443–58.

Malmstrom, T. (2009) *2008 Saline Wetlands Conservation Partnership Progress Report*, Lincoln, NE: Saline Wetlands Conservation Partnership.

Mandell, M. and Steelman, T. (2003) 'Understanding What Can be Accomplished Through Interorganizational Innovations', *Public Management Review*, 5(2): 197–224.

Manpower Demonstration Research Corporation (MDRC) (2002) *What Works in Welfare Reform - The Future of Welfare Reform*, New York: MDRC.

Margolis, H. (1982) *Selfishness, Altruism and Rationality*, Cambridge: Cambridge University Press.

Mariotti, J. (1996) *The Power of Partnerships: The Next Step beyond TQM, Reengineering and Lean Production*, Cambridge: Blackwell Business.

Mascini, P. and Van Wijk, E. (2009) 'Responsive Regulation at the Dutch Food and Consumer Product Safety Authority: An Empirical Assessment of Assumptions Underlying the Theory', *Regulation and Governance*, 3(1): 27–47.

Maslow, A. (1954) *Motivation and Personality*, New York: Harper.

May, E. (1997) 'The Evolving Scope of Government', in J. Nye, P. Zelikow and D. King (eds), *Why People Don't Trust Government*, Cambridge, MA: Harvard University Press.

May, P. (2002) 'Social Regulation', in L. Salamon (ed.) *The Tools of Government; A Guide to the New Governance*, New York: Oxford University Press.

May, P. and Winter, S. (1999) 'Regulatory Enforcement and Compliance: Examining Danish Agro-Environmental Policy', *Journal of Policy Analysis and Management*, 18(4): 625–51.

McAfee, R. and McMillan, J. (1986) 'Bidding for Contracts: A Principal-Agent Analysis', *Rand Journal of Economics*, 17(3): 326–38.

McCarthy, J. (2000) *Wild Logging: The Rise and Fall of Logging Networks and Biodiversity Conservation Projects on Sumatra's Rainforest Frontier*, Bogor, Indonesia: Center for International Forestry Research.

McKie, J. (1974) *Social Responsibility in the Business Predicament*. Washington, DC: Brookings.

McKinley, J. (2011) 'Police Departments Turn to Volunteers', *The New York Times*, 1 March.

Mead, L. (1986) *Beyond Entitlement: The Social Obligations of Citizenship*, New York: Free Press.

Meals Victoria (2008) *Provider Survey*, Victoria: Meals Victoria Incorporated.

Megginson, W. and Netter, J. (2003) 'History and Methods of Privatization', in D. Parker and D. Saal (eds), *International Handbook on Privatization*, Cheltenham: Edward Elgar.

Melhuish, E., Belsky, J. and Barnes, J. (2010) *Sure Start and its Evaluation in England, Institute for the Study of Children, Families and Social Issues*, Birkbeck: University of London, accessed on 15 January 2011 at http://www.child-encyclopedia.com/documents/Melhuish-Belsky-BarnesANGxp.pdf.

Milgrom, P. and Roberts, J. (1992) *Economics, Organization and Management*, London: Prentice-Hall.

Millar, J. (2000) *Keeping Track of Welfare Reform: The New Deal Programmes*. York: The Joseph Rowntree Foundation.

Millward, R. (1986) 'The Comparative Performance of Public and Private Ownership', in J. Kay, C. Mayer and D. Thompson (eds), *Privatization and Regulation*, Oxford: Clarendon Press.

Minahan, S. and Inglis, L. (2008) 'Organisational Decline and Renewal in an Australian Voluntary Association', Working Paper 2/08, Department of Management Working Paper Series, Faculty of Business and Economics, Monash University.

Mintzberg, H. (1979) *The Structuring of Organizations*, Englewood Cliffs, NJ: Prentice-Hall.

Moe, T. (1984) 'The New Economics of Organization', *American Journal of Political Science*, 28: 739–75.

Moore, M. (1995) *Creating Public Value: Strategic Management in Government*, Cambridge, MA: Harvard University Press.

Moore, M. (2000) 'Managing for Value: Organizational Strategy in For-Profits, Nonprofit, and Governmental Organizations', *Nonprofit and Voluntary Sector Quarterly*, 29(1): 183–208.

Morley, E. (1989) 'Patterns in the Use of Alternative Service Delivery Approaches', in *Municipal Year Book, 1989*, Washington, DC: International City Management Association.

Morrison, E. and Robinson, S. (1997) 'When Employees Feel Betrayed: A Model of How Psychological Contract Violation Develops', *Academy of Management Review*, 22(1): 226–56.

Moyle, P. (ed.) (1994) *Private Prisons and Police*, Sydney: Pluto Press.

Mulgan, G. (2005) 'Joined-Up Government: Past, Present and Future', in V. Bogdanor (ed.), *Joined-Up Government*, Oxford: Oxford University Press.

Mulgan, R. (1997) 'Contracting Out and Accountability', *Australian Journal of Public Administration*, 56(4): 106–16.

Mulgan, R. (2000a) ' "Accountability": An Ever-Expanding Concept?' *Public Administration*, 78: 555–73.

Mulgan, R. (2000b) 'Comparing Accountability in the Public and Private Sectors', *Australian Journal of Public Administration*, 59(1): 87–97.

National Audit Office (2001) *Joining Up to Improve Public Services*, Report by the Comptroller and Auditor General, HC 383 Session 2001–2002, London.

National Council of Nonprofits (2010) *Costs, Complexification, and Crisis: Government's Human Services Contracting 'System' Hurts Everyone*, Washington.

National Head Start Association (NHSA) (2011) 'Basic Head Start Facts', accessed 11 October 2011 at http://www.nhsa.org/files/static_page_files/48BADE30-1D09-3519-ADED347C39FA16A4/Basic_Head_Start_Facts_rev02212011.pdf.

Ng, Irene C.L. and Tseng, L.M. (2008) 'Learning to be Sociable: The Evolution of Homo Economicus', *American Journal of Economics and Sociology*, 67(2): 265–86.

Nielsen, V. and Parker, C. (2009) 'Testing Responsive Regulation in Regulatory Enforcement', *Regulation & Governance*, 3(4): 376–99.

Niskanen, W. (1971) *Bureaucracy and Representative Government*, Chicago: Rand McNally.

Noble, G. and Jones, R. (2006) 'The Role of Boundary-Spanning Managers in the Establishment of Public-Private Partnerships', *Public Administration*, 84(4): 891–917.

NSW Commission for Children and Young People and Commission for Children and Young People QLD (2004) *A Head Start for Australia: An Early Years Framework*. accessed on 14 August 2010 at http://www.kids.nsw.gov.au/uploads/documents/headstart_full.pdf.

O'Faircheallaigh, C., Wanna, J. and Weller, P. (1999) *Public Sector Management in Australia: New Challenges, New Directions*, Melbourne: MacMillan.

O'Flynn, J. (1999) *Controlling Common Law Liability Costs in the Transport Accident Commission (A)*, Melbourne: Melbourne Business School.

O'Flynn, J. (2008) 'Elusive Appeal or Aspirational Ideal?: The Rhetoric and the Reality of the "Collaborative Turn" in Public Policy', in J. O'Flynn and J. Wanna (eds), *Collaborative Governance: A New Era of Public Policy in Australia?*, Canberra: ANU E-Press.

O'Flynn, J. and Alford, J. (2008) 'The Separation/Specification Dilemma in Contracting: The Local Government Experience in Victoria', *Public Administration*, 86(1): 205–24.

O'Flynn, J., Buick, F., Blackman, D. and Halligan, J. (2011) 'You Win Some, You Lose Some: Experiments with Joined-Up Government', *International Journal of Public Administration*, 34(4): 244–54.

O'Neill, J and Hill, M. (2001) 'Gaining Ground? Measuring the Impact of Welfare Reform on Welfare and Work', Civic Report No. 17, New York: Center for Civic Innovation at the Manhattan Institute.

OECD (1997) *Contracting out Government Services: Best Practice Guidelines and Case Studies*, Public Management Occasional Papers No. 20, Paris: OECD.

OECD (2001) *Government of the Future*, OECD Public Management Policy Brief, PUMA Policy Brief No. 9, Paris: OECD.

OECD (2005) *Modernising Government: The Way Forward*, Paris: OECD.

OECD (2010) *Contracting Out Government Functions and Services in Post-Conflict and Fragile Situations,* Paris: OECD.

OECD (2011) *Innovation in Public Service Delivery: Context, Solutions and Challenges*, Paris: OECD.

Office of the Inspector of Custodial Services (2004) 'Inspection of the Interim Arrangement at the Supreme Court Following the Escape of Nine Prisoners from the Custody Area on 10th June 2004', Report No. 25, Government of Western Australia, Perth, Australia.

Ogawa, R. and Bossert, S. (1995) 'Leadership as an Organizational Quality', *Educational Administration Quarterly*, 31(2): 224–43.

Oldham, G. and Cummings, A. (1996) 'Employee Creativity: Personal and Contextual Factors at Work', *Academy of Management Journal*, 39(3): 607–34.

Oliver, C. (1990) 'Determinants of Interorganizational Relationships: Integration and Future Directions', *Academy of Management Review*, 15(2): 241–65.

Olson, M. (1965) *The Logic of Collective Action: Public Goods and the Theory of Groups*, Cambridge, MA: Harvard University Press.

Osborne, D. and Gaebler, T. (1992) *Reinventing Government: How the Entrepreneurial Spirit is Transforming the Public Sector*, New York: Addison-Wesley Publishing Company.

Osborne, S. and Murray, V. (2000) 'Understanding the Process of Public-Private partnerships', in S. Osborne (ed.), *Public-Private Partnerships: Theory and Practice in International Perspective*, Oxford: Routledge.

Ostrom, E. and Walker, J. (2003) *Trust and Reciprocity*, New York: Russell Sage Foundation.

Ostrom, V. and Ostrom, E. (1971) 'Public Choice: A Different Approach to the Study of Public Administration', *Public Administration Review*, 31(2): 203–16.

Oullier, O. and Sauneron, S. (2010) *Improving Public Health Prevention with Behavioural, Cognitive and Neuroscience*, Paris: Centre for Strategic Analysis.

Padula, M. (2004) *The Australia Competition and Consumer Commission and Video Ezy*, Melbourne: The Australia and New Zealand School of Government Case Library.

Padula, M. (2008) *Regulation Reform in the Australian Road Transport Industry (A)*, Melbourne: The Australia and New Zealand School of Government, ANZSOG case library, 2008/71.1.

Parasuraman, A., Zeithaml, V. and Berry, L. (1985) 'A Conceptual Model of Service Quality and its Implications for Future Research', *Journal of Marketing*, 49(4), 41–50.

Parker, C. (2000) 'Reinventing Regulation within the Corporation: Compliance-Oriented Regulatory Innovation', *Administration & Society*, 32(5): 529–65.

Parker, R. and Bradley, S. (2000) 'Organisational Culture in the Public Sector: Evidence from Six Organisations', *International Journal of Public Sector Management*, 13(2): 125–41.

Parsons, W. (1995) *Public Policy*, Lyme: Edward Elgar.

Parston, G. and Timmins, N. (1998) *Joined-up Management*, London: Public Management Foundation.

Paternoster, R. and Simpson, S. (1996) 'Sanction Threats and Appeals to Morality: Testing a Rational Choice Model of Corporate Crime', *Law & Society*, 30(3): 549–84.

Pavetti, L., Derr, M., Kauff, J. and Kirby, G. (2005) 'Universal Engagement in Practice: Lessons from the Implementation of the Pathways Case Management System', *Lessons from the Field – Information for Evaluators, Program Leaders, and Policymakers*, Mathematica Policy Research, Amend Inc., accessed on 8 September 2010 at http://www.pmatch.org/pathways.pdf.

Peacock, A.E. (1984) 'The Successful Prosecution of the Factory Acts', *Economic History Review*, 37: 197–210.

Perry, J. (1996) 'Measuring Public Service Motivation', *Journal of Public Administration Research and Theory*, 6: 5–24.

Perry, J.L. (2000) Bringing Society In: Toward a Theory of Public-Service Motivation, *Journal of Public Administration Research and Theory*, 10(2): 471–88.

Perry, J.L. and Hondeghem, A. (2008) 'Building Theory and Empirical Evidence about Public Service Motivation', *International Public Management Journal*, 11(1): 3–12.

Perry, J.L., Hondeghem, A. and Wise, L.R. (2010) 'Revisiting the Motivational Bases of Public Service: Twenty Years of Research and an Agenda for the Future', *Public Administration Review*, 70(5): 681–90.

Perry, J. and Kraemer, K. (eds) (1983) *Public Management: Public and Private Perspectives*, Palo Alto, CA: Mayfield Publishing.

Perry, J.L. and Porter, L.W. (1982) 'Factors Affecting the Context for Motivation in Public Organizations', *The Academy of Management Review*, 7(1): 89–98.

Perry, J. and Rainey, H. (1988) 'The Public-Private Distinction in Organization Theory: A Critique and Research Strategy', *Academy of Management Review*, 13(2): 182–201.

Perry, J. and Wise, L. (1990) 'The Motivational Bases of Public Service', *Public Administration Review*, 50: 367–73.

Peters, T. and Waterman, R. (1982) *In Search of Excellence: Lessons from America's Best-Run Companies*, New York: Harper & Row.

Petty, R. and Cacioppo, J. (1981) *Attitudes and Persuasion: Classic and Contemporary Approaches*, Dubuque, IA, W.C. Brown.

Phillips, R. and Rowley, S. (2011) *Bringing it Home: Using Behavioural Insights to Make Green Living Policy Work*, London: Green Alliance.

Phillips, Y. (2010) 'Aboriginal Ward Family get $3.2m for Prison Van Death', *PerthNow*, 29 July.

Pickles, E. (2010) 'We'll boost recycling with a gentle nudge', in *Guardian*, 8 June 2010, accessed on 13 July 2011 at http://www.guardian.co.uk/commentisfree/cif-green/2010/jun/08/recycling-reward-scheme.

Piliavin, J. and Charg, H. (1990) 'Altruism: A Review of Recent Theory and Research', *Annual Review of Sociology*, 16: 27–65.

Piliavin, J.A. (2001) 'Sociology of Altruism and Prosocial Behavior', in N. Smelser and P. Baltes (eds), *International Encyclopaedia of the Social and Behavioral*, pp. 411–15.

Podolny, J. and Page, K. (1998) 'Network Forms of Organization', *Annual Review of Sociology*, 24(1): 57–76.

Pollitt, C. (2003) 'Joined-Up Government: A Survey', *Political Studies Review*, 1: 34–49.

Pollitt, C. (2007) 'New Labour's Re-disorganization: Hyper-modernism and the Costs of Reform – A Cautionary Tale', *Public Management Review*, 9(4): 529–43.

Pollock, A., Price, D. and Liebe, M. (2011) 'Private Finance Initiatives during NHS Austerity', *British Medical Journal*, 342, 19 February: 417–19.

Pollock, A., Price, D. and Player, S. (2007) 'An Examination of the UK Treasury's Evidence Base for Cost and Time Overrun Data in UK Value-for-Money Policy and Appraisal', *Public Money & Management*, 27(2): 127–34.

Porter, M. (1985) *Competitive Advantage: Creating and Sustaining Superior Performance*, New York: Free Press.

Powell, W., Koput, K. and Smith-Doerr, L. (1996) 'Interorganizational Collaboration and the Locus of Innovation: Networks of Learning in Biotechnology', *Administrative Science Quarterly*, 41: 116–45.

Prager, J. (1994) 'Contracting Out Government Services: Lessons from the Private Sector', *Public Administration Review*, 54(2): 176–84.

Prahalad, C. and Hamel, G. (1990) 'The Core Competence of the Corporation', *Harvard Business Review*, May–June: 79–91.

Pressman, J. and Wildavsky, A. (1973) *Implementation: How Great Expectations in Washington are Dashed in Oakland; Or Why It's Amazing That Federal Programs Work At All*, Berkeley: University of California Press.

PriceWaterhouseCoopers (2006) *Trendsetter Barometer*, released 10 January.

Putnam, R. (1995) 'Bowling Alone: America's Declining Social Capital', *Journal of Democracy*, 6(1): 65–78.

Quiggin, J. (1994) 'The Fiscal Gains from Contracting Out: Transfers or Efficiency Improvements', *Australian Economic Review*, 3rd quarter: 97–102.

Quinn, J. and Hilmer, F. (1994) 'Strategic Outsourcing', *Sloan Management Review*, summer: 43–55.

Rainey, H. (1982) 'Reward Preference Among Public and Private Managers: In Search of the Service Ethics', *American Review of Public Administration*, 16(4): 288–302.

Rainey, H. (2003) *Understanding and Managing Public Organizations*, 3rd edn, San Francisco: Jossey-Bass.

Rainey, H., Backoff, R. and Levine, C. (1976) 'Comparing Public and Private Organizations', *Public Administration Review*, 36(2): 233–44.

Ramarajan, L., Bezrukova, K., Jehn, K.E. and Euwema, M. (2011) 'From the Outside In: The Negative Spillover Effects of Boundary Spanners' Relations with Members of Other Organizations' relations with members of other organizations', *Journal of Organizational Behavior*, 32(6): 886–905.

Ranade, W. and Hudson, B. (2003) 'Conceptual Issues in Inter-Agency Collaboration', *Local Government Studies*, 29(3): 32–50.

Raven, B. (1992) 'A Power/Interaction Model of Interpersonal Influence: French and Raven Thirty Years Later', *Journal of Social Behavior and Personality*, 7(2): 217–44.

Rawls, J. (1972) *A Theory of Justice*, Oxford: Oxford University Press.

Rawsthorne, M. and Christian, F. (2005) 'Government/Community Sector Compacts: Real Engagement?', in D. Gardiner and K. Scott (eds), *Proceedings of International Conference on Engaging Communities*, Brisbane (14–17 August): pp. 1–20.

Reeson, A.F. and Tisdell, J.G. (2008) 'Institutions, Motivations and Public Goods: An Experimental Test of Motivational Crowding', *Journal of Economic Behavior & Organization* 68(1): 273–81.

Rege, M. and Telle, K. (2004) 'The Impact of Social Approval and Framing on Cooperation in Public Good Situations', *Journal of Public Economics*, 88 (7–8): 1625–44.

Reiss A.J. (1984) 'Consequences of Compliance and Deterrence Models of Law Enforcement for the Exercise of Police Discretion', *Law and Contemporary Problems*, 47: 91–102.

Rhodes, R. (1997) 'It's the Mix that Matters: From Marketisation to Diplomacy', *Australian Journal of Public Administration*, 56: 40–53.

Riccio, J., Friedlander, D., Freedman, S., Farrell, M., Fellerath, V., Fox, S. and Lehman, D. (1994) 'GAIN: Benefits, Costs, and Three-Year Impacts of a Welfare-to-Work Program', New York: Manpower Demonstration Research Corporation.

Rijksoverheid (2007) 'Samen' werken, samen leven 2007–2011 [To live and work together 2007–2011], Dutch national government, accessed on 10 February 2011 at http://www.rijksoverheid.nl/ regering/het-kabinet/regeerakkoord-oude/ samen-werken-samen-leven.

Ring, P. and Van de Ven, A. (1992) 'Structuring Co-operative Relationships between Organizations', *Strategic Management Journal*, 13: 483–98.

Ring, P. and Van de Ven, A. (1994) 'Developmental Processes of Co-operative Interorganizational Relationships', *Academy of Management Review*, 19(1): 90–118.

Riordan, M.H. and Williamson, O.E. (1985) 'Asset Specificity and Economic Organization', *International Journal of Industrial Organization*, 3: 365–78.

Robens, A. (1972) *Safety and Health at Work: Report of the Committee, 1970–72*, London: HMSO.

Roberts, N.C. (2000) 'Wicked Problems and Network Approaches to Resolution', *International Public Management Review*, 1(1): 1–19.

Rochester, C., Hutchison, R., Harris, M. and Keely, L. (2002) 'A Review of the Home Office Older Volunteers Initiative', Home Office Research Study 248, London: Home Office Research, Development and Statistics Directorate.

Rohrer, F. (2008) 'Will We Eat Wonky Fruit and Veg?', BBC News, published 11 December 2008, accessed on 20 July 2010 at http://news.bbc.co.uk/2/hi/7724347.stm.

Romzek, B. and Johnson, J. (2005) 'State Social Services Contracting: Exploring the Determinants of Effective Contract Accountability', *Public Administration Review*, 65(4): 436–49.

Roth, J., Scholz, J. and Witte, A. (1989) *Taxpayer Compliance Volume 1: An Agenda for Research*, Philadelphia: University of Pennsylvania Press.

Rowson, J. (2011) Nudge is Not Enough, It's True. But We Already Knew That, *Guardian*, 19 July 2011, accessed on 20 August 2011 at http://www.guardian.co.uk/commentisfree/2011/jul/19/nudge-is-not-enough-behaviour-change.

Rumsfeld, D.H. (1995) *Thoughts from the Business World on Downsizing Government*, Chicago: The Heartland Institute, 25 August.

Saadé, C., Bateman, M., Bendahmane, D.B. (2001) *The Story of a Successful Public-Private Partnership in Central America: Handwashing for Diarrheal Disease Prevention*, Arlington, VA: Basic Support for Child Survival Project (BASICS II), the Environmental Health Project, the United Nations Children's Fund, the United States Agency for International Development, and The World Bank.

Safrilsyah, Jusoof, K. and Fadhill, R. (2009) 'Prosocial Behavior Motivation of Acheness Volunteers in Helping Tsunami Disaster Victims', *Canadian Social Science*, 5(3): 50–5.

Salamon, L. (1981) 'Rethinking Public Management', *Public Policy*, 29(1): 255–575.

Salamon, L. (1989) *Beyond Privatization: The Tools of Government Action*, Washington, DC: The Urban Institute.

Salamon, L. (ed.) (2002) *The Tools of Government: A Guide to the New Governance*, New York: Oxford University Press.

Salamon, L.M. and Sokolowski, W.S. (2001) 'Volunteering in Cross-National Perspective; Evidence From 24 Countries', in *Working Papers of The Johns Hopkins Comparative Nonprofit Sector Project*, Baltimore, MD: Johns Hopkins University.

Sandfort, J. and Milward, H.B. (2008) 'Collaborative Service-Provision in the Public Sector', in S. Cropper, M. Ebers, C. Huxham and P. Ring (eds), *The Oxford Handbook of Inter-Organizational Relations*, New York: Oxford University Press.

Satow, K.L. (1975) 'Social Approval and Helping', *Journal of Experimental Social Psychology*, 11 (6): 501–9.

Saunders, T., Stone, V. and Candy, S. (2001) *The Impact of the 26 Week Sanctioning Regime*, London: Working Age Research and Analysis Publications, Department for Work and Pensions.

Savas, E. (1977) 'An Empirical Study of Competition in Municipal Service Delivery', *Public Administration Review*, 37(6): 717–24.

Savas, E.S. (1982) *Privatizing the Public Sector: How to Shrink Government*, Chatham, NJ: Chatham House Publishers.

Savas, E. (1987) *Privatization: The Key to Better Government*, Chatham, NJ: Chatham House Publishers.

Savas, E. (2000) *Privatisation and Public-Private Partnerships*, New York: Chatham House.

Scahill, J. (2007) *Blackwater: The Rise of the World's Most Powerful Mercenary Army*, New York: Nation Books.

Schaeffer, P. and Loveridge, S. (2002) 'Toward an Understanding of Types of Public-Private Cooperation', *Public Performance and Management Review*, 26(2): 169–89.

Schein, E.H. (2003) *Organisational Culture and Leadership*, San Francisco, CA: Jossey-Bass.

Schein, E. (2004) *Organizational Culture and Leadership*, San Francisco: Jossey-Bass.

Schmolders, G. (1970) 'Survey Research in Public Finance: A Behavioural Approach to Fiscal Theory', *Public Finance*, 25: 300–6.

Scholz, J. (1984) 'Voluntary Compliance and Regulatory Enforcement', *Law and Policy*, 6 (October): 385–404.

Scholz, J. (1994) 'Managing Regulatory Enforcement in the United States', in David Rosenbloom and Richard Schwartz (eds), *Handbook of Regulation and Administrative Law*, New York: Marcel Dekker, Inc.

Schwartz, R. and Orleans, S. (1967) 'On Legal Sanctions', *University of Chicago Law Review*, 34: 274–300.

Schwass, M. (2007) 'Offering Help: The Ministry of Social Development and Marlborough's Viticulture Industry', Australia and New Zealand School of Government, Case Program, 2007–72.5.

Scott, C. and Baehler, K. (2010) 'Adding Value to Policy Analysis and Advice', Sydney: UNSW Press.

Seddon, N. (2004) *Government Contracts: Federal, State and Local*, 3rd edn, Sydney: The Federation Press.

Segal, D.R., Bachman, F.G., Freedman-Doan, P. and O'Malley, P.M. (1999) 'Propensity to Serve in the U.S. Military Temporal Trends and Subgroup Differences', *Armed Forces and Society*, 25(3), spring: 407–27.

Selsky, J. and Parker, B. (2005) 'Cross-Sector Partnerships to Address Social Issues: Challenges to Theory and Practice', *Journal of Management*, 31(6): 849–73.

Selznick, A. (1957) *Leadership in Administration: A Sociological Interpretation*, New York: Harper & Row.

Severson, K. (2011a) 'A Scandal of Cheating, and a Fall From Grace', *The New York Times*, 7 September 2011, accessed on 8 October 2011 at http://www.nytimes.com/2011/09/08/us/08hall.html?emc=eta1.

Severson, K. (2011b) 'Systematic Cheating is Found in Atlanta's School System', *The New York Times*, 5 July 2011, accessed on 8 October 2011 at http://www.nytimes.com/2011/07/06/education/06atlanta.html?_r=1&emc=eta1.

Shaoul, J. (2005) 'The Private Finance Initiative or the Public Funding of Private Profit?', in G. Hodge and Greve C. (eds), *The Challenge of Public-Private Partnerships: Learning from International Experience*, Cheltenham: Edward Elgar.

Shaw, J. and Baker, M. (2004) ' "Expert Patient" – Dream or Nightmare', *BMJ*, accessed on 15 March 2010 at http://www.bmj.com/content/328/7442/723.

Sheffrin, S. and Triest, R. (1992) 'Can Brute Deterrence Backfire? Perceptions and Attitudes in Taxpayer Compliance', in J. Slemrod (ed.), *Why People Pay Taxes: Tax Compliance and Enforcement*, Ann Arbor: University of Michigan Press.

Sheinin, A.G. (2009) 'Why License Librarians? Some Regulation Called Outdated', *The Atlanta Journal-Constitution*, 27 November.

Sheppard, B. and Sherman, D. (1998) 'The Grammars of Trust: A Model and General Implications', *Academy of Management Review*, 23(3): 422–37.

Sigler J.A. and Murphy J.E. (1988) *Interactive Corporate Compliance*, New York: Quorum Books.

Sigmund, K. (2007) 'Punish or Perish? Retaliation and Collaboration Among Humans' *Trends in Ecology and Evolution*: 593–600.

Simon, H. (1957) *Models of Man Social and Rational: Mathematical Essays on Rational Human Behavior in a Social Setting*, New York: Wiley.

Sinclair, A. (1991) 'After Excellence: Models of Organisational Culture for the Public Sector', *Australian Journal of Public Administration*, 50(3): 321–32.

Six, F. (2011) 'Trust in Regulatory Relations: How New Insights from Trust Research Improve Regulation Theory', paper presented at the Public Management Research Association Conference, June 2–4, Syracuse University, USA.

6, Perri (1997) *Holistic Government*, London: DEMOS.

6, Perri (2004) 'Joined-Up Government in the Western World in Comparative Perspective: A Preliminary Literature Review and Exploration', *Journal of Public Administration Research and Theory*, 14(1): 103–38.

Sjoquist, D.L. (1973) 'Property Crime and Economic Behaviour: Some Empirical Results', *American Economic Review*, 63(3), June: 439–46.

Skelcher, C. (2005) 'Public-Private Partnerships and Hybridity', in E. Ferlie, L. Lynn and C. Pollitt (eds), *The Oxford Handbook of Public Management*, Oxford: Oxford University Press.

Slemrod, J. (1989) 'Tax Effects Of Foreign Direct Investment in the U.S.: Evidence from a Cross-Country Comparison', Research Seminar in International Economics, University of Michigan, accessed on 12 March 2009 at http://ideas. repec.org/p/mie/wpaper/254.html.

Smith, A. (1986) *The Wealth of Nations*, London: Penguin Classics.

Smith, S. and Lipsky, M. (1993) *Non-profits for Hire: The Welfare State in the Age of Contracting*, Cambridge, MA: Harvard University Press.

Smith, S.R. (2007) 'NGOs and Contracting', in E. Ferlie, L.E. Lynn and C. Pollitt (eds), *The Oxford Handbook of Public Management*, Oxford University Press, Oxford: 591–614.

Sobel, R. (1999) *The Pursuit of Wealth*, New York: McGraw-Hill.

Sommer, J. (2009) 'When Humans Need a Nudge Toward Rationality', *The New York Times*, 8 February 2009, accessed on 6 June 2010 at http://www. nytimes.com/2009/02/08/business/08nudge.html.

Sparrow, M. (1994) *Imposing Duties: Government's Changing Approach to Compliance*, Westport, CT: Praeger.

Sparrow, M.K., Moore, M.H. and Kennedy, D.M. (1990) *Beyond 911: A New Era for Policing*, New York: Basic Books.

Spekman, R.E., Kamauff, J.W. and Myhr, N. (1998) 'An Empirical Investigation into Supply Chain Management: A Perspective on Partnerships', *Supply Chain Management: An International Journal*, 3(2): 53–67.

Spicer, M. and Lundstedt, S. (1976) 'Understanding Tax Evasion', *Public Finance*, 31(2): 295–305.

Star, S.L. and Griesemer, J.R. (1989) 'Institutional Ecology, "Translations" and Boundary Objects: Amateurs and Professionals in Berkeley's Museum of Vertebrate Zoology, 1907–39', *Social Studies of Science*, 19(3): 387–420.

Steele, J. (1999) *Wasted Values: Harnessing the Commitment of Public Managers*, London: Public Management Foundation.

Stewart, J. (1996) 'A Dogma of our Times: The Separation of Policy-making and Implementation', *Public Money & Management*, 16(3): 33–40.

Stewart, J. and Ranson, S. (1988) 'Management in the Public Domain', *Public Money & Management*, 8(spring/summer): 13–19.

Stoker, G. and Moseley, A. (2010) *Motivation, Behaviour and the Microfoundations of Public Services*, London: 2020 Public Services Trust.

Stokey, E. and Zeckhauser, R. (1974) *A Primer for Policy Analysis*. New York: W.W. Norton.

Stone, D. (2002) *Policy Paradox: The Art of Political Decision Making*, New York: W.W. Norton.

Stone, M.M. (2000) 'Exploring the Effects of Collaborations on Member Organizations: Washington County's Welfare-to-Work Partnership', *Nonprofit and Voluntary Sector Quarterly*, 29(supp. 1): 98–119.

Streitfeld, D. (2010) 'A City Outsources Everything. Sky Doesn't Fall', *The New York Times*, 19 July.

Stukas, A.A., Worth, K.A., Clary, E.G. and Snyder, M. (2009) 'The Matching of Motivations to Affordances in the Volunteer Environment. An Index for Assessing the Impact of Multiple Matches on Volunteer Outcomes', *Nonprofit and Voluntary Sector Quarterly*, 38(1): 5–28.

Sturgess, G. (1996) 'Virtual Government: What Will Remain Inside the Public Sector?', *Australian Journal of Public Administration*, 55(3): 59–73.

Sturgess, G. (2002) 'Private Risk, Public Service', *Policy*, 18(1): 3–7.

Sullivan, H. and Skelcher, C. (2002) *Working Across Boundaries: Collaboration in Public Services*, Basingstoke: Palgrave Macmillan.

Sundeen, R.A (1990) 'Citizens Serving Government: The Extent and Distinctiveness of Volunteer Participation in Local Public Agencies', *Nonprofit and Voluntary Sector Quarterly*, 19: 329–44.

TAC (2009) 'Lowest Road Toll on Record but the Campaign Goes On', media release, accessed on 2 February 2010 at http://www.tac.vic.gov.au/jsp/content/NavigationController.do?areaID= 23&tierID= 1&navID= 63CC12CD7F0000 0101A5D19311EC6AC2&navLink= null&pageID= 1922.

Talbot, C. (2004) 'Executive Agencies: Have They Improved Management in Government?', *Public Money & Management*, 24(2): 104–12.

Talbot, C. (2005) *The Paradoxical Primate*, Exeter: Imprint Academic.

Taylor, P. (2004) 'Prisoner Bust Costs Firm Contract', *The Australian*, 15 June.

Teece, D., Pisano, G. and Shuen, A. (1997) 'Dynamic Capabilities and Strategic Management', *Journal of Strategic Management*, (1997): 509–33.

Teisman, G. and Klijn, E.H. (2002) 'Partnership Arrangements: Governmental Rhetoric or Governance Scheme?' *Public Administration Review*, 62(2): 197–205.

Thaler, R.H. and Sunstein, C.R. (2008) *Nudge. Improving Decisions about Health, Wealth and Happiness*, New Haven, CT: Yale University Press.

The Australian (2010) US Intelligence Reliant on 'Contractors', *The Australian*, 21 July.

The Scottish Government, accessed http://www.scotland.gov.uk/About/Directorates.

Thomas, J.C. (1995) *Public Participation in Public Decisions: New Skills and Strategies for Public Managers*, San Francisco: Jossey-Bass.

Thornton, D., Gunningham, N.A. and Kagan, R.A. (2005) 'General Deterrence and Corporate Environmental Behavior', *Law and Policy*, 27(2): 262–88.

Thurow, L. (1983) *Dangerous Currents: The State of Economics*, Oxford: Oxford University Press.

Titmuss, R.M. (1970) *The Gift Relationship – From Human Blood to Social Policy*, London: Allen & Unwin.

Tittle, C.R. (1980) *Sanctions and Social Deviance*, New York: Praeger.

Todd, L. (2008) 'EU Bans Peking Duck Forcing Council Snoopers to Shut Down Restaurant Ovens in Chinatown', *Mail Online*, 19 July 2008, accessed on 6 October 2010 at http://www.dailymail.co.uk/ news/article-1036578/EU-bans-Peking-Duck-forcing-council-snoopers-shut-restaurant-ovens-Chinatown.html.

Toppe, C.M., Kirsch, A.D. and Michel, J. (2002) *Giving and Volunteering in the United States 2001: Findings from a National Survey*, Washington, DC: Independent Sector.

Triggle, N. (2010) 'Fears over £65bn "NHS mortgage"', BBC News, 13 August.

Trouton, A., Kavanagh, J., Oakley, A., Harden, A. and Powell, C. (2005) *A Summary of Ongoing Activity in the Use of Incentive Schemes to Encourage Positive Behaviours in Young People*, London: EPPI-Centre, Social Science Research Unit, Institute of Education, University of London.

Tushman, M.L. and Scanlan, T.J. (1981) 'Boundary Spanning Individuals: Their Role in Information Transfer and Their Antecedents', *Academy of Management Journal*, 24(2): 289–305.

Tversky, A. and Kahneman, D. (1981) 'The Framing of Decisions and the Psychology of Choice', *Science*, 211(4481): 453–8.

Tyler, T.R. (1990) *Why People Obey The Law*, New Haven, CT: Yale University Press.

UNDP (2006) 'Incentive Systems: Incentives, Motivation, and Development Performance', Conference Paper 8, Capacity Development Group, Bureau for Development Policy, United National Development Programme.

UNISON (2011) 'Insourcing Update: The Value of Returning Local Authority Services In-house in an Era of Budget Constraints', report by Association of Public Service Excellence for UNISON, London.

United Nations (2005) *Unlocking Human Potential for Public Sector Performance*, *World Public Sector Report 2005*, New York: United Nations.

United States Government Accountability Office (GAO) (2011) 'Private Fund Advisers: Although a Self-Regulatory Organization Could Supplement SEC Oversight, It Would Present Challenges and Trade-Offs', report to Congressional Committees, Washington, USA.

Upton, W. (1973) 'Altruism, Attribution and Intrinsic Motivation in the Recruitment of Blood Donors', *Selected Readings on Donor Motivation and Recruitment*, Vol. III, ed. by American Red Cross.

Uzzi, B. (1997) 'Social Structure and Competition in Interfirm Networks: The Paradox of Embeddedness', *Administrative Science Quarterly*, 42: 35–67.

Van de Ven, J. (2001) 'Social Approval as a Motivation to Give', *Journal of Institutional and Theoretical Economics*, 158(3): 464–82.

Van Slyke, D.M. (2002) 'The Public Management Challenges of Contracting with Nonprofits for Social Services', *International Journal of Public Administration*, 25(4): 489–517.

Van Slyke, D.M. (2005) 'Agents or Stewards: How Government Manages its Contracting Relationships with Nonprofit Social Service Providers', in K. Mark Weaver (ed.), *Proceedings of the Sixty-Fifth Annual Meeting of the Academy of Management* (CD), ISSN 1543–8643.

Van Slyke, D.M. (2007) 'Agents or Stewards: Using Theory to Understand the Government-Nonprofit Social Service Contracting Relationship', *Journal of Public Administration Research and Theory*, 17(2): 157–87.

Vandenbergh, M. (2003) 'Beyond Elegance: A Testable Typology of Social Norms in Corporate Environmental Compliance', *Stanford Environmental Law Journal*, 22(2): 55–144.

Varley, P. (1994) 'High Stakes and Frightening Lapses: DSS, La Alianza Hispana and the Public-Private Question in Child Protection Work', Parts A and B and Epilogue, Kennedy School of Government Case Program, C16-94-1265-6, Cambridge, MA: Harvard University.

Vincent, A. (2008) 'Incentives and Prosocial Behavior in Democratic Societies', *Journal of Economic Psychology*. 29(2008): 849–55.

Vincent, J. (1998) *Jobseeker's Allowance Evaluation: Qualitative Research on Disallowed and Sanctioned Claimants Phase Two: After Jobseeker's Allowance*, Research Report, London: DfEE.

Volunteering Australia (2009) '2009 National Survey of Volunteering Issues', Melbourne: Volunteering Australia Inc.

Volunteering England (2010) 'Public Sector Volunteering – Overview', available at www.volunteering.org.uk accessed 31 October 2010.

Walker, K. (1977) 'Concepts of Industrial Democracy in International Perspective', in R. Pritchard (ed.), *Industrial Democracy in Australia*, Sydney: CCH.

Wallschutzky, I. (1988) *The Effects of Tax Reform on Tax Evasion*, Sydney: Australian Tax Research Foundation.

Walsh, J. and O'Flynn, J. (2000) 'Managing Through Contracts: The Employment Effects of Compulsory Competitive Tendering in Australian Local Government', *Industrial Relations Journal*, 31(5): 454–69.

Watts, T. (2004) 'The Privatisation of Melbourne's Public Transport System', Case Program, Case No. 2004-3.1, Melbourne: The Australia and New Zealand School of Government.

Weaver, D. and Hasenfeld, Y. (1997) 'Case Management Practices, Participants' Responses, and Compliance in Welfare-to-Work Programs', *Social Work Research*, (21): 92–100.

Webb, R. and Pulle, B. (2002) 'Public Private Partnerships: An Introduction', Research paper no. 1 2002–03, Department of the Parliamentary Library, Commonwealth of Australia.

Weber, L. (2003) 'Down the Wrong Road: Discretion in Decisions to Detain Asylum Seekers Arriving at UK Ports', *The Howard Journal*, 42(3): 248–62.

Weber, M. (1966) *The Theory of Social and Economic Organization*, New York: Free Press.

Weill, P. and Ross, B. (2004) *IT Governance; How Top Performers Manage IT Decision Rights for Top Performance*, Cambridge, MA: Harvard Business School Press.

Weimer, D. and Vining, R. (2004) *Policy Analysis: Concepts and Practice*, 4th edn, New Jersey: Prentice-Hall.

Weiner, M.J. and Mander, A.M. (1978) 'The Effects of Reward and Perception of Competency on Intrinsic Motivation', *Motivation and Emotion*, 2(1), 67–73.

Wenseleers, T. and Ratnieks, F.L.W. (2006) 'Comparative Analysis of Worker Reproduction and Policing in Eusocial Hymenoptera Supports Relatedness Theory', *American Naturalist*, 168(2006): E163–E179.

Wettenhall, R. (2000) 'Reshaping the Commonwealth Public Sector', in G. Singleton (ed.), *The Howard Government: Australian Commonwealth Administration 1996–1998*, Sydney: University of New South Wales Press.

Whitaker, G. (1980) 'Co-production: Citizen Participation in Service Delivery', *Public Administration Review*, 40(May/June): 240–6.

White, S. (2005) 'Cooperation Costs, Governance Choice and Alliance Evolution', *Journal of Management Studies*, 42(7): 1383–412.

White, S., Hall, C. and Peckover, S. (2008a) 'The Descriptive Tyranny of the Common Assessment Framework: Technologies of Categorisation and Professional Practice in Child Welfare', *British Journal of Social Work Advance Access*, 10.1093/bjsw/bcn053.

White, S., Wastell, D., Broadhurst, K., Peckover, S., Hall, C. and Pithouse, A. (2008b) 'Managing Risk in a High Blame Environment: Making a 'Flight Deck' Simulation in Childcare Social Work', in Interim Meeting of the International Sociological Association Research Committee 33(RC33).

Whitely, R. (2006) 'Project-Based Firms: New Organizational Form or Variations on a Theme?', *Industrial and Corporate Change*, 15(1): 77–99.

Williams, P. (2002) 'The Competent Boundary Spanner', *Public Administration*, 80(1): 103–24.

Williams, P. (2010) 'Special Agents: The Nature and Role of Boundary Spanners', paper presented to the ESRC Research Seminar Series 'Collaborative Futures: New Insights from Intra and Inter-Sectoral Collaborations', University of Birmingham, February.

Williams, T.P. (2003) *Moving to Public-Private Partnerships: Learning from Experience Around the World*, Arlington, VA: IBM Endowment for The Business of Government.

Williamson, O.E. (1975) *Markets and Hierarchies: Analysis and Antitrust Implications*, New York: Free Press.

Williamson, O.E. (1979) 'Transaction-Cost Economics: The Governance of Contractual Relations', *Journal of Law and Economics*, 22, (October): 233–61.

Williamson, O.E. (1981) 'The Economics of Organization', *American Journal of Sociology*, 87: 548–77.

Williamson, O.E. (1985) *The Economic Institutions of Capitalism*, New York: Free Press.

Williamson, O.E. (1991) 'Comparative Economic Organization: The Analysis of Discrete Structural Alternatives', *Administrative Science Quarterly*, 36(2): 269–96.

Wilson, J. (1973) *Political Organization*, New York: Basic Books.

Wilson, J. (1989) *Bureaucracy: What Government Agencies Do and Why They Do It*, New York: Basic Books.

Wilson, T.D. (1984) 'The Cognitive Approach to Information-Seeking Behaviour and Information Use', *Social Science Information Studies*, 4: 197–204.

Winterbotham, M., Adams, L. and Hasluck, C. (2001) *Evaluation of New Deal for Long Term Unemployed People Enhanced National Programme*, Report ESR82. Sheffield: Employment Service.

Wintour, P. (2010) 'David Cameron's "Nudge Unit" Aims to Improve Economic Behavior', *The Guardian*, 9 September 2010, accessed on 19 July 2011 at http://www.guardian.co.uk/society/2010/sep/09/cameron-nudge-unit-economic-behaviour?intcmp=239.

Wolf, C. (1988) *Markets or Governments: Choosing Between Imperfect Alternatives*, Cambridge, MA: MIT Press.

Zand, D. (1997) *The Leadership Triad: Knowledge, Trust, and Power*, New York: Oxford University Press.

Zimmeck, M. (2001) *The Right Stuff: New Ways of Thinking about Managing Volunteers*, London: Institute for Volunteer Research.

Index of Names

Index of Subjects